Judaic Studies

*Global Publications*

Binghamton University

State University of New York at Binghamton

*General Editor*

Jacob Neusner

# JEWISH LAW ASSOCIATION STUDIES XII

The Zutphen Conference Volume

# JEWISH LAW ASSOCIATION STUDIES

ISSN: 7552-0890

Jewish Law Association Studies I: The Touro Conference Volume
B.S. Jackson, Editor

Jewish Law Association Studies II: The Jerusalem Conference Volume
B.S. Jackson, Editor

Jewish Law Association Studies III: The Oxford Conference Volume
A.M. Fuss, Editor

Jewish Law Association Studies IV: The Boston Conference Volume
B.S. Jackson, Editor

Jewish Law Association Studies V: The Halakhic Thought of R. Isaac Herzog
B.S. Jackson, Editor

Jewish Law Association Studies VI: The Jerusalem 1990 Conference Volume
B.S. Jackson and S.M. Passamaneck, Editors

Jewish Law Association Studies VII: The Paris Conference Volume
S.M. Passamaneck and M. Finley, Editors

Jewish Law Association Studies VIII: The Jerusalem 1994 Conference Volume
E.A. Goldman, Editor

Jewish Law Association Studies IX: The London 1996 Conference Volume
E.A. Goldman, Editor

Jewish Law Association Studies X: The Jerusalem 1998 Conference Volume
H.G. Sprecher, Editor

Jewish Law Association Studies XI: Law, Judicial Policy and Jewish Identity in the State of Israel
D.B. Sinclair, Editor

Jewish Law Association Studies, XII

# The Zutphen Conference Volume

Edited by

Hillel Gamoran

Global Publications
State University of New York at Binghamton
2002

Printed in the United States of America

ISBN 1-58684-180-7

Published and Distributed by:
Global Publications
LNG99, State University of New York at Binghamton
Binghamton, New York, USA 13902-6000
Phone (607) 777-4495 or 6104; Fax: (607) 777-6132
E-mail: pmorewed@binghamton.edu
http://ssips.binghamton.edu

# The Jewish Law Association Officers 2000/2002



The Association seeks to promote the research and study of Jewish law through biennial international congresses, the publication of a newsletter and of a yearbook series, *Jewish Law Association Studies,* and making other publications in Jewish law available to its members at concessionary rates. For further details of membership, please contact the appropriate membership secretary:

*For Israel:* Prof. Nahum Rakover, P.O. Box 7286, Jerusalem 91074, Israel.

*For the rest of the world:* Prof. Peter S. Zaas, Siena College, 515 Loudon Road, Loudonville, NY 12211, USA

http://www.mucjs.org/jlas/

This volume is dedicated to the memory of

R. Daniel ben R. Jochanan

in appreciation of

the work of his father, Joop Al

in organising the Zutphen Conference, 2000

CONTENTS


1: JACOB BAZAK, Compromise vs. Adjudication in Jewish Law 1

2: J. DAVID BLEICH, Constructive Agency in Religious Divorce: An Examination of *Get Zikkuy* 7

3: SHERMAN L. COHN, Teaching Jewish Law in a Secular American Law School 37

4: JONATHAN FISHER, Entrapment in Jewish Law 51

5: JOSEPH FLEISHMAN, A Father's Versus a Husband's Authority to Annul a Vow (*Numbers* 30:4-17) 71

6: HILLEL GAMORAN, Lending - No, Investing - Yes: Development of the *Iṣḳa* Law from the 12th to the 15th Centuries 79

7: MOSHE ISH-HOROWICZ, Some Aspects of Theodicy: The Flood and the Holocaust 95

8: BERNARD S. JACKSON, *Moredet*: Problems of History and Authority 103

9: STEPHEN M. PASSAMANECK, The *Shoṭer* 125

10: NAHUM RAKOVER, Should Transgression Disqualify One from Public Office? 141

11: STEVEN H. RESNICOFF, Jewish Fraudulent Transfer Law 159

12: YOSEF RIVLIN, Incarceration for Non-Payment of Debts 193

13: ELIMELECH WESTREICH, The Rise and Decline of the Law of the Rebellious Wife in Medieval Jewish Law 207

14: SAMUEL WOLFMAN, Mental Disease in Divorce Law in the Responsa Literature and in Rabbinical Court Rulings in Israel 219

1

# COMPROMISE VS. ADJUDICATION IN JEWISH LAW

by

JACOB BAZAK[a]

The word פשרה, the Hebrew equivalent for "compromise", originates from מים פושרים, פושרים — not warm nor cold.

In common parlance the metaphoric meaning of the word "compromise" carries with it a negative sense, an attitude of disrespect and contempt. For people prefer and appreciate more a clear-cut standing, an emphatic and unequivocal decision — white or black, right or wrong. People dislike an attitude which is "neither this nor this" or an attitude of "this *as well as* this". The *Brisker Rov*, R. Velvel Soloveitchik, used to say that people on the road use the *sides* of the road, the right side or the left side. Going in the middle of the road, neither right nor left, is the habit of animals, not of human beings. Vacillating (פסיחה על שני הסעיפים) is interpreted as a sign of weakness, weakness either of character or of intellect, or of both.

There is an inherent contradiction between compromise and legal adjudication. For adjudication represents an effort to arrive at the true factual as well as at the precise legal solution of the conflict, while compromise is patently a conscious waiver of legal rights, an explicit deviation from the true strict legal solution. Indeed we find in *Tosefta (Sanhedrin (1, 2); Bavli, Sanhedrin* 6b) two dichotomous opinions regarding the value of compromise in the legal process. R. Elazar, son of R. Yose Ha'Glili sharply criticizes compromise solutions in legal disputes, saying: "Any (judge) who makes a compromise (in legal proceedings) is a transgressor and any one who blesses such a judge is indeed blaspheming G-D, for judgment belongs to G-D." R. Elazar goes further to say that one should not deviate from the strict legal solution even in cases where it necessitates the piercing of a mountain (יקוב הדין את ההר, a metaphoric expression meaning: even if it necessitates radical actions).

[a] Judge (retired). Prof. of Law, The Academic Center, Kiryat Ono, Israel.

On the other hand we find the opinion of R. Yehoshua Ha'Glili who holds that compromise is not only not prohibited, but that it is rather commendable and is a *Mitzvah*. The *Tosefta* goes on to say that these two contradicting opinions reflect the two different approaches of Moses and Aaron respectively. Moses used to say: "Let the law pierce the mountain" (i.e., the full rigor of law should be applied, justice should be done whatever the outcome will be) while Aaron used to mediate between the contesting parties and would convince them to agree to a compromise solution.

Can these two contradicting opinions regarding compromise be reconciled? Can these two most basic norms — law on the one hand and peace on the other hand — live together? A most interesting answer to this problem can be found in the commentary *Ha'ameḳ Davar* by Naftali Zvi Yehuda Berlin on Exodus.

But before discussing this interesting commentary of Berlin, let us first deal briefly with some of the limits of the law. There is no doubt that legal adjudication helps in educating the contesting parties as well as society at large to adhere to the norms of the law. That outcome depends however on one important condition and that is — that the judgment of the court is indeed the correct one, both legally and factually. For if the judgment is a mistaken one, then the outcome will not help in educating the contesting parties as well as society at large to adhere to the norms of the law but will have quite the opposite effect, the court's decision will give legal effect to an erroneous view and will in fact become a tool in educating the public to injustice and to disrespect for law. In cases like this, the outcome will be, as is expressed in the sad verse in Ecclesiastes (3,16): "... in the place of justice — wickedness was there." That is also the background to the famous apparently paradoxical saying of R. Yohanan in *Bava Metzia* (30b): "The destruction of Jerusalem would not have come about if not for the fact that they adjudicated according to strict Torah law and were not willing to act in an equitable way." Law is inherently *a priori* and general. In some practical instances therefore there is, sometimes, a need to make some divergence from the strict letter of the law in order to achieve a real just and satisfactory solution.

The outcome of all this therefore is that adjudication would have been the only right way to deal with legal disputes, were it not for the fact that one can never be completely sure that the adjudication in each specific case would be based on the correct understanding of both law and fact. Taking into consideration the shortcomings of human nature, a compromise solution, to which both sides consent, is therefore preferable.

Accordingly it was held (see *Shulḥan Arukh, Ḥoshen Mishpaṭ,* 12,2) that at the outset of each legal proceedings the court should try to convince the litigating parties to agree to a compromise solution through mutual concessions. However, no coercion should be used to achieve this, just פיוסים ופיתויים, "appeasement and temptation" (*Shilṭei Ha'giborim, ad loc.*) If the parties, or even just one of them, are reluctant to accept a compromise, then the court should immediately turn to the hearing of the case and decide it boldly according to the merits of the case and the relevant principles of law. The court is however not precluded from further suggesting a compromise solution again and again throughout the hearing of the case. Once however the parties have concluded their arguments and the court can already see what the final decision is going to be, in such a case the court is not allowed anymore to suggest a compromise, for this would not be fair to the party who was about to win the case.

We can now come back to the commentary *Ha'ameḳ Davar* by Naftali Zvi Yehuda Berlin regarding the two conflicting views of Moses and Aaron regarding conflict resolutions. Moses — as beforehand mentioned — used to say: "Let the law pierce the mountain," while Aaron used to mediate between the contesting parties and convince them to accept a compromise solution. The reason for it, according to Berlin, is that *Moshe Rabeinu*, because of his immense erudition in *halakhah* and great understanding of human nature, could see immediately, right at the beginning of the hearing of the case, who is going to win the case. Therefore he was precluded from suggesting a compromise, for that would be unfair to that party. While Aaron, who did not have that deep insight of human nature and that extremely wide erudition in *halakhah*, could not arrive at any clear conclusion before completely hearing the whole case. Therefore he *was* allowed to persuade both parties to agree to a compromise solution until the last stage of the case.

All these halakhic views were authoritatively settled by Maimonides (in the introduction to his *Commentary on the Mishnah*, tractate *Zeraim*, part V, *Abot*) in the following words: "Every judge should make all efforts possible to mediate between the contesting parties. If he will manage not to adjudicate all through his life by convincing always the disputing parties to agree to compromise solutions, how good and how pleasant, if however this is not possible, then he should cut it down and proclaim his judgment."

As stated above, compromise solutions cannot be *forced* upon the litigant parties. The parties must priorly give their willful consent to it, either consent to the concrete compromise solution proposed by the court or consent to the principle of accepting any compromise solution that the court will decide upon.

There are however in Jewish law three exceptions, where the court is authorized to impose a compromise solution even without the agreement of the parties. These exceptions are as follows:

A. Where the court is under a duty to impose an oath (*shvu'ah*) on one of the litigants.
B. When the truth cannot be ascertained.
C. According to some sources the court is entitled under certain circumstances to force a rich party to act equitably towards the poor party.

Let us deal shortly with each of these three instances.

## A. *Where the Court is under a Duty to Impose an Oath*

When the court, after hearing all the witnesses and arguments comes to the conclusion that the plaintiff (or the defendant) is entitled to a judgment in his favor, but on condition that he makes a declaration under oath to substantiate his version, then the court is entitled to impose a compromise solution in order to avoid the need for such an oath. This principle was acted upon by the Rabbinical Court in Jerusalem in the following case (*PDR* Vol.4 p.318) (the *Dayanim* in that case were Rabbi Eliezer Waldenberg, Rav Ovadya Yosef, and Rav Y. Kappach, each of whom were among of the leading and respected *Dayanim* of the State of Israel). A grocery owner sued a customer for a debt of 343.80 Li, basing herself on the entries in her ledger. The defendant denied the claim arguing that her debt amounted to 9 Li only. The Court explained at the beginning of its judgment that there is a common error amongst some people, holding that under halakhah a shopkeeper is entitled to base his claim on the entries in his ledger. The court cited a famous responsum of Yeheskel Landau (*Noda BiYehuda,* Second Volume, *Ḥoshen Mishpaṭ,* 15) in which he stated that any judge who holds that a shopkeeper is entitled to base his claim on the entries in his ledger, even under oath, does not understand elementary principles of Jewish civil law and is completely mistaken in his interpretation of the Mishnah. In the present case however, the defendant admits part of the claim, though a very minimal part of it, therefore the Talmudic principle that applies in such a case is that the defendant — who is מודה במקצת — must first substantiate his version under oath in order that the court will decide in his favor, i.e., that he must pay the plaintiff only 9 Li. However, under the rule stated in *Ḥoshen Mishpaṭ* 12,2, when the Court decides to impose an oath on one of the litigants, the court is entitled to make a compromise decision in order to evade the penalty of a severe Shvu'ah. Therefore the court in the present case decided to hand down a compromise judgment, which, under the present circumstances, is considered strict law not just "compromise". "We hold therefore that the defendant must pay the plaintiff 150 Li."

## B. *When the Truth Cannot Be Ascertained*

The second instance where the court is entitled to impose a compromise judgment is when the truth can not be ascertained. The principle is that a judge is under obligation to give judgment in any case within his jurisdiction that was duly brought to him. The fact that it is a very complicated case, legally or factually, can not serve as an excuse to exempt him from that duty. If the truth cannot be ascertained, the court will decide that the plaintiff, on whom, in most cases, the burden of proof lies, has not succeeded in convincing the court, and therefore his claim will be dismissed, not necessarily because the court came to the conclusion that the defendant was right, but because of the rule that the onus of proof is on the plaintiff. In Jewish Law however the court is entitled in several instances where the truth can not be ascertained, to give a compromise judgment. The rule in such cases, as laid down in *Ḥoshen Mishpaṭ* 12, 5, is as follows: "A judge is entitled to make a compromise judgment where the truth can not be ascertained. And he is *not* entitled to leave the case open without any final decision." This rule is based on a responsum of R. Asher b. Yeḥiel (*Responsa of Rabeinu Asher* (107,4) regarding a very complicated case that had been referred to him by "The Countess." *Rabeinu Asher* deals extensively with the relevant facts and with the law citing many sources from the Talmud, and concludes his responsum in the following words: "I have explained very extensively all this, in order to make it clear that a judge is not entitled to leave a case open without a final decision. The judge is bound to conclude each case and to make a final decision in order to put an end to the litigation and to make peace in the world. For that end the Sages empowered the judge to make a judgment according to what he thinks fit, where the truth can not be ascertained through proof and evidence, either by assessment (see *Ḥoshen Mishpaṭ* 15, 5), or according to his full discretion without basing himself on evidence or on any reasoning[1] or by giving a compromise judgment (*Ḥoshen*

1 *Shuda De'Dainei*. According to *Rashi* (*Ketubot* 85b), *Ṭur* and *Rambam* the judge must, even under such circumstances, base himself on logical consid-

*Mishpaṭ* 12). A judge is however not entitled, so is expressly stated in *Ḥoshen Mishpaṭ* 12,5, to leave the case open without a final decision (so is the rule at least in monetary disputes. Regarding divorce cases — see *Yad Ha'Ḥazaḳah, Ishut*, 14, 17, and see also *PDR*, vol.4, p.267).

C. *Compromise on Equitable Grounds*

Some authorities hold that in cases where the strict law is on the side of the wealthy litigant, although on equitable grounds one could expect the wealthy party to be generous and not to act according to the strict letter of the law, the court, in such cases, is entitled to force the wealthy party to act equitably (see *B.M.* 24b, *Bach, Ḥoshen Mishpaṭ* 12, 4). This however is a minority view only, while the majority hold that a court is not entitled to act in this way. (*Rama, Ḥoshen Mishpaṭ* 12,2; see also *Shav Ya'aḳov* (by R. Ya'aḳov b. Binyamin Ha-Kohen*) Even Ha'ezer* 29 cited in *Pitḥai Teshuva, Shulḥan Arukh, Ḥoshen Mishpaṭ* 12, 6: "God forbid that a court of law would be allowed to enforce the winning party to act equitably contrary to the strict letter of the law which is on his side.")

To sum up: Jewish law highly praises compromise solutions to legal disputes for it enhances peace in the world. The court should therefore start every case by trying to convince the parties in the merits of a willful compromise solution. If however this is not acceptable to one of the parties, the court should decide the case on its merits according to law even if the outcome needs the "piercing of the mountain." In addition to the duty of the court to start every legal proceedings with efforts to achieve a willful compromise solution, there are certain exceptional cases where the court, under Jewish law, is entitled to impose a compromise solution.

These exceptional cases are as follows:

A. Where the court is under a duty to impose an oath (*shvu'ah*) on one of the litigants.
B. When the truth cannot be ascertained.
C. According to some minority views, the court is entitled under certain circumstances to force a rich party to act equitably towards a poor party.

---

erations, while *Rabeinu Tam*, *Rabeinu Asher* and *Ran* (see: *SMA, Ḥoshen Mishpaṭ*, 240,3) hold that under such circumstances the judge is entitled to make a decision according to his feeling without even basing himself on any logical considerations.

2

# CONSTRUCTIVE AGENCY IN RELIGIOUS DIVORCE: AN EXAMINATION OF *GEṬ ZIKKUY*

by

J. DAVID BLEICH[*]

The problem of the modern-day *agunah* resulting from the refusal of the husband to cooperate in the execution of a religious divorce on behalf of his wife despite the irreversible breakdown of their marriage has long plagued, and continues to plague, rabbinic decisors. Over the years, a series of proposals for remedying the situation has been advanced, examined, debated and, for the most part, rejected because of compelling halakhic objections. Some few proposals involving antenuptial agreements of one form or another have been adopted in some circles but remain the subject of controversy. For reasons that are difficult to identify, proposals that have been advanced for antenuptial agreements to which no halakhic objections have been voiced have yet to gain universal endorsement and hence have not been implemented.

Within recent years a small number of individuals have donned the mantle of authority and have assumed upon themselves responsibility for permitting wives of recalcitrant husbands to remarry on the basis of halakhic considerations rejected as spurious by recognized halakhic authorities. The expedient of *ḳiddushei ta'ut*, i.e. annulment of the marriage *ab initio*, was addressed by this writer in the Fall, 1998 issue of *Tradition*. Some have also sought to resolve the problem by invoking the concept of *geṭ zikkuy*, i.e. a *geṭ* executed by the *bet din* on its own motion, contrary to the expressed desire of the husband, on the grounds that an act performed for the benefit of another does not require that party's consent.

[a] A *Rosh Yeshivah* at Yeshiva University and Professor of Jewish Law and Ethics at Benjamin Cardozo School of Law.

Unfortunately, this expedient falls far short of halakhic acceptability. The attempt to resolve the *agunah* problem in this fashion can, at best, be described as an endeavor based upon misunderstanding and misapplication of halakhic concepts and precedents. Nevertheless, those who have an interest in *Halakhah* and in the halakhic process undoubtedly wish to understand the underlying principles and why they do or do not serve as a basis for ameliorating the plight of the *agunah*. Such an understanding requires elucidation of the difficult and complex halakhic concept of *zekhiyyah* and its ramifications.

## I. *The Principle of Zekhiyyah in Jewish Law*

### A. Third Party Beneficiaries

"*Zekhiyyah*", as an operative legal concept, is unique to Jewish law. The translation of "*zekhiyyah*" as "constructive agency" is somewhat misleading in that the translation implies adoption of one of two competing theses advanced as descriptive hypotheses upon which the biblical institution may rest. Those competing hypotheses will be discussed at a later point. Nevertheless, putting aside the question of the legal rationale that actually serves as the formal cause of the halakhic institution of *zikkuy*, the term "constructive agency" effectively and accurately describes its *telos* or final cause, i.e. the operational effect of employing the halakhic construct known as *zekhiyyah*.[1]

The term "constructive agency" is unknown in legal parlance. Indeed, in describing the operation of other legal systems, the term would be akin to an oxymoron. Agency, in other legal systems, requires designation, or at least a presumption of actual intent, on the part of the principal. Other legal systems may indeed recognize a principle of implied agency, e.g. a situation in which an employee routinely conducts business on behalf of his employer, but that is because the circumstances give rise to the presumption that the employee acts with the knowledge and authority of the employer and hence the implication is that the employer actually intends the employee to serve as his agent. The crucial distinction between implied agency and constructive agency is that in instances of implied agency the principal is presumed to

1 Indeed, this is essentially how R. Chaim Soloveichik categorizes *zekhiyyah* according to those authorities who do not regard *zekhiyyah* as a simple form of agency. See *infra*, note 21.

have had prior intent to create the agency whereas constructive agency implies neither intent nor prior cognition of *any* kind on the part of the principal.

The legal construct most clearly akin to that of constructive agency, and one that for certain purposes achieves the same effect, is that of a third party beneficiary. To the extent that such claims are recognized, the rights of third party beneficiaries arise as a construct of contract law. And it is precisely because the concept arises in contract law that some other legal systems have had difficulty acknowledging such rights. The enforceability of a contract hinges upon privity between the contracting parties. Applying conventional legal principles, two parties cannot by contract create rights in a third person when there is no privity of contract between them and the third party. Accordingly, in some jurisdictions it became necessary to enact statutes in favor of certain classes of beneficiaries, such as beneficiaries of insurance policies or mortgages. In other jurisdictions, courts give effect to such contracts by finding a fictitious "privity" or "trust" relationship or by ruling that the claim of a third party may properly be recognized in equity if not in law.[2]

The earliest recognition of the rights of a third person to sue as a beneficiary of a contract to which that person was not a party was in a 1677 decision by the King's Bench in *Dutton v. Poole.*[3] A father sought to sell wood to raise a dowry for his daughter. The elder son, who wanted to inherit the wood, promised the father to pay the daughter £1,000 if the father would refrain from selling the wood. Upon failure of the son to pay the agreed-upon sum, the daughter brought suit. The son sought to have the case dismissed on the grounds that "the action ought not to be brought by the daughter but by the father ... for the promise was made to the father, and the daughter is neither privy nor interested in the consideration."[4] The Court rejected that argument but without necessarily affirming the standing of all third party beneficiaries. Instead, the Court found that consideration for a promise may be given by a third person, i.e. that a party (in this case the daughter) may be a promisee of the one who will be benefited by dependence on the contract and yet not be the one who gave the consideration. In effect, such a promisee is not a third-party beneficiary; he or she is the direct

2 See Arthur L. Corbin, "Contract for the Benefit of Third Persons", *Yale Law Journal* 27/8 (1918), 1008-1029.

3 83 Eng. Rep. 523 (K.B., 1677).

4 *Ibid.,* at 523, 524.

beneficiary of the party who gave the consideration. Privity is established by the fact that the promise is directed to the promisee. Hence the only problem is whether consideration can move from a person and it was only this point that was settled in the affirmative in *Dutton*.

Even that limited recognition of the rights of third party beneficiaries was rejected in 1861 in *Tweddle v. Atkinson* with the observation that the promisee cannot bring an action unless the consideration moved from him.[5] In 1915, in denying recovery to a third party in *Dunlop Pneumatic Tyre Co. v. Selfridge & Co.*, one of the Lords declared the notion that "only a person who is a party to a contract can sue on it to be a fundamental principle of the law of England."[6] That principle was reaffirmed by the House of Lords as recently as 1968 in a decision handed down in *Beswick v. Beswick.*[7] In some subsequent cases, English courts, although upholding this rule in principle, have recognized a cause of action based upon an expanded notion of the concept of trust. Thus, for example, if A promises B that he will pay a sum of money to C, the promisee, B, may be regarded as holding the claim against A, the promisor, as trustee for C.[8]

American courts, for the most part, have upheld rights of third part beneficiaries. As early as 1825, in *Farley v. Cleveland*,[9] a New York court ruled that the promisee need not himself provide consideration. Since the major case in this area, *Lawrence v. Fox*,[10] was decided by the New York Court of Appeals in 1859, two years before *Tweddle v. Atkinson*, it may be fair to say that American courts adopted the doctrine announced in *Dutton v. Poole* before its reversal in *Tweddle* and in later decisions declined to follow *Tweddle* in reversing American precedents.[11]

In *Lawrence*, the New York court went beyond the principle enunciated

5 121 Eng. Rep. 762, 764 (Q.B., 1861, Crompton, J.).

6 [1915] App. Cas. 847, 853 (H.L., 1915, Lord Haldane).

7 [1968] App. Cas. 58 (H.L., 1867, Lord Reid).

8 See E. Allan Farnsworth, *Contracts*, 3rd ed. (New York: Aspen Law and Business, 1999), 675 n.8.

9 4 Com. 432 (N.Y. 1825), *aff'd*, 9 Com. 639 (N.Y. 1827).

10 20 N.Y. 268 (1859). For an analysis of this case see Anthony Jon Waters, "The Property in the Promise: A Study of the Third Part Beneficiary Rule", *Harvard Law Review* 98/6 (1985), 1109-1210.

11 For a study of the impact and influence of *Lawrence* see M.H. Hoefflich and E. Perelmutter, "The Anatomy of a Leading Case: *Lawrence v. Fox* in the Courts, the Casebooks and the Commentaries", *University of Michigan Journal of Law Reform* 21/4 (1988), 721-744.

in *Farley* in ruling that not only may consideration be provided by the beneficiary himself, but that the beneficiary may recover even though he is not the promisee. The principle developed in *Lawrence* was gradually accepted by other states as well, although Massachusetts did not generally permit recovery by contract beneficiaries until 1979.[12] Although the pioneer in the development of this legal doctrine, New York did not explicitly abandon the requirement of a family relationship between a donee beneficiary and the promisor until 1985.[13] *Restatement Second* §302 limits the right to an "intended beneficiary"as opposed to an "incidental beneficiary" described in *Restatement Second* §315.

The rights of third party beneficiaries do not present a similar issue in Jewish law for the simple reason that the issue is one of contract and because Jewish law, strictly speaking, does not recognize the enforceability of contracts *qua* contracts. That is to say that Jewish law does not distinguish contracts from promises. Hence, words of contract do not generate legal obligations any more so than do words of promise. Certainly, moral obligations of greater or lesser degree can arise from such undertakings, but moral obligations are not enforceable in the manner of legally valid undertakings. But, of course, Jewish legal practice does employ and validate contracts. The enigma is resolved upon recognition that contracts are valid and enforceable in Jewish law only if entered into pursuant to *ḳinyan*, a formal act usually in the form of delivering a *ṣuddar* or "kerchief". Technically, the purpose of *ḳinyan* is not to generate an obligation but to effect a conveyance. Transfer of title to any property, real or personal, requires an appropriate act of *ḳinyan*. The *ḳinyan* giving effect to a contract also represents a conveyance, *viz*., conveyance of a *shi'bud ha-guf*, i.e. a lien *in personam*. A personal servitude represents a circumscribed property interest just as title to a slave represents a virtually unlimited property interest. A lien against property flows from the servitude by virtue of the doctrine that a person's property serves as his surety. The conveyance of a servitude *in personam* makes it possible to seize property in the event of non-performance of the contract. Absent valid reconveyance of a lien *in personam*, no cause of action can arise. Thus, in effect, contracts are reduced to conveyances.

A contract providing for a third party beneficiary is, in effect, a

12 *Choate, Hall & Stewart v. SCA Serv. Inc.*, 378 Mass. 535, 392 N.E.2d 1045 (Mass. 1979).

13 *Fourth Ocean Putnam Corp v. Interstate Wrecking Co.*, 66 N.Y.2d 38, 495 N.Y.S.2d 1, 485 N.E.2d 208 (N.Y. 1985).

conveyance by the promisor of a lien *in personam* directly to the beneficiary. There is no problem arising from lack of privity because, since the contract is not really a contract but a conveyance, there could not be a requirement of privity. Furthermore, the question of passing of consideration by the promisee, who is really a stranger to the contract *cum* conveyance, does not present the same problem as it does in other legal systems because consideration is not required to give effect to alienation of property or to generate a property interest in another party.[14] Hence, Jewish law does not require consideration in order to generate a binding contract. But it does require *ḳinyan*. *Ḳinyan* on the part of the promisee, who is really a stranger to the transaction, is efficacious on behalf of the beneficiary through operation of the principle of *zekhiyyah*, herein defined as constructive agency.

## B. *Zekhiyyah* As an Operative Principle

The Gemara, *Ḳiddushin* 42a, derives the principle of *zekhiyyah* from the biblical verse describing the apportionment of the Land of Israel: "And you shall take one prince from each tribe to take possession of the land" (*Numbers* 34:18).[15] The function of the designated princes was to take title and to apportion the land among the members of each tribe. The ordinary principles of agency do not seem to provide a legal basis for effecting those ends since, even assuming that there was formal appointment by the populace of the princes as agents, there were also minors among those

14 The absence of a requirement for consideration in order to consummate transfer of title is evidenced by the fact that title may be transferred by means of other forms of *ḳinyan* as well, e.g. a chattel may be transferred by "pulling" (*meshikhah*) or "lifting" (*hagbahah*) etc., and real property may be transferred by deed or *ḥazaḳah* (e.g. plowing a furrow in a field, the antecedent of livery of seisen in common law). Even *ṣuddar* (delivery of a "kerchief") does not function as a symbolic "peppercorn" consideration since, according to one opinion recorded in the Gemara, the *ṣuddar* is delivered by the person who alienates title rather than by the person coming into possession. Cf. Asher Gulak, *Yeṣodei ha-Mishpaṭ ha-Ivri* (Berlin: Dvir, 1922), II, 40ff. and Menachem Elon, "Contract", *Encyclopedia Judaica* (Jerusalem: Keter, 1992), V, 924f. Of course, *ḳeṣef,* i.e. payment of money, serves as a *ḳinyan* with regard to real property and, according to one opinion in the Gemara, for chattel as well.

15 For a discussion of the ramifications of this interpretive analysis of *Numbers* 34:18 see *Encyclopedia Talmudit*, XII (Jerusalem: Yad Harav Herzog, 5727), 135-136.

entitled to receive parcels of property and a minor lacks legal capacity to appoint an agent. That problem is resolved by the talmudic formulation of the notion of *zekhiyyah* as a biblical institution enabling an individual to act on behalf of another provided that the act redounds entirely to the latter's benefit.[16]

The simplest explanation of the theory underlying the principle of *zekhiyyah* is that it represents a form of agency[17] based upon the presumption that every person desires the unmitigated benefit accruing through operation of *zekhiyyah*, i.e. "we are witnesses" (*anan sahadi*) to the fact that, had the beneficiary been consulted he would happily have authorized the agent to act on his behalf[18] (and hence the principle of *zekhiyyah* may aptly be termed "constructive agency"). Alternatively, *zekhiyyah* may be understood as tantamount to agency simply by operation of law (*gezeirat ha-katuv*), i.e. the legal system itself, in appropriate circumstances, authorizes any person to act as an agent for another.[19] Among the authorities who propound a theory of agency in explaining *zekhiyyah*, some maintain that, in addition to serving as the agent of the beneficiary, the person performing the act of *zekhiyyah* also serves as an agent of the benefactor.[20] Other authorities maintain that *zekhiyyah* is a completely novel legal institution entirely distinct from the notion of agency,[21] at least in theory if not in effect.[22]

16 For amplification of this point insofar as apportionment of the Land of Israel is concerned see *Encyclopedia Talmudit, ibid.*, at 136 and 135 n.12.

17 For a list of authorities who subscribe to this view see *ibid.*, at 136 n.13.

18 See *ibid.*, n.14.

19 See *ibid.*, at 137 n.17, and n.26. This thesis was developed by, and is primarily associated with, *Ketsot ha-Ḥoshen* 105:1.

20 See *ibid.*, at 136 n.14.

21 See *ibid.*, at 137 and sources cited *ibid.*, nn.18 and 24. *Ketsot ha-Ḥoshen* 105:1 and *Ḥiddushei ha-Rim, Giṭṭin* 11b, categorize *zekhiyyah* according to these authorities as being in the nature of a "hand" (*mi-ṭa'am yad*), i.e. the benefactor's hand becomes, in effect, an extension of the hand of the beneficiary. R. Chaim Soloveichik, *Ḥiddushei ha-Grah al ha-Shas*, (Jerusalem, 5729), 191, asserts that, even according to these authorities, *zekhiyyah* is, in effect, a novel form of agency that is available even to minors who do not have the capacity to appoint an agent. The position of R. Chaim is cited and discussed by R. Baruch Ber Leibowitz, *Birkat Shmu'el, Ḳiddushin*, nos. 10 and 15. Cf. *Imre Binah, Hilkhot Gevi'at Ḥov*, no.29, sec.4 and *Ḥiddushei R. Shimon Shkop, Giṭṭin*, no.4.

22 See R. Chaim Halberstam, *Teshuvot Divrei Ḥayyim*, I, *Even ha-Ezer*, no.87,

Perhaps the most obvious application of the principle of *zekhiyyah* is with regard to taking title to abandoned property on behalf of another individual. For example, a man may chance upon an abandoned piece of jewelry that he deems to be appropriate for his wife. If, while picking up the jewelry, the husband declares, "I take title to this jewelry on behalf of my wife," title immediately vests in his wife and the husband cannot subsequently claim title for himself, as would be the case in other legal systems. Title vests in the wife immediately despite the fact that at no time did the wife appoint her husband as an agent to act on her behalf in taking title to chance findings and at no time did the husband enter into a contract with his wife to do so.

Historically, a concept essentially analogous to *zekhiyyah* appears in the principle of international law that provided that a subject may seize newly discovered territory in the name of his sovereign. Thus, for example, Sir Walter Raleigh laid claim to what was to become Virginia in the name of Queen Elizabeth I of England and the Queen thereby acquired sovereign rights. Sovereignty, however, is not to be equated with ordinary property interests. No concept analogous to *zekhiyyah* is found in any area of domestic common law.

## II. *Zekhiyyah of a Get on Behalf of a Wife*

The principle of *zekhiyyah* is operative only when the act redounds to the unmitigated benefit of the beneficiary, e.g. acquisition of property that is *res nullius* or performance of *ḳinyan* in property that is to vest as a gift.[23] Thus, in ordinary circumstances, *zekhiyyah* is of no avail in acceptance of a bill of divorce on behalf of a wife because, although delivery of the bill of divorce effects a release from marital bonds and engenders capacity to contract another marriage, divorce also serves to extinguish the husband's marital obligations with the result that the wife no longer has a claim for support

who asserts that this notion of *zekhiyyah* is not at all applicable to divorce since there is no financial interest involved "for the wife is not [the chattel] of the husband." According to *Divrei Ḥayyim*, *zekhiyyah*, to be relevant with regard to divorce, must be in the guise of agency.

23 For citation of conflicting authorities with regard to the efficacy of *zekhiyyah* in situations of immediate benefit but of consequential results that are not beneficial see *Sedei Ḥemed, Kellalim, ma'arekhet zayin,* sec.22 and *Encyclopedia Talmudit*, XII, 139, nn.40 and 41.

and maintenance and loses other marital benefits as well.[24] Even if it is known that the wife despises her husband, the benefit to her is not unmitigated. Hence no unauthorized person is empowered to accept a bill of divorce on her behalf.

The Gemara, *Yevamot* 118b, questions whether *zekhiyyah* may effectively be employed in executing a divorce in situations of marital discord in which the wife has actively sought a divorce. The Gemara's conclusion is apparently in the negative. However, some authorities[25] maintain that the Gemara leaves the question unresolved. Accordingly, those authorities rule that, if a divorce is executed on the basis of *zekhiyyah* in instances of marital discord in which the wife has demanded a divorce, it serves to engender a state of doubt, i.e. the validity of the divorce is doubtful, and hence the wife finds herself having the indeterminate status of a woman who is "doubtfully married, doubtfully divorced."

A wife's announced desire, or even persistent demand, that the husband grant her a divorce does not suffice to render the divorce an unmitigated benefit or an absolute *zekhut*. The Palestinian Talmud, *Giṭṭin* 6:1, explains that the principle of *zekhiyyah* cannot be invoked in such cases because the *geṭ* must be a benefit to the wife at the moment of its acceptance on her behalf. Thus, even if the wife had previously demanded a *geṭ*, she may have undergone a change of heart and have been in a different frame of mind at the time of its delivery. Subsequent reiteration of her earlier expressed desire to be divorced is not sufficient to establish that her frame of mind was constant throughout the intervening period.

The Gemara, *Yevamot* 118b, similarly questions whether a divorce executed on the basis of *zekhiyyah* is valid when it is motivated by the husband's desire to release his wife from the requirement of levirate marriage (*yibbum*). The situation discussed involved a childless and gravely ill husband. Since there always exists a possibility of recovery, and recognizing that in the event of the husband's recovery the divorce would not be to the wife's benefit, the Gemara outlines a procedure that calls for a conditional divorce to be effective only retroactively upon the death of the husband. The issue, according to *Rashi, ad locum*, and Rabbenu Nissim, *Giṭṭin* 11b, is whether or not a woman might prefer levirate marriage to widowhood or, according to *Toṣafot Yeshanim, ad locum*, whether the wife, in some

24 See *Encyclopedia Talmudit*, XII, 158 and sources cited *ibid.*, at n.231.

25 *Rabbenu Nissim*, *Giṭṭin*, 62b, cited by *Shulḥan Arukh*, *Even ha-Ezer* 140:5, as "some say."

particular situations, might not actually desire her brother-in-law as a marriage partner. If she does prefer marriage to her brother-in-law to widowhood, the divorce is not at all to her benefit. The Gemara leaves the matter unresolved. Accordingly, *Rambam, Hilkhot Geirushin* 9:21, and *Shulḥan Arukh, Even ha-Ezer* 145:10, rule that the *geṭ* is of questionable validity. Consequently, in such situations, marriage to the brother-in-law is forbidden because marriage between a woman and her former husband's brother is biblically prohibited other than in the presence of an unequivocal levirate obligation, but the wife nevertheless requires *ḥalitsah* in order to be free to contract a marriage with some other man. However, in our day, since levirate marriage is no longer practiced, many latter-day decisors rule that divorce under such circumstances is an unmitigated benefit.[26] That line of reasoning is particularly cogent if the brother-in-law is married since, subsequent to the edicts of Rabbenu Gershom, he can neither divorce his own wife against her will nor, according to many authorities, take a second wife even in fulfillment of the *mitsvah* of *yibbum*.[27]

As noted by *Bet Yoṣef, Even ha-Ezer* 140, and *Shulḥan Arukh, Even ha-Ezer* 140:5, some authorities maintain that *zekhiyyah* is operative with regard to a wife who has committed adultery. An adulteress is forbidden to consort with her husband, who does not have the option of condoning the adultery, and also forfeits any and all claims for further support and maintenance. Accordingly, those authorities regard divorce on behalf of an adulteress to be an unmitigated benefit. Other authorities, whose position is accepted by *Rema, ad locum*, maintain that *zekhiyyah* is of no avail even in such instances on the grounds that, although the divorce does not prejudice the wife's interests, it does not necessarily provide any benefit, particularly since she may have no desire to enter into another marital relationship. *Noda bi-Yehudah, Even ha-Ezer, Mahadura Ḳamma*, nos. 70 and 92, asserts that even in the case of an adulteress, divorce may be prejudicial to her interests since as a feme sole she may become subject to sexual harassment.

Nevertheless, *Rema* agrees that *zekhiyyah* may be employed to give effect to a divorce on behalf of a woman who has become an apostate and who "lives among the gentiles". In such a case it is presumed that the woman engages in adulterous sexual activity on an ongoing basis. Divorce, then, serves to rescue her from ongoing violations of the prohibition against

26 See sources cited in *Encyclopedia Talmudit*, XII, 162, nn.278 and 280.

27 For other situations of impending levirate obligation in which divorce may be an unmitigated benefit see *Encyclopedia Talmudit*, XII, 163.

adultery and, since she enjoys none of the legal or actual benefits of marriage, divorce, for such a woman, represents an absolute and unmitigated benefit.[28]

## III. *Zekhiyyah on behalf of a Husband in Executing a Geṭ*

### A. *Zakhin me-Adam*

Invocation of the principle of constructive agency in situations in which divorce is an unmitigated benefit for the husband is far more complex and of far more recent origin. The classic case involves a husband whose wife is mentally incompetent and hence cannot presently be divorced. The husband is prevented from marrying another woman by virtue of the edict of Rabbenu Gershom banning polygamy. The standard procedure in such cases is to grant a *hetter me'ah rabbanim*, i.e. dispensation to take a second wife, on the condition that the husband place the value of his mentally incompetent wife's *ketubah* in escrow, draft a bill of divorce and appoint an agent to deliver the instrument to his wife when and if she regains the requisite mental capacity to accept delivery of the *geṭ*.[29]

In the eighteenth century, the scholars of Lissa, citing *Mishneh le-Melekh, Hilkhot Geirushin* 6:3, raised an objection to the validity of such divorces. *Mishneh le-Melekh* rules that a divorce effected by an agent designated under such circumstances is invalid because of the principle governing agency formulated by the Gemara, *Nazir* 12b, declaring that an agent can be designated to perform only such acts as the principal himself has the capacity to perform at the time of designation. In effect, the halakhic rules governing agency stipulate that the power of an agent can be no greater than that enjoyed by the principal at the inception of the agency. Put somewhat differently, a principal can authorize an agent to act in his stead, but only to perform an act that the principal might himself validly perform at the time that he grants authority to the agent to do so. Thus, declares the Gemara, an agent cannot be designated for the purpose of contracting a marriage with a woman who is already married at the time of the inception of

28 For additional sources reflecting this controversy see *Encyclopedia Talmudit*, XII, 165f. See also sources cited in *Otsar ha-Poṣḳim*, I (Jerusalem: Defuṣ Bet Yetomim Diṣḳin, 5707), *Even ha-Ezer* 1:10, sec.73:2.

29 For a discussion of the purpose served by this practice and a survey of the authorities who required the procedure as well as of those who challenged the validity of such a *geṭ* see *Otsar ha-Poṣḳim*, I, *Even ha-Ezer* 1:10, sec.72:30-35. See also, *infra*, note 41 and accompanying text.

the agency with the result that even if the woman subsequently became widowed or divorced the agent lacks capacity to act on behalf of the principal. Although some authorities disagree, *Mishneh le-Melekh* asserts that the agent has no authority to act on behalf of the principal even if the principal expressly stipulates that the agency is to become effective only upon the woman's attainment of capacity to contract a valid marriage. The husband could not himself execute a divorce of his mentally incompetent wife; hence, argued the scholars of Lissa, the husband has no power to appoint an agent to act on his behalf until such time as his wife's mental health is restored.

As recorded by *Markevet ha-Mishneh* (Frankfurt am Oder, 5611), *Hilkhot Geirushin* 6:3, the practice of appointing an agent to effect a divorce of this nature was defended by a certain scholar described as the aged chief rabbi of Krotoszyn. That authority advanced an argument asserting that the normative rule is that designation of an agent is valid even if the agency cannot be carried out at the time of designation. Moreover, he contended that, even if it is conceded that a bill of divorce executed under such circumstances could not be regarded as valid on the basis of the rules of agency, it would nevertheless be valid by operation of the principle of *zekhiyyah*. He argued that, in designating an agent, the husband has signified his desire to be divorced and has indicated that he regards severance of the marital bonds to be beneficial to him. Thus, designation of an agent, although ineffective in accomplishing its avowed purpose, is nevertheless evidence of a mental state that enables the agent to act, not on the basis of his designation as an agent, but on the basis of the principle of *zekhiyyah*. Moreover, the divorce is objectively beneficial to the husband since the *hetter me'ah rabbanim* is valid only during the period of his wife's mental incompetence. Thus, with the recovery of mental capacity by the first wife, the husband, in the absence of a divorce, would be in transgression of the ban of Rabbenu Gershom.

*Markevet ha-Mishneh* dismisses this view with the argument that *zekhiyyah* operates only as a principle of vesture of title (*zakhin le-adam*) but is of no avail as a means of giving effect to an attempt to divest an individual of property or of a privilege (*zakhin me-adam lo amrinan*). The rationale underlying that distinction is that loss of any kind is, by definition, a disadvantage. On balance, the benefit of divestiture may outweigh the gain of continued possession; *zekhiyyah*, however, is operative only in situations of unmitigated benefit. *Teshuvot Ḥatam Ṣofer, Even ha-Ezer*, I, no.11, s.v. *naḥzor*, dismisses that contention with the observation that it is common practice[30] to invoke the principle of *zekhiyyah* in selling *ḥamets* belonging to others at the appropriate hour on the eve of Passover.

An alternative rationale for this distinction lies in the fact that although transfer of title does require *da'at* or intent, it does not always require the *da'at* or intent of the individual in whom title is vested. Thus, a minor, who by statute is regarded as lacking *da'at* or intellectual capacity for the requisite mental determination, can nevertheless be the beneficiary of a gratuitous transfer. In such instances the *da'at* or intent of the adult conveying title suffices (*da'at aḥeret maḳneh).* Similarly, in cases of *zakhin le-adam,* the self-appointed agent need perform only the physical act of *ḳinyan*; the requisite mental act is supplied by the person conveying title. In contradistinction, divestiture of title always requires *da'at* or intent on the part of the person transferring title. Accordingly, it has been argued that *zekhiyyah,* since it involves a self-designated agent, is available for physical acts but is not operative with regard to any act that requires a determinant mental state, e. g. conveyance of property or the granting of a *geṭ.* This distinction is reflected in the comments of *Ketsot ha-Ḥoshen* 105:1.

The issue of whether the principle of *zekhiyyah* is operative only for the purpose of vesting title or whether it is applicable to alienation of title (*zakhin me-adam*) as well and the circumstances in which it may be invoked in order to do so is a matter of considerable controversy among latter-day authorities.[31] A number of latter-day authorities maintain that resolution of that question is directly contingent upon the nature of the principle of *zekhiyyah*. They assert that, if the principle of *zakhin me-adam* is tantamount to constructive agency, it is available in all instances of benefit in which explicit agency itself is operative. If, on the other hand, *zekhiyyah* is a novel legal construct, it may be regarded as limited to matters similar to the biblical paradigm of "each prince", i.e. to acquisition of title as was the case with regard to division and apportionment of the Land of Israel.[32]

R. Isaac Elchanan Spektor, in both his *Be'er Yitsḥaḳ, Oraḥ Ḥayyim,*

30 Nevertheless, *Ḥatam Ṣofer, loc. cit.*, asserts that, the principle of *zekhiyyah* notwithstanding, a new bill of divorce must be drafted by the agent subsequent to the recovery of the wife because of a completely different consideration.

31 See, for example, *Zikhron Yonatan, Even ha-Ezer*, no.2, sec.57; *Ḥiddushei ha-Rim, Even ha-Ezer* 121; *Teshuvot Noda ba-She'arim*, no.9; and *Teshuvot Roshi ba-Shamayim*, no.16.

32 See *Encycolpedia Talmudit*, XII, 149-150 and accompanying notes as well as p. 167, nn.326 and 327.

no.1 and his *Ein Yitsḥaḳ*, *Even ha-Ezer*, no.2, sec.4 and no.51, sec.10, asserts that *zakhin me-adam* cannot serve to remedy defective agency. Thus, for example, if agency fails because of the principal's own lack of capacity to effect the desired end, the "agent" cannot give effect to his act on the basis of *zakhin me-adam*. R. Isaac Elchanan Spektor asserts that explicit appointment of an agent is tantamount to a declaration that the principal wishes to give effect to the specified act only through the instrumentality of agency and hence appointment of an agent constitutes a renunciation of any advantage that might accrue on the basis of *zakhin me-adam*.

Many latter-day scholars have refused to accept the concept of *zakkin me-adam* and to employ it in cases of divorce. In part, their position is based upon the comments of a highly respected authority, *Ketsot ha-Ḥoshen* 243:8, who completely dismisses the application of *zekhiyyah* in matters requiring a determinate mental state. Thus, for example, the editors of *Otsar ha-Poṣḳim* (Jerusalem, 5707), *Even ha-Ezer* 1:10, sec.70:31, cite *Ketsot ha-Ḥoshen* as well as others who accepted his view and, although declining to formulate a definitive position, conclude that one should not act in a manner contrary to that view.

That attitude notwithstanding, in the modern era the principle of *zakhin me-adam* was applied in the area of divorce by a noted scholar, R. Eliyahu Klatzkin of Lublin. In 1922, in the aftermath of World War I, Rabbi Klatzkin received a plea for help from R. Mordechai Horowitz of Zamosc in alleviating the plight of an *agunah*, a woman whose husband did not return from the war and was presumed to be dead but who lacked actual proof of his death. Mobilization of the Polish army took place in 1914. Conscripts from the surrounding area were brought to Zamosc. Recognizing the likelihood that not all of the soldiers would survive the armed conflict and concerned for the plight of their wives, Rabbi Horowitz, in accordance with sound halakhic practice, encouraged each of the soldiers to designate a scribe as his agent to draft a bill of divorce, witnesses to sign the instrument and yet another individual to serve as his agent for the delivery of the *geṭ* to his wife. The purpose of that procedure was to make it possible to draft a bill of divorce at some future time in the unfortunate eventuality that the husband would fail to return from battle but that no satisfactory evidence that he was killed in action would be forthcoming. It subsequently transpired that one of the soldiers who followed the instructions of Rabbi Horowitz, a resident of Traningrad, failed to return and was presumed to have perished but there was no evidence substantiating his death. Unfortunately, the person designated by that soldier as his agent for the delivery of the *geṭ* had also died in the early days of the war.[33]

R. Eliyahu Klatzkin, *Dvar Halakhah, milu'im*, no.93, accepts the notion that in instances of a *hetter me'ah rabbanim* involving a mentally incompetent wife, a *geṭ* can be drafted for the woman upon her recovery in reliance upon the principle of *zakhin me-adam*.[34] The problem is that, unlike instances involving a husband of a mentally incapacitated wife who has remarried on the basis of a *hetter me'ah rabbanim*, it is not immediately clear that, in the case confronting Rabbi Klatzkin, divorce would have been a benefit to the husband. Assuming that the husband was still alive — and, if not, the *geṭ* would have been entirely superfluous — he might well still have anticipated and desired resumption of the marital relationship at some point. Rabbi Klatzkin counters that argument by developing a novel thesis to the effect that, since the husband failed to return to his wife for a period of several years after cessation of hostilities and had provided no information with regard to his whereabouts, the husband thereby forfeited his right to demand that his wife fulfill any of her wifely duties and indeed he might be compelled by her to execute a *geṭ*. In such circumstances, argues Rabbi Klatzkin, the marriage no longer represents a benefit of any kind to the husband and hence the divorce represents an unmitigated benefit.

In a subsequent case reported in his *Milu'ei Even*, no.29, Rabbi Klatzkin went far beyond his original position.[35] The latter situation involved a

33 Assuming that the agent need not personally hear the husband appointing him, that problem might have been obviated by naming multiple agents. See R. Malki'el Zvi Tennenbaum, *Teshuvot Divrei Malki'el*, IV, no.156, who, in the case of soldiers conscripted in the army, advises appointing all inhabitants of a city as agents. R. Shiloh Rafael, *Torah she-be'al Peh*, XI (5729), 128, reports that during World War II it was the practice of the Chief Rabbinate of Palestine to have soldiers designate "each of the residents of Jerusalem" as an agent. See, however, *infra*, pp.22-27.

34 A letter authored by R. Yoṣef Shlomoh Shabbetai Horowitz, the chief rabbi of Zamosc, is also included in *Dvar Halakhah*. Rabbi Horowitz does not refer to the herein cited position of Rabbi Isaac Elchanan Spektor who maintains that designation of an agent is tantamount to disavowal of the advantages available through operation of *zakhin me-adam* but notes that, in the case presented for his consideration, the husband did not designate a specific agent, or even choose to avail himself of the expedient of agency, on his own accord, but was simply acquiescing in the instructions of the rabbi. Hence, he argues, there is no reason to assume that the husband desired a particular agent to act on his behalf to the exclusion of others who might act in reliance upon the principle of *zakhin me-adam*.

35 This position is reiterated by Rabbi Klatzkin and applied in yet another case

woman abandoned by her husband immediately after their wedding and whose subsequent whereabouts were unknown. Two years after her husband's disappearance the woman entered into a second marriage. Unbeknown to the wife, prior to the marriage the young man had, on occasion, behaved in a deranged manner. The possibility existed that the groom's mental illness was of sufficient gravity to constitute an undisclosed "grave defect" that would serve to void the marriage. Hence, the validity of the marriage was a matter of doubt. If the first marriage was a nullity, no *geṭ* would have been required. If, however, the first marriage was indeed valid, the second marriage was a nullity and constituted an adulterous relationship. Hence, as an adulteress, the woman was precluded from resuming a marital relationship with her first husband. Accordingly, argued Rabbi Klatzkin, the marital state no longer represented a benefit of any kind to the first husband. Consequently, Rabbi Klatzkin ruled that the principle of *zakhin me-adam* might be invoked in drafting and executing a *geṭ* to ameliorate the plight of the *agunah*.

### B. The Requirement that the Scribe and Witnesses Be Personally Instructed by the Husband

The additional barrier to be surmounted in this case lies in the fact that not only had the husband failed to designate an agent for delivery of the *geṭ*, but unlike the earlier case in which only the agent for delivery of the *geṭ* had died, the husband had not issued a face-to-face directive to the scribe to write the instrument on his behalf. The rule, as recorded in *Shulḥan Arukh, Even ha-Ezer* 120:4, is that the scribe and witnesses must hear directly from the husband that he instructs them to draft and sign the *geṭ*.[36] That provision reflects the requirement that a bill of divorce be written specifically on behalf of a particular husband and a particular wife. The halakhic presumption is that the requisite intent cannot be evoked unless the scribe and the witnesses actually hear the voice of the husband.[37] In the case of a husband who has absconded without issuing such instructions, it is of course impossible for

---

in his *Devarim Aḥadim*, sec.44.

36 For a survey of the various considerations involved and the differing opinions with regard to the validity of a *geṭ* executed other than in this manner see *Encyclopedia Talmudit*, V (Jerusalem, 5753), 570-574.

37 For a fuller discussion of the rationale underlying this requirement see *infra*, pp. 35-36.

the scribe or the witnesses to hear those instructions from the husband.

In deflecting that objection, Rabbi Klatzkin relies on a previous ruling of an earlier scholar, R. Israel Hapstein, popularly known as the Maggid of Koznitz (Kozienice) recorded in the latter's *Bet Yisra'el.* A young man, a native of Chmielnik, married and established residence in Staszow. A year later the husband left home, apparently to seek his fortune, and was not heard from for a period of twelve years. Some eight years after his departure, a contingent of Prussian soldiers were quartered in Jewish homes in Staszow for a period of time. A number of soldiers were quartered in the home of the wife and during their stay the soldiers became aware of the husband's disappearance. Some time later, one of the soldiers who was then stationed in Warsaw wrote that he had identified the husband as one of a group of prisoners under his supervision. The wife sent her brother to Warsaw to search for her husband but to no avail. Later, the same soldier wrote once again to inform the wife that her husband had escaped and crossed over to the foreign army.

Shortly afterwards, foreign soldiers passed through Staszow and remained in that city for a period of time. One of the soldiers conversed with the townspeople in Yiddish, a phenomenon that aroused a measure of curiosity. Upon closer scrutiny, one of the townspeople recognized the Yiddish-speaking soldier as a friend of his youth and as none other than the missing husband. Subsequently, other people, including his wife, claimed to recognize him. When confronted, he admitted only that he was a former resident of the area. As a test, some of the townspeople pointed to various women and asked with regard to each one whether the woman was his wife. Each time the soldier answered in the negative. Finally, they brought the abandoned wife and asked the same question. The soldier averted his face and refused to converse further in Yiddish but inquired in a foreign language after the welfare of the woman's sister. The matter was reported to the foreign officer in command of the soldiers who ordered two of his soldiers to examine the man in question in order to ascertain whether he was circumcised. Those soldiers claimed that he was not. Nevertheless, the townspeople persisted in demanding that the gentleman reveal the truth. Finally, on *Shabbat, erev Shevu'ot* 5559, shortly before leaving the city, the soldier acknowledged his identity and gave assurances that, if his wife would follow him to the next encampment, he would execute a *geṭ*.

Toward the end of that summer a letter addressed to the rabbi and officers of the community was received from the earlier-mentioned foreign officer. In that letter the officer identified the missing husband and described him as a

"Jewish apostate". The officer indicated that he was writing at the behest of the soldier who was seriously ill and feared that he would never return home. He further reported that the soldier had expressed a desire to execute a *geṭ* in order to enable his wife to seek another husband and had requested the officer to write to the Jewish community of Staszow to that effect. Later in the winter a second letter arrived. The soldiers had again approached the officer to ask if he had received any news from Staszow and if the divorce had been executed. Accordingly, the officer again requested that, if the communal officials had not already done so, they arrange the divorce without delay and inform him that the request had been honored. The officer's letter was countersigned in Hebrew script by the husband and bore the Hebrew signature of a witness. The communal leaders to whom the letter was addressed responded both with a letter to the officer requesting him to arrange for the soldier to present himself before the nearest rabbi and with an enclosed open letter soliciting the assistance of the local Jewish community. Seven weeks later a reply was received from the officer reporting that the letter of instruction arrived too late to be acted upon because the soldier had been shot and had died of his wounds immediately thereafter.

Of course, were the officer's letter to have been accepted as sufficient proof of the husband's death, no further action would have been required. Indeed, that issue is addressed in *Bet Yisra'el* but, for reasons beyond the scope of this discussion, the testimony regarding the husband's death was found to be inadequate. Nevertheless, since the husband had no issue, the Maggid of Koznitz as well as a number of renowned rabbinic scholars with whom he corresponded and whose responses are included in *Bet Yisra'el*, did require that, in addition to the execution of a *geṭ* in accordance with the husband's original instructions, the wife undergo *ḥalitsah* because of the possibility that the husband had indeed died.

The major issue addressed in *Bet Yisra'el* is whether the letter sent by the foreign captain and countersigned by the husband served as a valid appointment of an agent for execution of a *geṭ*. The letter could serve as the basis for such authorization only if it might be construed as a memorial of prior oral designation of a scribe and witnesses by the husband and, in addition, if it is agreed that oral designation of a scribe and witnesses is valid even if such designation takes place out of their earshot or, in the alternative, if the signature of the husband might itself be construed as designation of the scribe and witnesses and it is agreed that written authorization is equivalent to oral designation.[38] If written authorization is sufficient, it is because the reading of the letter and of the husband's signature by the scribe and witnesses is regarded as tantamount to the scribe and witnesses having heard the husband's oral designation. Also addressed by *Bet Yisra'el* is the evidentiary problem of the officer's probity as well as the authenticity of the letter and its appended signatures.

Rabbi Klatzkin cites *Bet Yisra'el* as precedent for the position that the scribe and witnesses can effectively perform their functions specifically on behalf of the husband (*le-shemo*) and wife (*le-shemah*) even if they do not actually hear the husband's command and applies that principle to instances of self-designation predicated upon the principle of *zakhin me-adam*. In point of fact, however, the thrust of *Bet Yisra'el*'s own responsum is that the act of writing is comparable to physical gesticulation. The Mishnah, *Giṭṭin* 67b, declares that designation of a scribe and witnesses may validly be accomplished on the basis of shaking of the head and the like. In effect, the Mishnah categorizes such physical gestures as "body language". The author of *Bet Yisra'el* equates penning a signature with body language which, in turn, is tantamount to speech. Thus, *Bet Yisra'el* does not assert that the written word is equivalent to the oral word but that the act of writing is a form of body language manifesting intent.

A responsum authored by R. Pinchas ha-Levi Horowitz, renowned as the author of the *Hafla'ah*, is incorporated by the Maggid of Koznitz in his *Bet Yisra'el*. *Bet Yisra'el* relies heavily upon *Hafla'ah* as a pre-eminent authority who endorsed his ruling. However, an examination of *Hafla'ah*'s responsum reveals that *Hafla'ah* regards equation of writing with body language to be a matter of doubt. *Hafla'ah* also assumes that the husband did indeed designate a scribe and witnesses orally and that the letter merely memorialized the antecedent oral designation. The validity of oral designation not actually heard by the scribe and witnesses is categorized by *Hafla'ah* as a matter of doubt. Nevertheless, he concurs in the Maggid of Koznitz's permissive ruling on the basis of a *ṣefeḳ ṣefeiḳa*, or "double doubt", i.e. although neither position, *viz*., neither equation of writing with body language nor the validity of oral designation not heard by the scribe and witnesses, can be accepted unequivocally, nevertheless, each of those positions is sufficiently authoritative so that, in combination, the two considerations can be relied upon in practice.

38 That view is reiterated by R. Eliyahu Klatzkin in his *Devarim Aḥadim*, sec.44, in a discussion of another case in which there was no oral designation.

Neither the reasoning of *Bet Yisra'el* nor the reasoning of *Hafla'ah* is applicable to the thesis propounded by Rabbi Klatzkin. Moreover, it is striking that nowhere in the entire collection of responsa presented by *Bet Yisra'el*, numbering well over one hundred pages, is there the slightest hint that the problem of the unfortunate woman, whose plight each of the respondents sought to alleviate, could be remedied by application of the principle of *zakhin me-adam.* To this writer, that absence is not a fallacious *argumentum ex silentio* but palpable evidence of rejection of that potential solution.

The question of whether the principle of *zakhin me-adam* fails as an expedient in facilitating execution of a *geṭ* by reason of the absence of a direct command by the husband to the scribe ordinarily mandated in order to fulfill the requirement of *le-shemah* is closely related to the issue of *kitvu u-tenu*, i.e. "write and give," a procedure in which the husband authorizes others to designate a scribe and witnesses on his behalf. The procedure of *kitvu u-tenu* is relied upon by many authorities in situations in which the husband is unable or unwilling to appear personally before the *bet din.* Other authorities, including *Ḥazon Ish, Even ha-Ezer*, no.85, rule that such a procedure should never be relied upon. *Ramban, Giṭṭin* 66b, and those early-day authorities who adopt his position maintain that a procedure of this nature is unacceptable because of the absence of what, to borrow a term from another area of law, may be termed "privity" between the husband and those subject to his directions.

If the rule that a husband cannot authorize others to designate a scribe and witnesses on his behalf reflects an irrebuttable principle of *Halakhah* to the effect that the quintessential nature of *le-shemah* requires an antecedent auditory event, it is obvious that a *geṭ* cannot be valid on the basis of *zakhin me-adam* by virtue of the fact that the requirement of *le-shemah* requires a direct command. If, however, as some scholars have argued, the problem lies in the mind-set of the scribe and witnesses who, in the absence of a personally received oral directive, are presumed to be less then fully convinced of the determination of the husband to give effect to the *geṭ*, that consideration assuredly does not pertain in situations of *zakhin me-adam.* The very concept of *zekhiyyah* is predicated upon the principle that "we are witnesses" (*anan sahadi*) to the fact that the effect accomplished is firmly and resolutely desired by the person on whose behalf the *geṭ* is performed. Although the underlying rationale is not elucidated by those authorities, apparently both the Maggid of Koznitz and *Hafla'ah* assumed the presumption of the absence of *le-shemah* to be blanket and irrebuttable in nature whereas R. Eliyahu Klatzkin seems to have regarded the presumption to be empirical and psychological in nature and hence not applicable in instances of *zakhin me-adam.*

C. Rejection of *Zakhin me-Adam* in the Execution of a *Geṭ*

Problems even more anguishing than those faced by Rabbi Klatzkin following World War I arose in the wake of World War II. In the post-World War II period the tragedy was not that of a limited numbers of soldiers missing in action but of countless individuals who disappeared during the upheavals of the Holocaust but whose death could not be established by credible evidence. As a result many women became *agunot.* A remedy for the surviving wives in the form of a *geṭ* executed in reliance upon the principle of *zakhin me-adam,* with Rabbi Klatzkin's rulings following World War I serving as a precedent, would certainly have been an enticing solution. It was precisely such a proposal that prompted an examination of Rabbi Klatzkin's earlier-advanced thesis by R. Israel Minzberg, *She'eirit Yisra'el, Even ha-Ezer,* no.8, sec.3.

Rabbi Minzberg curtly dismisses Rabbi Klatzkin's responsum with the comment: "Begging his pardon, he has committed to writing foolish and vacuous words that are inappropriate [even] for a person who knows and is familiar only with the outline of the topic." In demonstrating what he considers to be the untenability of Rabbi Klatzkin's thesis, Rabbi Minzberg points to the halakhic provisions governing situations in which the husband may be compelled to divorce his wife. In such cases, the husband may be coerced by means of physical force, if necessary, until he signals his acquiescence to execution of a *geṭ* by stating verbally, "I so wish" (*Rotseh ani*). All instances in which physical duress is available as a remedy involve situations in which the wife is relieved of all further marital obligations. Hence, in all such cases, religious divorce can only redound to the benefit of the husband by relieving him of all further financial obligations and by making it possible for him to enter into marriage with another woman. If so, queries Rabbi Mintzbeg, why is it necessary to go through the unpleasant process of applying physical force in order to obtain the husband's consent rather than simply executing the divorce by operation of the principle of *zakhin me-adam*? At the very minimum, the requirement for oral acquiescence in the form of "*Rotseh ani*" should indicate that the principle of *zakhim me-adam* is not operative in the face of the husband's previously announced unwillingness to divorce his wife. Moreover, Rabbi Minzberg endeavors to show that the husband's declaration "*Rotseh ani*" is required even in cases in which he has not previously voiced a lack of willingness to divorce his wife.

Absence of a doctrine of *zakhin me-adam* with regard to divorce may be inferred from other talmudic provisions as well. As stated by the Gemara, *Giṭṭin* 29a, the general rule is that an agent cannot appoint a sub-agent for execution of a *geṭ*. The Gemara records a controversy with regard to whether an agent may designate a sub-agent with the specific authorization of the husband. The Gemara, *Giṭṭin* 66b, records a further controversy with regard to whether a *bet din* that has been authorized to execute a *geṭ* may delegate that authority. The normative rule is that such authority can never be delegated. Putting aside the operation of rules of agency, in appointing an agent for the purpose of executing a *geṭ*, the husband has certainly evidenced his desire to be divorced from his wife. If so, why should others not have capacity to act on the husband's behalf on the basis of the principle of *zakhin me-adam*? The clear implication is that the principle of *zakhin me-adam* is of no avail in giving effect to an otherwise invalid divorce.

Rabbi Klatzkin, *Devarim Aḥadim*, sec.113, himself raises a similar objection. In the case of the classic *agunah*, *viz.*, a woman whose husband is missing and presumed dead, the Sages relaxed the rules of evidence and permitted remarriage on the basis of a single witness who testifies to the husband's demise. Why, questions Rabbi Klatzkin, did not the Sages simply advise execution of a *geṭ* on the wife's behalf on the basis of *zakhin me-adam*? Moreover, it may be added, if, as Rabbi Klatzkin maintains, absence for an extended period of time effectively extinguishes the husband's marital privileges, invocation of the principle of *zakhin me-adam* in executing a *geṭ* would eliminate the need for even a single witness and would effectively free many additional *agunot*. Rabbi Klatzkin responds that such a procedure would not be possible until such time as the husband has forfeited his marital prerogatives which, according to Rabbi Klatzkin, does not occur unless he is absent for a period of five years. The Sages, he claims, were concerned for the woman's welfare and did not want to compel her to wait such a long period of time. Rabbi Klatzkin also implies that the Sages did not wish the wife to be prohibited to a *kohen* as a divorcée. Moreover, Rabbi Klatzkin seems to suggest that the Sages feared that general and widespread reliance upon the expedient of *zakhin me-adam* in the case of a missing husband might lead to abuse of the principle by reliance upon *zakhin me-adam* in situations in which invocation of that principle is entirely inappropriate. Hence the Sages sought ways and means to establish a basis to substantiate the death of the husband in order to enable the wife to remarry as a widow.

Rabbi Minzberg further underscores the fact that the opinion of the Maggid of Koznitz does not serve as precedent for Rabbi Klatzkin's ruling. The situation addressed by the Maggid of Koznitz involved an apostate who, according to some authorities,[39] may be compelled to divorce his wife, and with whom, according to all authorities, continued marital relations are forbidden[40] and, moreover, in that instance, as certified by the military officer and evidenced by the husband's own signature, the husband orally requested that the officials of the Jewish community execute a *geṭ* on his behalf.

In his *Dvar Halakhah*, sec.93, Rabbi Klatzkin reports that he was consulted by the rabbi of Zamosc with regard to a woman whose husband had been conscripted at the beginning of World War I and who had not been heard from since that time. Before his induction into the army, the husband designated a scribe and witnesses to draft a *geṭ* as well as an agent to deliver the *geṭ* to his wife. Unfortunately, the agent died during the intervening period. Rabbi Klatzkin ruled that, in the light of the husband's expressed desire to divorce his wife, a substitute agent could be empowered to act on behalf of the husband by virtue of the principle of *zekhiyyah*. In his *Dvar Halakhah, milu'im*, no.122, Rabbi Klatzkin presents a responsum authored by R. Meir Arak concurring in his ruling. Even so, Rabbi Klatzkin was willing to rely upon the sources that he cites in permitting execution of a *geṭ* solely because of the existence of circumstantial evidence indicating that the husband had already died. Although the circumstantial evidence was not sufficiently strong to establish capacity to remarry as a widow and Rabbi Klatzkin was not willing to rely upon the principle of *zekhiyyah* in and of itself in order to validate a *geṭ*, he was willing to permit remarriage on the basis of both factors in combination.

One of the sources upon which Rabbi Klatzkin relies is *Teshuvot Ḥatam Ṣofer*, *Even ha-Ezer*, I, no.11 and *Even ha-Ezer*, II, no.43. As noted earlier, in instances in which a woman becomes mentally incompetent and cannot be divorced, the edict of Rabbenu Gershom banning polygamy is suspended upon issuance of a dispensation signed by one hundred rabbinic authorities. In such cases, the procedure is to draft a *geṭ* and to deposit it with an agent with instructions to deliver the *geṭ* to the wife when she regains the requisite

39 See *Rema*, *Even ha-Ezer* 154:1.

40 See R. Abraham of Regensberg cited in *Mordekhai*, *Yevamot*, sec.108, and *Terumat ha-Deshen*, no.219; see also *Matnot Kehunah*, *Va-Yikra Rabbah* 2:1 and *Shir-haShirim Rabbah* 4:20. Cf., however, *Mordekhai*, *Yevamot*, sec.109; *Teshuvot Maharik*, no.100, *Teshuvot Maharam Alshakar*, no.43; and *Teshuvot Bet Yoṣef* (Jerusalem, 5720), *Dinei Giṭṭin ve-Geirushin*, no.14.

mental capacity. But since the husband could not himself divorce his wife because of her lack of mental capacity, how can he validly appoint an agent to do so even at some future time? *Ḥatam Ṣofer* resolves the problem by postulating that the "agent" does not act in the guise of an agent governed by rules of agency. Rather, an attempt to appoint an agent, even if, in actuality, the appointment fails to establish agency because of some technical deficiency in the designation, is nevertheless conclusive evidence of the principal's desire. Consequently, argues *Ḥatam Ṣofer*, the designated individual may deliver the *geṭ* to the wife upon her recovery by virtue of the principle of *zakhin me-adam*.

Rabbi Minzberg writes that application of *Ḥatam Ṣofer*'s line of reasoning is limited to circumstances in which it is certain that the divorce remains a benefit to the husband at the time of its execution. Otherwise, evidence that the husband desired the *geṭ* at an earlier time is not evidence that he continues to desire a divorce. Accordingly, *Ḥatam Ṣofer* himself declares that the agent may deliver the *geṭ* to the wife upon her recovery only if the husband has remarried in the interim. In such cases it is certain that the *geṭ* remains a benefit for the husband because, absent the *geṭ*, upon recovery of his first wife, the husband, in remaining the consort of a second wife, is in violation of the edict promulgated by Rabbenu Gershom banning polygamy.[41] In all other cases, argues Rabbi Minzberg, there exists the definite possibility that, even if at one time the husband indicated a desire for divorce, he may have subsequently experienced a change of heart. If that did indeed occur, the *geṭ* is no longer a benefit and cannot be regarded as valid on the basis of *zakhin me-adam*.

Rabbi Minzberg reports that Rabbi Klatzkin himself reconsidered and rejected his earlier rulings regarding the *agunah* issue and that, subsequent to

41 This is indeed the position of R. Menachem Mendel Krochmal, *Teshuvot Tsemaḥ Tsedeḳ*, no.67, followed by *Bet Shmu'el*, *Even ha-Ezer* 1:23. There is however a considerable body of opinion that maintains that the husband, even without formally divorcing his first wife, may continue the second marital relationship without violating the edict of Rabbenu Gershom. See sources cited by *Pitḥei Teshuvah*, *Even ha-Ezer* 1:16 and *Otsar ha-Poṣḳim*, *Even ha-Ezer* 1:10, sec.72:17. Indeed, *Teshuvot R. Akiva Eger*, *Mahadura Tinyana,* no.44, and *Divrei Yissaskhar*, no.126, suggest that, if the first wife recovers, the husband may perhaps be permitted to live in a polygamous relationship with both wives. For a discussion of the conflicting opinions regarding the husband's obligation to divorce the first wife upon her recovery and of her obligation to accept a *geṭ*, see *Otsar ha-Poṣḳim* 1:10, secs.72:14 and 72:18.

his emigration to *Erez Yisra'el*, Rabbi Klatzkin requested that Rabbi Minzberg compose and publicize a responsum rebutting those rulings in order that they not be relied upon in future situations.

D. Spiritual Benefit As an Absolute Benefit

It has been argued by some that fulfillment of a halakhic obligation represents an absolute benefit and hence the principle of *zekhiyyah* can be invoked in such cases as a matter of course. The notion that spiritual benefit arising from fulfilling a halakhic obligation to execute a *get* in and of itself constitutes a benefit of a magnitude that renders the principle of *zekhiyyah* operative is asserted in a ruling recorded in *Teshuvot R. Eliyahu Mizrahi* (*Teshuvot ha-Re'em*), no.87. The problem addressed in that responsum concerns a woman whose husband became an apostate. R. Eliyahu Mizrahi rules that a *get* may be accepted in her behalf even though there is no indication that she actually wishes to be divorced. Indeed, *zekhiyyah* is operative despite the talmudic presumption of "*Tav le-meitav tan du mi-le-meitav armelu* -- Better to dwell as two than to dwell alone" (*Bava Kamma* 111a). *Teshuvot ha-Re'em* declares that the divorce is a *zekhut* for the wife of an apostate in that it precludes the possibility of prohibited cohabitation with an apostate, who is treated as a gentile for such purposes, and also greatly diminishes the likelihood that the woman will be enticed to commit other transgressions. *Teshuvot ha-Re'em* regards those benefits to be of utmost significance and to constitute an "absolute benefit" in the sense that, compared to that benefit, the loss of any incidental mundane benefit she may derive from the marriage pales into insignificance. R. Eliyahu Mizrahi maintains that, in such situations, the principle of *zakhim le-adam* is applicable even if the wife refuses a *get* and professes a desire to remain married to the apostate.

In support of that conclusion, R. Eliyahu Mizrahi cites the comment of *Rambam*, *Hilkhot Geirushin* 2:20, explaining why a *get* executed under duress at the command of the *bet din* is valid. In certain limited circumstances, the *bet din* may, if necessary, compel a divorce by beating the husband, if necessary, until he declares, "*Rotseh ani* — I wish it." The conceptual problem is obvious: if, in the enumerated circumstances, the husband's voluntary acquiescence is not needed, why must he declare "*Rotseh ani*?" If, on the other hand, even in such circumstances the *get* must be the product of the husband's free will, how does a declaration made under physical duress satisfy that requirement? *Rambam* explains that every Jew, in his innermost being, wishes to do as the *Torah* commands. At times, however, he may fail to do so because his "evil inclination" gains mastery over him. The evil inclination is concerned only with sensual and mundane pleasure and is quite prepared to renounce such pleasure if the cost is a disproportionate degree of pain. In effect, pleasure and pain are antagonistic vector forces with the result that pain of a sufficient degree causes pleasure to dissipate. Thus, when a person is beaten to the point that his evil inclination is neutralized and he signifies his assent, it is the person's unimpeded "inner will" that is asserting itself. Accordingly, a *geṭ* executed under such circumstances is a product of the husband's free will. Similarly, concludes R. Eliyahu Mizraḥi, in the case of a woman married to an apostate, since separation from her husband is demanded by *Halakhah*, it is certainly a benefit for her to be divorced in order to be preserved from transgression.

R. David ha-Kohen of Corfu, *Teshuvot Redakh, bayit 9, ḥeder* 12, raises an obvious objection to the comparison of the situation of the wife of an apostate to that of a recalcitrant husband. In the latter case, *Halakhah* demands that the husband declare "*Rotseh ani*", i.e. the person's "evil inclination" must also signify acquiescence and, until such a mental state is reached, the *geṭ* cannot be executed. In the case of a third party who accepts a *geṭ* on behalf of the wife who wishes to remain married to her apostate husband there is no declaration of "*Rotseh ani*" and hence there is no evidence of the requisite mental state. Quite to the contrary of the conclusion of *Teshuvot ha-Re'em*, the requirement for a declaration of "*Rotseh ani*" establishes that "spiritual benefit" does not in and of itself constitute an absolute benefit; the requirement of "*Rotseh ani*" demonstrates that in its absence the mundane counterbenefit diminishes the spiritual benefit at least to the point that the principle of *zekhiyyah* is rendered inapplicable.

A Sephardic scholar, R. Moshe Raphael Bula, *Zekhut Mosheh*, no.7, explains that *Teshuvot ha-Re'em* espouses the view of *Rashba*, *Ḳiddushin* 23a, who maintains that a third party may accept a bill of manumission on behalf of a slave even in the face of the slave's announced refusal to be emancipated. *Rashba* maintains that acquiring both the status of a full-fledged Jew with regard to *mitsvot* and the right to marry a Jewess constitutes an "absolute benefit" and is regarded in that light by all people. Hence the slave's protestations to the contrary are to be dismissed as an aberration. To this *Rashba* adds the observation that, were the slave physically present, his master could present him with the bill of manumission even against his will. Therefore, since emancipation is deemed an absolute benefit, other persons can similarly act on his behalf even against his desire. By the same token, maintains R. Eliyahu Mizraḥi, since a woman can be divorced by delivery of a *geṭ* directly to her, even against her will, others can similarly act on her behalf in circumstances in which divorce constitutes an absolute benefit.

E. Consent of the Husband As an Absolute Requirement

Quite obviously, even *Zekhut Mosheh*'s elucidation of R. Eliyahu Mizraḥi's line of reasoning does not serve to establish that *Teshuvot ha-Re'em* may be considered an authoritative precedent for executing a *geṭ* on behalf of a husband on the basis of the principle of *zakhin me-adam*. It is abundantly clear that *Zekhut Mosheh*'s citation of *Rashba* in demonstrating that *zekhiyyah* is operative even against the announced wishes of the person "benefited" thereby serves to demonstrate that *zekhiyyah* can be invoked contrary to the desire of the beneficiary only if the act in question is one that can in some manner be carried out without the beneficiary's consent. That is never the case with regard to a husband's role in execution of a *geṭ*. Even in situations in which coercion of the husband is halakhically mandated, the declaration "*Rotseh ani*" remains a requirement. Hence a divorce is never permissible on the basis of *zakhin me-adam* when such divorce is contrary to the husband's announced wishes.

Methodologically, it is readily demonstrable that any argument that might be formulated to establish the possibility of a divorce without the actual consent of the husband is doomed to failure. *Toṣafot*, *Zevaḥim* 2a, observes that there must always be active intent to write a bill of divorce *le-shemah* because there is no situation whatsoever in which the wife is "*le-geirushin omedet*", i.e. in which dissolution of the relationship must be assumed as a foregone conclusion and hence the marriage is, as it were, "programmed" for divorce. That statement is problematic because there are circumstances in which a wife may demand a *geṭ* and hence, in such situations, divorce is assured by virtue of prescription of law. Hence, at least in such cases, it would appear that *le-shemah* should not be a requirement. R. Akiva Eger, in a responsum appended to his *Drush ve-Ḥiddush*, vol.I,[42] observes that, even in instances in which the husband can be compelled to divorce his wife, the wife enjoys the option of foregoing that prerogative and hence, even in such circumstances, divorce is not a foregone conclusion.

However, the case of the wife of an apostate presents an additional complexity that challenges the statement of *Toṣafot*. The identical

42 See *Drush ve-Ḥiddush R. Akiva Eger* (Brooklyn, 5709), I, 182, s.v. *amnam*.

complexity exists with regard to any other marriage in which the couple is not permitted to live as man and wife. The wife is not entitled to waive her "right" to a divorce and, indeed, both parties may be compelled by the *bet din* to cooperate in the execution of a *geṭ*. Thus it would appear that, in instances in which cohabitation between the marriage partners is forbidden, the wife is indeed *le-geirushin omedet* and the *geṭ* need not be explicitly drafted *le-shemah*. Yet, *Tosafot* declare that the *geṭ* must be explicitly drafted *le-shemah* in all cases without exception. The explanation must be that, when the parties do not desire a *geṭ* and duress must be applied by the *bet din* to effect the *geṭ*, the marriage *qua* marriage cannot be categorized as "*omed le-geirushin*", i.e. dissolution of the marriage cannot be regarded as foregone and inevitable. If, however, acquiescence of the husband is redundant because of the feasibility of a third party acting on his behalf by operation of the principle of *zekhiyyah*, every such marriage would constitute an instance in which the woman is "about to be divorced" and positive intent of *le-shemah* in writing the bill of divorce would be unnecessary. But, since such intent is always required, it must be concluded that there is never a case in which actual consent of the husband is not required.

The question of executing a *geṭ* without the consent or knowledge of the husband on the basis of the principle of *zakhin me-adam* arose again in 1957. The case involved four Yemenite women whose husbands became apostates to Islam and sought to force their wives to convert as well. The women and their children succeeded in escaping to Aden and from there made their way to Petach Tikvah. Since there was no way to obtain *giṭṭin* from their husbands who remained in Yemen, the women became *agunot*. The then Chief Rabbi of Israel, Rabbi Isaac ha-Levi Herzog, sought a basis upon which to permit the women to remarry and sent his written examination of the issues to Rabbi Yechiel Ya'akov Weinberg with a request for the latter's response. That exchange of correspondence is published in Rabbi Weinberg's *Seridei Esh*, III, no.25.

In the course of his discussion, Rabbi Herzog refers to the permissive view of Rabbi Klatzkin. He further writes that, some time earlier, a *bet din* in Italy had ruled that a *geṭ* might be issued on behalf of a recalcitrant husband who refused to heed a decision of the *bet din* ordering him to execute a *geṭ*. Rabbi Herzog reports that he sent a telegram to the Italian authorities admonishing them not to persevere in carrying out their intention to issue such a *geṭ*, lest any subsequent issue of the woman be deemed *mamzerim*.

Rabbi Weinberg dismisses the notion of invoking the principle of *zakhin me-adam* for this purpose and explicitly rejects the earlier-cited thesis of

*Zekhut Mosheh* to the effect that spiritual benefit is regarded as an absolute benefit. Rabbi Weinberg cites the statement of the Gemara, *Ketubot* 11a, declaring that conversion to Judaism on the part of an adult who has already experienced the "taste of sin" is not an unmitigated benefit. The spiritual benefit attendant upon conversion is clearly not regarded as necessarily constituting an absolute benefit. Similarly, argues Rabbi Weinberg, the spiritual benefit that would accrue to the husband in alleviating the plight of an *agunah* by freeing her from the marital bonds does not represent an unmitigated benefit to the husband. Although, in the case of an apostate who abandoned his wife, divorce is in no way detrimental to the husband, it nevertheless does not represent a benefit in the positive sense. The principle of *zakhin me-adam*, contends Rabbi Weinberg, cannot be invoked other than in instances of a positive benefit that is unmitigated in nature.

In an addendum to his responsum, Rabbi Weinberg presents some support for Rabbi Klatzkin's novel view on the basis of the comments of *Petaḥ ha-Bayit*, no.21, sec.6, who similarly maintains that a *geṭ* can be *delivered* to a wife without the consent of the husband in situations in which *zakhin me-adam* is applicable. However, Rabbi Weinberg notes that *Petaḥ ha-Bayit* makes no such statement with regard to the *writing* of the *geṭ*, possibly because of the many authorities who maintain that the scribe must hear the directive to draft a *geṭ* directly from the husband.

Rabbi Weinberg offers his own explanation of the position of the early-day authorities who require that the scribe hear the husband's directions to draft the *geṭ* personally from the latter's mouth because of the requirement that the *geṭ* be written *le-shemah*. Although the *geṭ* must be written on behalf of a particular husband and for the specific purpose of divorcing his wife, it is far from clear why this cannot be accomplished without the scribe actually hearing the husband's directive. Rabbi Weinberg explains that since, in the normal course of events, a husband does not divorce his wife, a scribe is not ordinarily in a position to draft a *geṭ* for purposes of divorce, i.e. such a document cannot be deemed to have been written specifically for the requisite purpose. It is only the declaration of intent on the part of the husband that renders the woman a candidate for divorce which, in turn, makes it possible for the scribe to write the bill of divorce *le-shemah*. Rabbi Weinberg maintains that, unless he hears directly from the husband or his agent, the scribe is uncertain with regard to the status of the document that he is writing because, although the husband may have announced his intention to others, he may nevertheless have changed his mind. A *geṭ* written with that uncertainty, claims Rabbi Weinberg, is not written *le-shemah*.[43]

However, contends Rabbi Weinberg, if the *geṭ* represents an unmitigated benefit for the husband there is no reason to suspect that he may have undergone a change of heart. Accordingly, maintains Rabbi Weinberg, in situations in which the *geṭ* is an unmitigated benefit for the husband, all authorities would agree that it can be drafted *le-shemah* even if the scribe does not receive instructions directly from the husband.

## IV. *Conclusion*

The rulings of the Maggid of Koznitz, R. Meir Arak and R. Eliyahu Klatzkin, whatever their merits, are not at all germane to the problem of the modern-day *agunah* and do not serve as precedent for the actions of those individuals who execute *giṭṭin* on behalf of recalcitrant husbands. Those rulings provide no basis for a *geṭ* executed on the basis of constructive agency (*geṭ zikkuy*) even in the relatively rare situations in which the husband might legitimately be compelled by means of physical force to authorize the execution of a *geṭ*. A declaration of "*Rotseh ani*" on the part of the husband remains the *sine qua non* of the validity of any divorce executed in conformity with Jewish law. Each of the cited rulings of the Maggid of Koznitz, R. Meir Arak and R. Eliyahu Klatzkin involves a situation in which the husband, in one way or another, had signified his desire for the execution of a *geṭ*. The issue in each of the cases was whether the existence of *gilluy da'at*, or signification of desire to execute a *geṭ*, provided sufficient grounds to proceed with the execution of a *geṭ* in the absence of the usual form of authorization. In none of those sources is there the slightest hint that signification of assent on the part of the husband may be dispensed with, much less so is there any intimation that a *geṭ* can be executed in the face of the husband's recalcitrance. Small wonder then that no recognized rabbinic authority has endorsed the expedient of *geṭ zikkuy* as a remedy for the problem of the recalcitrant husband, and not a few authorities have vociferously denounced such action as a charade that can only lead to increased instances of *mamzerut*.

43 See also the explanations advanced by R. Eliezer Menachem Mann Shach, *Avi Ezri, Mahadura Ḳamma, Hilkhot Ishut* 3:18 and *Mahadura Ḥamisha'ah, Hilkhot Geirushin* 7:22; and R. Moshe Feinstein, *Iggerot Mosheh, Even ha-Ezer*, I, no.166.

3

# TEACHING JEWISH LAW IN A SECULAR AMERICAN LAW SCHOOL

by

SHERMAN L. COHN*

*Introduction*

A revolution of sorts has occurred in the American law school. Forty, fifty years ago, the only courses taught were those of practical importance: Procedure, Evidence, Contracts, Taxation, Corporations, and the like. More recently, the focus widened to include courses that are not of immediate practical importance, that give the student breath and depth. At the Georgetown University Law Center we term these "perspective" courses. We offer many such courses ranging from Law and Literature, through various History of Law and Sociology of Law offerings, to a whole range of ethnic law courses. It is in this context, that we look at the teaching of Jewish Law in the modern American law school.

Jewish Law, *Mishpaṭ Ivri,* is now being taught at approximately forty American law schools. When we speak of law schools in this context, we exclude *yeshivot,* which teach exclusively Jewish religious subjects. Rather, we are speaking of those law schools which are teaching and training persons to become secular American lawyers and are accredited by the American Bar Association to accomplish this task. While two of these law schools, the Cardozo School of Law of Yeshiva University and the Fuchsberg School of Law of Touro College, are Jewish-sponsored institutions, the remainder of the schools are either purely secular or sponsored by other religious groups. Thus, you will find Jewish law courses at the law schools of Georgetown University, Fordham University, St. Johns University, St. Louis University, and the Catholic University of America, which are all sponsored by the

* Professor of Law, Georgetown University Law Center, Washington, D.C. Some of the information in this paper is taken from responses by eleven teachers of Jewish law to a survey sent out by the author.

Roman Catholic church or some Roman Catholic religious order. Other Jewish law courses are offered at the law schools of Harvard, Yale, Columbia, New York University, University of California at Los Angeles, University of California at Davis, Emory University, and other schools that are sponsored by states or by other purely secular institutions. And other courses are offered at schools that are sponsored by other religious movements, such as Brigham Young University, which is sponsored by the Mormon Church.

The number of law schools offering courses could be higher. The problem is the availability of teachers. Some of the teachers are regular fulltime faculty members. Others are adjuncts. Still others are visitors. No regular fulltime faculty member known to me teaches Jewish Law fulltime. All teach other subjects as well. For example, Professor Neil Hecht at Boston University teaches evidence and property courses, Professor Steven Resnicoff at DePaul teaches in the contracts and commercial law fields, and Professor David Cobin at Hamline teaches in the civil procedure and constitutional law areas. All also teach Jewish Law; Even Professor J. David Bleich at Cardozo School of Law of Yeshiva University teaches comparative law in addition to Jewish Law and teaches Talmud in the Yeshiva as well as law at the law school. Some, such as Professor Bleich and Professor Michael Broyde at Emory University, hold appointments in another school or direct a separate program at the same University. Professor Broyde, for example, directs the Law and Religion Program at Emory in addition to teaching Jewish law and other subjects at the school of law.

Among the visitors there are professors who teach nothing but Jewish Law while they are in residence. Professors Menachem Elon and Aaron Kirschenbaum are prime examples. And when they are not in residence, Jewish law courses are generally not offered. Many of the offerings in Jewish law are by adjuncts, persons who come to teach only the one course, which is offered at most during one of the two semesters and, indeed, may not be offered every year. Some of these persons are local rabbis. For example, at Yale the course has been offered by Rabbi Michael Whitman, an adjunct at Yale, who fulltime has occupied the pulpit at Young Israel of New Haven.[1] Another example is Samuel J. Levine, who taught a course in Jewish Law at St. Johns University law school part time while fulltime he was a law clerk to a federal judge.

1 Unfortunately for Yale, Rabbi Whitman has accepted a new pulpit in Quebec, Canada, and, as of this writing, there is no prospect known to me of anyone else picking up his course.

Those of us who have been teaching Jewish law have heard often from deans of other law schools seeking assistance in finding a person qualified and willing to teach the course. They are not always easy to find.[2] One solution is a joint teaching arrangement. For example, at the University of California at Los Angeles, a course is offered by fulltime Professor Arthur Rosett and adjunct Professor Elliott Dorff, who fulltime is the President of the University of Judaism. At Georgetown the course is taught by myself, a fulltime member of the faculty, along with adjunct Professors David Saperstein and Barry Freundel. Professor Saperstein's fulltime position is the director of the Religious Action Center of the Union of American Hebrew Congregation. Professor Freundel occupies the pulpit at Kesher Israel Synagogue in Washington.

There are two reasons for the heavy use of adjuncts. First, these courses are never required and do not draw large numbers of students. And, second, there are some, but not many, fulltime faculty who are capable of teaching such courses. Among those who do teach Jewish law, there are only a few who have made the subject a significant area of their academic and scholarly work. This, however, is beginning to change.

In recent years, Jewish law has become recognized as a serious academic and scholarly subject. The Association of American Law Schools, which is the organization of all of the accredited law schools and of the many thousands of fulltime teachers in those schools, has Sections in various subject areas. Those Sections are the focal point for teachers of those subjects to come together, to share their experiences, and to learn from each other. About a decade ago, the Association, upon the petition of twenty or so teachers of Jewish Law, created a Section of Jewish Law, with Professor J. David Bleich as its first chair. This Section meets every year at the Association's Annual Meeting. At those meetings, teachers of Jewish Law present panels on how to teach the subject and also on various areas within Jewish Law. At times, these programs are presented in conjunction with other Sections, such as the Section on Family Law, and the Section on Medicine and Law, so that the programmatic presentation on Jewish Law is presented to a larger audience.

Moreover, there are now tenured professors in American law schools whose scholarship on Jewish Law is counted among their scholarly

2 E.g., Professor David A. Funk reports that he taught Jewish Law at Indiana University School of Law (Indianapolis), as a part of a World Legal History course, but since his retirement in June 1997, no one has taught such a course at the school.

achievements. For an American law professor to become tenured at any accredited law school, he or she is expected to produce published scholarship, which is then reviewed by his or her peers at other academic institutions. Law school tenure committees are sending out, for peer review, the writings of scholars in Jewish law and, thus, are recognizing its significance in the scholarly world. This scholarship is aided by the fact that law reviews, which are published at every law school in the nation, will publish articles on Jewish law. Unfortunately, there is not today a law review that is dedicated to Jewish law topics, though for a time the National Jewish Law Students Association sponsored the National Jewish Law Review. Five annual issues were published before the journal disappeared. The annual Jewish Law Association Studies does provide a significant avenue of publication, particularly for papers that are delivered at its biennial conferences.

With this as a background, we should turn to an examination of the Jewish law courses that are now being offered. Who takes courses in Jewish law? What do the courses look like? And what has spawned this development?

### A. *Who Takes Courses in Jewish Law?*

Professor Edward Rabin of the University of California at Davis reports that some years almost fifty percent of the students in his Jewish law course are not Jewish.[3] This is somewhat higher than my experience, which is that typically 1/4 to 1/3 of the students are not Jewish. Others report various percentages of non-Jewish students, from 90% to 10%, as their usual enrollment.[4] Why do non-Jewish students take such courses? There are many reasons. Sometimes it is because the person is Mormon, and, since the Mormon religion deems itself to be a descendent of the Jewish religion,

3 Edward Rabin, "Symposium: The Evolution and Impact of Jewish Law, Forward," 1 *U.C. Davis J. Int'l. L. & Policy* 49 (1995).

4 E.g., Professor Dellas Lee at Texas Tech generally has one or two Jewish students out of an enrollment of 15. Professor Whitman reports that typically at Yale 40% of his students were not Jewish. Professor Stephen Werber at Cleveland State puts his experience at 50% non-Jewish, though some years the "clear majority" are not Jews. Professor Yale Rosenberg puts the figure at University of Houston as 50% to 67% non-Jewish. On the other hand, Professor Neil Hecht at Boston University finds that typically 85% of his classes are Jewish.

with the originals being a part of the tribe of Levi, they consider that they are studying their own background. Thus, the longest, continuously running course in Jewish law appears to be at Brigham Young University, where the teachers (for many years Douglas Parker and now John Welch) report that, as far as they know, they have never had a Jewish student in their classes.[5]

Other reasons given by non-Jewish students for taking a course in Jewish law are equally interesting. Some take the course because they have a particular interest in religion and the law such as the law student who already had advanced degrees in Moral Theology and, in fact, had taught the subject at a major university, and was now in law school. Some, take a course in Jewish law because they grew up in a Jewish area and thus were exposed to much of Judaism and wish to learn more. Occasionally, persons take the course to explore a particular issue of great interest with the hope of finding support for their position from this exploration. For example, a student who is a devout Roman Catholic and is very pro-life on the abortion issue, took such a course in order to explore what she hoped would be Jewish support for her position. Of course, there are always students who just need the credit, or, in the case of a seminar, perhaps the writing credits, and the time of the course just fits. But they seem to be a distinct few in the larger picture.

The Jewish students who take these courses are also a mixed lot. Some come to the law school with fine *yeshivot* backgrounds, sometimes ordained rabbis. They come to learn the familiar from a different perspective. Others come with very little or no background, most having ceased any formal Jewish education at the time of their bar or bat mitzvah. They seem to find the course to be a way of approaching Judaism again now that they are adults; there is a legitimate adult way back home. There are a few who take the course for particular reasons, for example, the young man who was born of a Jewish father and a non-Jewish mother who is exploring how he can be Jewish, or the young lady who was adopted and is very concerned about the impact of Jewish law upon her. In recent years there seem to be more students who have fine non-*yeshivot* Jewish day school education, perhaps with a Jewish studies exposure at the college level, and who now wish to continue that education in a positive mode.

5 The courses at University of California at Berkeley and at Temple University probably started at an earlier date, but they were offered only when a teacher was available.

### B. *What is the Course in Jewish Law?*

Samuel Levine has described four models for the study of Jewish law in American law schools:[6]

(1) *Comparative Jewish Law*: Comparing American law with Jewish law, focusing on subjects that find parallels in the American legal system. In this model, students' and teachers' knowledge of American law becomes a real asset. The largest drawback to this model is that a suitable teacher must have a strong knowledge of both systems. But it is also its strength, for it gives the student with no background a comparative handle on which to grasp the Jewish law. As Samuel Levine points out, "one of the aims of this model is for students to appreciate the way a study of each legal system can illuminate an understanding of the other."[7] This type of course fits well within the general comparative-law offerings of the law school. Probably all law schools today have at least one general comparative-law course that focuses heavily on comparing the civil and common law systems, and probably bringing in some comparison of what was once called socialist or communist law of Russia or China.

(2) *Comparative Israeli Law*: With an emphasis on Israeli law, one can compare two modern secular states, that of the United States and Israel, and their various struggles. For example, a study can be made of how each handles the relations between organized religion and the State and how each handles law and security. The comparison of the United States written constitution and the Israeli system of basic or fundamental laws but without a written constitution is also of much interest. Of course, within the Israeli system there is the role of Jewish law within the family-law setting as well as under the Foundations of Law Act of 1980, requiring that lacunae be filled "in the light of the principles of freedom, justice, equity, and peace of the Jewish heritage." This type of course would require a teacher who is steeped in Israeli law, with Jewish law playing its role within that system, as well as in American law. There are a few law schools which offer such a subject.

(3) *Jewish Law*: Exclusively examining Jewish law, with little, if any, reference to other legal systems, including that of the United States. This approach probably results in the greatest depth of learning of Jewish law. It requires a teacher with significant depth in Jewish law, though his or her

6 Samuel J. Levine, "Teaching Jewish Law in American Law Schools: an Emerging Development in Law and Religion," 26 *Fordham Urb. L.J.* 1041 (1999).

7 *Ibid.*

knowledge of American law is not as significant. Such a course may be more difficult for the student who has some knowledge of American law but no background in Jewish law. Such a course would fit into a curriculum that offers other such courses, such as Islamic Law, Japanese Law, Chinese Law, Native American Law, African Law, Civil Law, and Canon Law. Such a course would not be offered in a comparative mode, though it is difficult not to compare the new with the familiar, but rather would look at the Jewish legal system on its own terms.

A course that focuses on Jewish law as a subject can be taught in various ways. How it is taught depends not only on the background and interest of the teacher, but also on the background level of the class. A class with non-Jewish students or with Jewish students who have little or no previous background must focus on basics, even definitions of fundamental terms such as "Torah," "Talmud," etc. It also must focus on sources and jurisprudential concepts, at least as a foundation to go on and examine a single topic in depth, or a series of substantive topics. Even those who take one substantive topic to explore throughout the course must integrate into the teaching of that subject the definitional, jurisprudential, and source material so that the student with little or no background can understand a context of what is being taught.

(4) *A synthesis of the first three*: This is Professor Levine's approach at St. John's University School of Law, and is probably more or less the approach of most of the courses. As Professor Levine points out, this approach begins with a discussion of sources and structure, from both a historical and a conceptual perspective. I would add that it must also include some broad sweep of Jewish history, for a context in which to view the sources and development of the law. After this foundation, there can then be explored various topics, both on their own terms in Jewish law, and in a comparative basis. Some focus on the use of Jewish law in Israel may also fit this development.

I would add that the exposure of the student to the jurisprudence of the Jewish legal system is very valuable. First, we have a system in which for 2,000 years there has been no sovereign authority enforcing Jewish law, no policeman on the corner. Yet, the system has survived and grown. How that has occurred is an important jurisprudential study, as well as an important foundation of the Jewish legal system.

Secondly, in modern western jurisprudence there is a debate as to how law evolves. What is the force that drives evolution of law? Economics, sociology, history, natural-law principles are offered. An acceptable answer is that there is no rational force; it just is what it is at this moment. Jewish law begins with the giving of the law by the ultimate law-giver, who stated, "This is the entire law. You shall not add to it, nor subtract from it." Yet, the agrarian society of the Biblical age, the society of living in a sovereign land, gave way to a varied history and urbanism and diaspora. Adaptation had to occur without destroying the foundation of the system. To me, this is the real meaning of the Talmudic lesson of the Oven of Akhnai. It also makes pertinent the work by historians such as Jacob Katz about social and economic influence in halakhic decisions.[8]

In our course at Georgetown, we assume no familiarity with Jewish law, history or sociology. We must introduce basic definitions to students who have never heard of "Torah" or "Talmud" or "Mishnah," as well as fundamental authorities to students who have never heard of Hillel or Maimonides or *Rashi*. And we find it good to give a large-sweep historical and sociological perspective of Biblical, Talmudic, and diaspora times, explaining the significance of the destruction of the Temple and the end of the Sanhedrin. We then focus on the moving ascendancy in the Jewish legal system of Persia, Spain, North Africa, and Rhineland, Eastern Europe, and finally the United States and Israel. We examine the significance of the Geonim of Persia and the development of responsa literature up through and including modern *poṣḳim*. We discuss the identity and importance of early commentators such as *Rashi* and the Tosafists, and the codes of Maimonides and Joseph Caro, the formation of schools and academies in these and other diverse contexts, including the formation of the Ashkenazic and Sephardic traditions.

From there we go on to the jurisprudence of Jewish law. We explore Jewish law's foundation in the thunder and lightening at Sinai and the significance of the Talmudic era and particularly the teaching of the Oven of Akhnai. We look at the importance of dispute resolution in Jewish law, from the pre-Sinai Noahite requirement through the action of Moses creating the courts of the hundreds, of the clans, and of the tribes, and from there to the era of the Sanhedrin and the Bet Din, and how this commandment was carried out in the *shtetles* of Europe and in the United States today. An exploration of the role of lawyers and judges and the ethics of each is included in this survey.

Two seeming digressions then occur. One explores the influence of

8 See, e.g., *The "Shabbes Goy": A Study in Halakhic Flexibility* (Philadelphia, Jerusalem: Jewish Publication Society, 1989).

Jewish law on the development of Anglo-American law, including the explicit influence in the early legislation of the Massachusetts Bay Colony and in the United States Constitution, the United States Supreme Court's occasional reference to Jewish law, and the apparent strong influence in the development of the Anglo-American law of mortgages and probably of liens. The other explores the role of Jewish law in Israel today, including the Foundations of Law Act of 1980 and the reference of all family law matters involving Jewish citizens to the Rabbinical courts.

We then turn to various topics, spending a class session on each. This list varies, but has included Family Law, Bioethics, Privacy, Tort Law, Property Law, Environmental Law, Government Ethics, Law and the Welfare System, among others. The specific topics depend on the amount of time we have, the interest of the instructors, and the apparent interest of the students from year to year.

Jewish law courses are taught as didactic classes or as seminars. The number of credit hours allotted varies from one to three, with the majority being for three credits, according to my survey. In only a very few schools can one find advanced courses that build upon the first, survey course.

A word should be said about teaching materials. Of course, each teacher chooses that teaching text most appropriate to his or her style and to his or her aim in the course. Having been weaned on the American case method of teaching, and having a style in which student participation and discussion is an important factor, I have found two books appropriate for assignment. The first of these books to be published is Elliott Dorff & Arthur Rosett, *A Living Tree*.[9] While the book is text in form, it has sufficient actual examples, following a basic theme, to be usable in lieu of a casebook. The second, which appeared in 1999, is the first real casebook as American law schools would recognize a casebook, Professor Menachem Elon's *Jewish Law (Mishpat Ivri): Cases and Materials*.[10] The strength of this book is that it is a casebook, setting forth real cases involving Jewish Law. The weakness is that all but a few of the cases are decisions by Professor Elon while on the Supreme Court of Israel, along with excerpts from any opinions disagreeing with him. It is a regret that the book does not contain a significant number of responsa from the vast literature that exists, though of course many responsa as well as talmudic passages are referred to and quoted.

9 Published 1988 by State University of New York and the Jewish Theological Seminary of America.

10 Published by Matthew Bender, co-authored by Professor Bernard Auerbach, Daniel D. Chazin, Esq., and Melvin J. Sykes, Esq.

In addition, the Institute of Jewish Law at Boston University has produced several teaching booklets.[11] And Professor Jeffrey Roth has published a model chapter for a Jewish law casebook.[12]

I have found other materials to be valuable resources for reference by myself and my students. Other teachers may find, however, that these materials are indeed teaching texts appropriate to their styles of teaching and the aims that they have for their courses. One such book is the *Introduction to the History and Sources of Jewish Law*,[13] a 1996 publication of the Jewish Law Association, in which 15 distinct periods are treated (each by a specialist in that period), in a common plan covering the political and jurisdictional background, the character (literary and legal) of the sources, legal practice, the principal authorities, and characteristic features of the substantive law (with special emphasis on family law). Other valuable books are Aaron Schreiber's really monumental work, though in a single volume, *Jewish Law and Decision Making (Criminal Law): A Study Through Time,*[14] George Horowitz, *The Spirit of Jewish Law,*[15] Louis Jacobs, *Jewish Law,*[16] and Menachem Elon, ed., *Principles of Jewish Law.*[17] Finally, special attention must be given to the 1994 translation into English, in four volumes, of Professor Elon's *magnum opus, Jewish Law (Ha-Mishpat Ha-Ivri): History, Sources, Principles*,[18] which provides an account of the history of Jewish law in terms largely of its legal and literary

11 H. Ben-Menahem and N.S. Hecht, *Selected Topics in Jewish Law* (Tel Aviv: Open University of Israel; Boston: Institute of Jewish Law, Boston University School of Law, 1987-): Vol. 1: H. Ben Menahem, *Legal Formalism in the Halakha*, 1987; Vol. 2: H. Ben Menahem, *Exigency Authority of Courts,* 1987; Vol. 3: H. Ben Menahem, *Law and Equity in Jewish Law*, 1993; Vol. 4: D.B. Sinclair, *Abortion*, 1994; Vol. 5: D.B. Sinclair, *Treating the Critically Ill*, 1994; Vol. 6: S. Ettinger, Self-Help in Jewish Law, 1993; Vol. 7: I. Waraftig, *Unjust Enrichment,* 1999.

12 "Fraud on the Surviving Spouse in Jewish and American Law: A Model Chapter for a Jewish Law Casebook," 28 *Case W. Res. J. Int'l L.* 101(1996).

13 N.S. Hecht, B.S. Jackson, S.M. Passamaneck, D. Piattelli and A.M. Rabello, eds., *An Introduction to the History and Sources of Jewish Law*, Oxford: The Clarendon Press, 1996.

14 Published 1979 by Temple University Press.

15 Published 1953 by Central Book Company.

16 Published 1968 by Berman House, NY.

17 Published 1975 by Keter. This work is a valuable compendium of the law subjects of the *Encyclopedia Judaica.*

18 Published 1994 by the Jewish Publication Society.

sources and concludes with a volume devoted to Jewish Law in the State of Israel.

Beyond these materials, a teacher must compile materials. We have found it very useful to use some Talmudic material (in translation, of course), as well as material borrowed from law reviews and from some more specialized texts. Each teacher will have brought together material that is most meaningful to his or her method of teaching.[19]

For a course to really succeed, particularly a seminar, the student should have available library material on the subject. Thus, law schools where courses in Jewish law have been offered have had to acquire books on the subjects, some starting from practically no holdings. Of course, the number of titles acquired has varied depending on the amount of resources devoted and the amount of time that the library has been engaged in the acquisitions. It also seems to vary with whether the course is taught by a fulltime faculty member or by an adjunct. Some schools have sought and obtained grants to aid in the task.

### C. *Why There Has Been This Growth of Jewish Law Courses*

As was pointed out at the beginning of this paper, there has been an evolution in law teaching in the United States, at least at most law schools. Until the 1970s, the emphasis was almost exclusively upon those practical courses that were needed for the successful practice of law, including the passing of the bar examination. Courses such as ethics, jurisprudence, history of law, and the like were considered oddities if offered at all.

But the academic legal community has undergone drastic change. In the first half of the 20th century, law schools were almost completely under the influence of the Realist and Positivist schools of jurisprudence. These schools maintained that the law is what has been duly enacted, and in a common-law system, what the judge says that it is. Leading law schools taught solely positive law. Indeed, there was no need to teach jurisprudence as there was no issue to be discussed. The same was true of legal ethics: ethics explores values, and the Realist school was not interested in a value discussion within the law, though it would look at policy outside of the law in terms of arriving at certain results. Georgetown, a Jesuit school, was

19 Some teachers, such as Professor Benjamin Mintz at Catholic University and Professor Stephen Werber at Cleveland State, use only materials that each has compiled from various sources.

looked down upon by the leading law schools even into the 1950s and 1960s because it offered, and required, courses in legal ethics and jurisprudence, where principles of natural law were explored. But with the study of what happened in Europe in the 1940s, there was a realization that Germans accomplished the Holocaust within duly enacted German law. It is said that the Realist school floundered upon the shoals of Auschwitz. And Nuremberg helped foster a concept that there is a law of general principles, perhaps call it natural law, that trumps positive law when they are in conflict.

Thus, in the 1960s and 1970s, there was a rediscovery of values in the law. Law school faculties began to ask the question "why?" Watergate furthered this process of self-examination, for many of those involved were graduates of first-rank law schools. For the first time, the self-appointed leading law schools began to explore values and offer courses to their students in which values were explored. And the students of the 1970s were open to such courses, for they too were questioning and exploring, not willing to just accept what is.

Thus, attitudes changed. Today ethics of law practice is a must in the studies of the student. But, more, today most law schools offer perspective courses that look at the history of the law as well as the legal profession, the sociology of the law, and subjects as diverse as Law and Literature, Law in Literature, Law in Music. As a part of this broadening, there came an opening for other courses that gave breadth and depth, though of no practical importance. Larger law schools particularly, tout to their applicants the breadth of their offerings.

As noted earlier, Jewish law fits into this picture. But more was happening. For one thing, law schools, which had been quite isolated, began to find significance in other disciplines. Economics came to be a recognized area for exploration, as did, to a less extent, psychiatry, psychology and philosophy. Science and courses in law schools utilizing those disciplines began to appear. Joint teaching with members of those disciplines became a sign of maturity. Law schools began to add non-lawyers to their faculty, and many of the newer recruits had Ph.Ds in other disciplines along with their law degrees. Further, many schools began to develop joint degree programs with all sorts of other disciplines, bringing into their student bodies young people with different foci than the usual law student of old and exposing faculty to other disciplines in a meaningful way. This made the introduction of non-traditional subjects easier to accomplish.

Still another influence affects this evolution. Before the 1970s, the focus was upon assimilation. Historically, legal studies were pursued by the establishment (generally, White, Anglo-Saxon Protestant and male). Then between the First and Second World Wars came the Roman Catholics from southern and eastern Europe as well as Jews, largely from eastern European backgrounds. The emphasis, however, was largely upon assimilation. There just was no recognition in American university education as a whole, and certainly not in legal education, of any value to ethnic studies. This began to change. We must admit that the push came largely from the Afro-Americans and the Black Pride movement. It also came from the Women's movement. So we began to see at the undergraduate, college level Black studies and Women's studies programs. This made it possible for the Jews, too, to speak of wanting to study their own heritage, and Jewish studies programs began.

Thus, we found in the past three decades that it was possible to be openly ethnic and still be American. Perhaps because assimilation progressed sufficiently, it was now acceptable to want to look at one's own group and preserve the values within that group. Thus, it became acceptable for Jews too to want to study something of Jewish Law and to do so within the umbrella of the secular law school.

Finally, there is another movement, small but important. This is the growth of what Professor Russell Pearce has termed the "religious lawyering movement."[20] In the 1970s Professor Thomas Schaffer of Notre Dame first looked at being a lawyer from the Roman Catholic perspective.[21] Professor Shaffer explored what it means to be a Roman Catholic lawyer; what values does a lawyer who happens to be a Roman Catholic bring to the practice of law? Others joined in from various Christian perspectives.[22] This led Jewish academics and lawyers to begin exploring what does it mean to be a Jewish lawyer. Professors Russell Pearce,[23] Howard Lesnick,[24] Monroe

20 Russell G. Pearce, "Symposium Forward: The Religious Lawyering Movement: An Emerging Force in Legal Ethics and Professionalism," 66 *Fordham L.Rev.* 1075 (1998).

21 See, e.g., "The Practice of Law as Moral Discourse," 55 *Notre Dame L. Rev.* 231 (1979), and his book *On Being a Christian Lawyer: Law for the Innocent* (Provo, Utah: Brigham Young University Press, 1981).

22 See, e.g., Joseph G. Allegretti, *The Lawyer's Calling* (New York: Penlist Press, 1996); Milner S. Ball, *The Word & the Law* (Chicago: University of Chicago Press, 1993).

23 See, e.g., John D. Feerick, Russell G. Pearce, Ismar Schorsch, "Symposium: Rediscovering the Role of Religion in the Lives of Lawyers and Those They Represent," 26 *Fordham Urb. L.J.* 821 (1999).

24 See, e.g., "Symposium: Attorney Well-Being in Large Firms: Choices Facing

Freedman,[25] Michael Broyde,[26] and Steven Resnicoff,[27] as well as Samuel Levine[28] began to think and write on the subject. This paper is not the place to explore this fascinating subject in depth.[29] I use it solely to show that it became respectable in academic legal circles to be a Jew openly and to explore Jewish subjects as a legitimate academic and scholarly subject.

It is in this changing atmosphere that Jewish Law has been welcomed to the general curriculum of law schools all over the country. From my experience, this has resulted in faculty discussions of the teaching of Jewish law on various topics. It has also resulted in students who first became familiar with Jewish law and its richness in our course and who then continued their studies in succeeding years.

All of this has been a tremendous change in the professional lives of most of us. And, I suggest, a change for the better.

---

Young Lawyers: Speaking Truth to Powerlessness," 52 *Vand. L. Rev.* 995 (1999).

25 See, e.g., "Legal Ethics From a Jewish Perspective," 27 *Tex. Tech L. Rev.* 1131 (1996).

26 *The Pursuit of Justice and Jewish Law: Halakhic Perspectives on the Legal Profession* (Hoboken, N.J.: Michael Scharf Publication Trust of the Yeshiva University Press; KTAV Publishing House, 1996).

27 See, e.g., Steven Resnicoff, "The Attorney-Client Relationship: A Jewish Law Perspective," 14 *Notre Dame J.L. Ethics & Pub. Pol'y* 349 (2000).

28 "The Broad Life of the Jewish Lawyer: Integrating Spirituality, Scholarship and Profession", 27 *Texas Tech. L. Rev.* 1199 (1996).

29 See "Symposium, Faith and the Law," 27 *Texas Tech L. Rev.* 911 (1996), and "Symposium, The Relevance of Religion to a Lawyer's Work," 66 *Fordham L. Rev.* 1075 (1998), for two collections of views from the viewpoint of a large variety of faiths.

4

# ENTRAPMENT IN JEWISH LAW

by

JONATHAN FISHER*

*Introduction*

With entrapment[1] becoming an increasingly common feature of policing in modern society, contemporary legal systems have struggled to balance the public interest in favour of the detection of crime against an equally strong public interest in favour of protecting a citizen's fundamental rights, and in particular, a citizen's right against self-incrimination. This paper considers how the tension between these competing public interests is addressed in Jewish law.[2] The European Court of Human Rights has recently drawn the

* Barrister, 18 Red Lion Court, London. The author is grateful to his family and friends, most notably Rabbi Eli Salasnik and Professor (Rabbi) Steven Resnicoff, for their comments and encouragement when reviewing a draft of this paper.

1 The UK Royal Commission on Police Powers, (Cmd 3297, 1929) defined (at p.40) entrapment as occurring when an instigator or a person commonly known as an *agent provocateur* "entices another person to commit an express breach of law which he would not otherwise have committed, and then proceeds or informs against him in respect of such offence." Although the *agent provocateur* is often a police officer or some other person acting as his agent or with his approval, any person can undertake to perform this role. In recent times, newspaper reporters have acted as *agents provocateurs* in cases where famous people have been the subject of entrapment. See, for example, *R* v. *Shannon*, 14.9.00, CA, unreported, and *R* v. *Hardwicke & Thwaites*, 10.11.00, CA, unreported. The word "entrapment" is derived from the French verb *entrapper*, meaning to beguile or catch in a trap. The word entered the English language in the mid 16th century.

2 For papers on entrapment in Jewish law written in Hebrew, see A. Kirschenbaum, "Entrapment in Jewish Law," (1989-90) 15 *Dinei Israel* 39, and E. Lederman, "Israeli Criminal Law Perspective on the Jewish Law of Entrapment," (1989-90) 15 *Dinei Israel* 105.

line between the use of entrapment where an undercover police officer participates in an on-going criminal enterprise, and the situation where an undercover officer instigates the commission of a criminal offence which would not have been committed without his / her intervention. Entrapment is permitted where the undercover officer participates in an on-going criminal enterprise, but not where he / she instigates the enterprise. This is not a distinction recognised in Jewish law.

### *Entrapment in Contemporary Secular Legal Systems*

#### 1. English Common Law

Although the police frequently utilized entrapment in the first half of the 20th century,[3] the English courts did not conclusively reject entrapment as a defence until the late 1970's when the issue finally came before the House of Lords in a landmark case, *R* v. *Sang*.[4] As Glanville Williams pointed out,[5] the English distrust an informer and a plain-clothes detective because, if their use is taken to extreme, it destroys confidence within the community. "Foreign examples, and, indeed, the lessons of our own history, show how vital it is to maintain a vigilant attitude of suspicion towards anything like a secret police." Lord Goddard, then Lord Chief Justice, echoed this distrust of informers and plain-clothes detectives in the years immediately following the second world war. During the course of a judgement delivered in a case involving a breach of road traffic regulations, Lord Goddard CJ noted that:

> No court in England has ever liked what are generally called *agents*

3 The UK Royal Commission on Police Powers noted that it was sometimes necessary for the police to take part in criminal offences, personally or through agents, in order to bring offenders to justice. The Royal Commission gave an example (at 42) where the police received information that a person was dishonestly obtaining money from ignorant girls by acting as a fortune teller. "It is impossible for any policeman or policewoman to be present ... when these fortunes are told, and the only way in which the evidence necessary to institute a prosecution can be obtained is by sending a constable in plain clothes, or even an agent on their behalf, to the fortune teller to have his or her fortune told." In contemporary times evidential problems are particularly acute in drugs cases, where the supply often takes place secretly in private places.

4 [1980] AC 402.

5 *Criminal Law, The General Part,* 2nd Edition, London, 1961, 782, at para. 256.

*provocateurs* resulting in imposing criminal liability.[6]

In so far as there might have been any residual doubt that entrapment could provide a defence in English law, this doubt was firmly laid to rest by the House of Lords in *R* v. *Sang* where the defendant had been induced by an informer acting on police instructions to commit a criminal offence involving forged United States banknotes. At the start of his trial the defendant sought to exclude the informer's evidence on the basis of entrapment. In addition to declaring that there was no doctrine of entrapment in English law, the House of Lords held that it was permissible for an *agent provocateur* to give evidence of a criminal offence, the commission of which he had induced. As Lord Salmon succinctly explained:

> A man who intends to commit a crime and actually commits it is guilty of the offence whether or not he has been persuaded or induced to commit it, no matter by whom.[7]

The effect of entrapment was reconsidered in England following the enactment of the Police and Criminal Evidence Act 1984 which contained a provision codifying the judicial discretion to exclude evidence having an adverse effect on the fairness of proceedings.[8] A number of cases came before the Court of Appeal (Criminal Division) concerning the exercise of this judicial discretion where evidence had been obtained by entrapment.[9] In exercising its discretion, the court is obliged to have regard to "all the circumstances, including the circumstances in which the evidence was obtained." Applying this discretion, the courts have held that evidence will be excluded only where a law enforcement officer "incites, instigates, persuades, pressurises or wheedles" a person into committing an offence. If none of these characteristics are present, English law regards it as "unobjectionable if a law enforcement officer gives a defendant an opportunity to break the law, of which the defendant freely takes advantage, in circumstances where it

6 *Browning* v. *J W H Watson Ltd* [1953] 2 All ER 775 at 779A.

7 [1979] 2 All ER 1222 at 1235h.

8 Section 78(1) of the Police and Criminal Evidence Act 1984 reads as follows: "In any proceedings the court may refuse to allow evidence on which the prosecution proposes to rely to be given if it appears to the court that, having regard to all the circumstances, including the circumstances in which the evidence was obtained, the admission of the evidence would have such an adverse effect on the fairness of the proceedings that the court ought not to admit it."

9 See, in particular, *R* v. *Smurthwaite & Gill* [1994] 98 Cr App R 437, *per* Lord Taylor CJ at 440.

appears that the defendant would have behaved in the same way if the opportunity had been offered by anyone else."[10]

## 2. Entrapment in European Human Rights Law

English common law today broadly accords with the law expounded by the European Court of Human Rights on the issue of entrapment. In European jurisprudence the seminal case is the decision of the European Court of Human Rights in *Teixeira de Castro* v. *Portugal*[11] where the court decided that use of undercover agents must be restricted and safeguards put in place. The court held that where police exercised an influence such as to initiate the commission of an offence and there is nothing to suggest that without their intervention it would have been committed, this was a breach of a person's fundamental rights under Article 6(1) of the European Convention.[12]

## 3 Entrapment in the United States

The law on entrapment has developed in the United States along similar lines. Initially there was a division of opinion concerning the limits of entrapment,[13] focussing principally upon whether entrapment should be seen from an objective or subjective point of view. The objective perspective concentrated on the conduct of law enforcement officers, whilst the subjective perspective looked at the defendant's predisposition to commit a criminal offence. The consensus of opinion broadly supports the subjective view. On the one hand, as the Supreme Court made clear long ago, the police may not originate a criminal design by implanting in the mind of an innocent person the disposition to commit a criminal offence and induce its commission in order that they may prosecute.[14] On the other hand:

> Where the government has induced an individual to break the law and the defence of entrapment is at issue ... the prosecution must prove beyond

10 *Nottingham City Council* v. *Amin*, [2000] 2 All ER 946 at 949j-950b.

11 [1998] 28 EHRR 101.

12 Article 6(1) provides *inter alia* that "in the determination ... of any criminal charge against him, everyone is entitled to a fair and public hearing within a reasonable time by an independent and impartial tribunal established by law." The right to a fair trial is violated by "active" entrapment.

13 *Sherman* v. *US* [1958] 356 US 369.

14 *Sorrells* v. *US* [1932] 287 US 435.

reasonable doubt that the defendant was disposed to commit the criminal act prior to first being approached by government agents.[15]

Accordingly:

when the government's quest for conviction leads to the apprehension of an otherwise law-abiding citizen who, if left to his own devices, would likely never run afoul of the law, the courts should intervene.[16]

## *Entrapment in Talmudic Law*

The approach taken by Jewish law towards entrapment is very different. Far from supporting the use of entrapment as a device in the detection of crime, Jewish law prohibits the use of entrapment to catch an offender who has committed a capital crime,[17] except in just one case where a number of stringent requirements have to be satisfied.

### *The Mishnah*

The principal source of Jewish law on the use of entrapment is found in the Mishnah.[18] A cursory reading of the Mishnah reveals that entrapment is generally prohibited in Jewish law, with one exception where an instigator incites another person to commit idolatry. It is only in this rare circumstance that Jewish law permits an offender to be entrapped. A careful reading of the Mishnah reveals the extent to which the application of this exception is severely limited.

The Mishnah reads as follows:

"The instigator *[ha'meiṣit]* — is a layman who incites [another] layman;
[The instigator] said to [the other layman], "There is a deity in such-a-such a place; thus it eats, it drinks, it does good, it does harm."
We do not conceal witnesses to entrap *[makhmeenin]* anyone punishable by death according to the Torah except for this one.
If [the instigator] spoke to two, and they are his witnesses, they bring him to

15 *Jacobson* v. *US* [1992] 503 US 540 at 547.

16 *Jacobson* v. *US* [1992] 503 US 540 at 554.

17 For a definition of a capital crime in Jewish law, see S. Mendelsohn, *The Criminal Jurisprudence of the Jews*, (New York: Sepher-Hermon Press, 1991), 53, para. 30. Capital crimes include offences of murder, rape, bestiality, incest, kidnapping, blasphemy and idolatry.

18 *Ṣanhedrin* 7:10.

the Court and stone him.
If [the instigator] spoke to one, [the layman] says: "I have friends who desire this."
If [the instigator] is clever and says that he is unable to speak before them, they conceal witnesses behind a partition, and [the layman] says to [the instigator]: "Say what you said to me in private."
[The instigator] says it to [the layman], to which [the layman] says to [the instigator] in reply: "How can we abandon our G-d in heaven and go and worship wood and stones?"
If [the instigator] retracts, it is good.
If [the instigator] says: "This is our obligation, it is proper for us," those standing behind the partition bring [the instigator] to Court and stone him.
Included in this [exception] is anyone who says:
"I shall serve, I shall go and serve, let us go and serve;
"I shall slaughter an offering, I shall go and slaughter an offering, let us go and slaughter an offering;
"I shall burn an offering, I shall go and burn an offering, let us go and burn an offering;
"I shall pour a libation, I shall go and pour a libation, let us go and pour a libation;
"I shall bow down, I shall go and bow down, let us go and bow down."
One who leads astray — is one who says "Let us go and serve idols."

### *(i) The General Rule Prohibits an Offender to Be Entrapped*

The Mishnah specifically records that as a general rule Jewish law does not permit the practice of concealing witnesses to entrap a person into committing a capital offence.[19] This accords with the position set out in the Jerusalem Talmud, in the following passage:

> Said Rabbi Abahu in the name of Rabbi Joḥanan: "To place witnesses behind a wall so that they may confirm any admission made privately is of no value."[20]

### *(ii) The Exception Applies Only in the Case of Incitement to Idolatry*

The Mishnah makes clear that entrapment can be utilised only where there is a frontal challenge to the unity and supremacy of Almighty G-d.

19 Use of entrapment, whether in capital or non-capital cases, offends the principle of *lifnei eever, post*, section 5.

20 Jerusalem Talmud, *Ṣanhedrin* III, 8

The instigator denies the unity and supremacy of G-d by positing that there is a deity in another place taking a physical form, which has the capacity to do good as well as harm. The instigator proposes to worship this deity and perceives that it is proper to do so.[21] To avoid misunderstanding about what qualifies, the Mishnah presents five different ways in which idol worship can be manifested. It is axiomatic that the prohibition against idolatry is paramount in the Mosaic Code. The prohibition is established in the second commandment[22] of the Ten Commandments; the supremacy of G-d as the fundamental tenet of Judaism has been highlighted throughout the ages.

### *(iii) The Exception Applies Only Where an Instigator Incites Another Person, in the Singular*

It is clear from the Mishnah that the exception does not apply where the instigator incites more than one person. The reason for this limitation is given in the Mishnah itself, because where there are at least two witnesses[23] who observe the incitement, the instigator can be punished and convicted by due process of law. Tangentially, the Mishnah implies an additional relaxation of Jewish criminal law and procedure where the capital offence of inciting idolatry is concerned. In addition to the stipulation that two witnesses must have observed the crime, Jewish law normally requires the witnesses to administer a warning to a defendant before he proceeds to commit a capital offence that he will be subject to the death penalty if he continues with his course of conduct.[24] The Mishnah implies by its terms

21 The conduct involves the articulation of words, rather than conduct by deeds. Performance of an idolatrous act is not required. The exception applies where an instigator incites idolatry, in circumstances where his incitement is unsuccessful.

22 *Exodus* 20:3-6.

23 It is a basic requirement in Jewish law that two witnesses are required to give evidence before a person can be convicted of a crime — *Deuteronomy* 19:15; TB *Ṣanhedrin* 30a; TB *Sotah* 2b.

24 Mishnah, *Ṣanhedrin* 5:1. Z. Falk, *Introduction to Jewish Law of the Second Commonwealth*, Part 1, (Leiden: E.J.Brill, 1972), 119, doubted whether this rule was effective at the time when Jewish courts dealt with capital cases, for no one would agree to risk the death penalty by expressly disregarding a caution. Falk suggested that the rule regarding cautioning during the Second Commonwealth resembled the concept of previous convictions in modern criminal law, indicating that in regard to certain offences the accused would be convicted and sentenced to death only if he repeated the offence.

that no warning needs to be given in the case of inciting idolatry. Not only is inciting idolatry the only capital offence a person can be entrapped to commit; it is also the only offence where the administration of a warning before the commission of a capital offence is not required.

*(iv) The Exception Requires the Layman to Play a Passive Role in Providing the Instigator with an Opportunity to Incite Idolatry*

Even where the entrapment procedure commences with the concealment of witnesses behind a partition, Jewish law remains concerned to ensure that the layman does not play any active role in the instigation of the commission of a capital offence. The Mishnah requires the layman to ask the instigator to repeat what he had said to him previously, so as to make sure that there has been no mistake. The layman's role is essentially passive. The language to be used by the layman is anodyne, viz: "Say what you said to me before, in private."

*(v) The Exception Applies Only Where the Instigator Has Been Given an Opportunity to Retract His Incitement*

Once the instigator has repeated what he had said previously, Jewish law requires the layman to try and dissuade the instigator from committing the capital offence. Although he does not warn the instigator of the consequences of his actions, the layman challenges the action proposed by the instigator and confronts him with the enormity of what he is saying. The Mishnah requires the layman to ask the instigator: "How can we abandon our G-d in heaven and worship wood and stones." Abrogative rhetoric is invoked, to stress the far-reaching significance of the actions proposed by the instigator. The choice of language is provocative and emotive, with its reference to the abandonment of Almighty G-d in preference to the worship of inanimate objects. If the instigator retracts his incitement to idolatry, he is not punished for his conduct. The Mishnah proceeds on the basis that if the instigator is silent, there is no basis to doubt the sincerity of his retraction.

*The Gemara*

The Mishnah is discussed at some length in the Gemara, TB *Ṣanhedrin* 67a. One interesting detail is added about the way in which the act of entrapment is to be performed:

> What do we do to him? We kindle a light for him in an inner room and place witnesses in a nearby outer room so that they can hear his voice but he cannot see them. The other (i.e. the target of the incitement) says to him, "Repeat privately what you have said to me before. The instigator says it to him, and the other replies, "How can we forsake our G-d in heaven and worship an idol?" If the instigator retracts, that is good. But if he says "This is our obligation," or "This is favourable for us," the witnesses who are listening from outside bring him into Court and stone him.

Whereas the Mishnah is silent on this point of detail, the Gemara requires a light to be kindled for an instigator who is inciting a layman to idolatry in an inner room. It seems that a candle would have been required to enable the witnesses to see the instigator, even though the instigator could not see them. Although the Gemara does not state that the witnesses must be able to see the instigator, this is implicit because otherwise the witnesses would not have been able to identify the person instigating the idolatry. Evidence of voice recognition is not admissible in Jewish law.[25]

There has been some discussion in the Talmudic commentaries about whether there is a conflict between the Mishnah and the Gemara on this point of detail. One suggestion is that the additional detail presented in the Gemara is easily reconciled with the Mishnah if the latter is treated as dealing with the situation where the entrapment takes place during the day in a secluded outdoor location. In contrast, the Gemara is positing a situation where an instigator is brought to a deserted house at night; rather than listening to the instigator behind a partition, the witnesses are located in an outer room.[26]

Although the Talmud refers to witnesses (in the plural) behind the partition or in the outer room, it might be thought that it would be sufficient compliance with Jewish law if just one witness was present since the layman speaking with the instigator could constitute the second witness. This would be erroneous because in a capital case Jewish law requires both witnesses to observe the conduct on a par with each other.[27]

There are six other references in the Gemara to the exceptional way in which the capital offence of inciting idolatry is treated in Jewish law, as follows:

25 *Yad Ramah, Ketzot HaḤoshen* 81:13.

26 See the commentary of the *Yad Ramah* on TB *Ṣanhedrin* 67a.

27 Compare the position in a case involving a monetary obligation: TB *Ṣanhedrin* 30a.

*(i) TB Ṣanhedrin 8b*

In TB *Ṣanhedrin* 8b it is explained that there are three requisites for conviction and punishment in a case involving a capital offence:

> Regarding all others mentioned in the Torah as liable to the death penalty, they cannot be put to death without trial by a court of 23, witnesses to the transgression and legal warning having been given before the capital offence was committed.

*Rashi*[28] comments that a legal warning is not required in the case of a person who incites idolatry. *Tosafot*[29] record that unlike other capital cases witnesses can be hidden in a case of inciting idolatry so that they may observe the crime unnoticed.

*(ii) TB Ṣanhedrin 29a*

The Gemara confirms in TB *Ṣanhedrin* 29a that the normal procedural rules to protect the interests of a defendant accused of committing a capital offence do not apply to a person accused of inciting idolatry.

> ... in capital cases, even if the defendant does not advance a plea to exonerate himself, the court pleads on his behalf. But the court does not plead on behalf of an instigator to idolatry, even though his is a capital case. What is the difference between an instigator to idolatry and defendants in other capital cases? R. Ḥama bar Ḥanina said: From the lectures of R. Ḥiyya bar Abba I learned the following reason — an instigator is different because G-d has stated regarding the instigator: "You shall not be compassionate to him, and you shall not conceal him.[30]

The Gemara continues to present an extraordinary illustration of the application of this rule by reference to Adam and Eve, and the serpent. The serpent is treated as an instigator to idolatry because he incited Eve to rebel against G-d:

> R. Shmuel bar Naḥman said in the name of R. Yonatan, "From where do we learn that one does not plead on behalf of an instigator? From the primordial serpent, who instigated Eve to eat from the Tree of Knowledge." As R. Simlai said, "There were many pleas that the serpent could have advanced to

28 R. Shelomo Yitsḥaḳi, 1040-1105, leading French commentator.

29 Recorded discussions of French and German scholars in the 12th & 13th centuries.

30 *Deuteronomy* 13:7-12. *Rashi* comments on this verse that a person must not search for the instigator's merits.

exonerate himself, but he did not advance them. And why did G-d not plead on the serpent's behalf? Because the serpent did not plead by himself, and being an instigator, he was not afforded the privilege of having a plea considered on his behalf.

*(iii) TB Ṣanhedrin 33b*

In TB *Ṣanhedrin* 33b the Gemara states that the rule in capital cases permitting verdicts of guilty to be revoked in favour of acquittal does not apply in the case of a person who incites another to idolatry.

*(iv) TB Ṣanhedrin 36a*

The Gemara records in TB *Ṣanhedrin* 36a that a judge is disqualified from judging a capital case where he is an old man or someone who does not have children, except in the case of an instigator who incites others to worship idols.

*(v) TB Ṣanhedrin 85b*

In TB *Ṣanhedrin* 85b it is stated that although it is forbidden for a son to be appointed an agent of the court for the purposes of administering judicial punishment to his father, this rule does not apply in the case of a father who has incited others to commit idolatry. This is because the Torah states regarding an instigator that "You shall not be compassionate to him, and you shall not conceal him."[31]

*(vi) TB Ṣanhedrin 88b*

The earlier formulation that a person who incites idolatry does not require a warning that he is liable to incur the death penalty is repeated in TB *Ṣanhedrin* 88b.

Interestingly, notwithstanding these references in TB *Ṣanhedrin* to the procedures for investigating an instigator who incites idolatry, one recent commentator[32] has noted that Jewish history does not record a single use of entrapment to secure evidence of religious seduction by a false prophet or a

31 *Deuteronomy* 13:7-12.

32 Rabbi Dr. J.H. Hertz, *The Pentateuch and Haftorahs*, 2nd edition (London: Soncino Press, 1965), 807.

member of one's family.[33]

*Entrapment in the Bible*

The exceptional circumstances in which entrapment is permitted by Jewish law can be traced to verses in the Mosaic Code in Deuteronomy 13:7-12 which stipulate, *inter alia*, that "your eye shall not pity [the instigator], nor shall you spare him."[34] These verses refer to an instigator who incites another person to serve other gods secretly. The Bible states that as a result of such abhorrent conduct a person forfeits every claim to mercy. In modern parlance, he loses the protection of due process. The full text of the passage in Deuteronomy 13:7-12 reads as follows:

> If your brother, the son of your mother, or your son or your daughter, or the wife of your bosom, or your friend who is like your own soul will entice you secretly, saying: "Let us go and worship the gods of others" — that you did not know, you nor your forefathers, from the gods of the peoples that are

33 It seems that Dr. Hertz must have doubted the authenticity of the last passage in TB *Ṣanhedrin* 67a suggesting that entrapment was utilised to catch an idolator prior to the destruction of the Second Temple. The passage states:

> It was related that this is precisely what they did to the well known inciter, the son of Setada in the city of Lod, who was hanged for his crimes on the eve of *Pesach*. [The Gemara raises a question about this anecdote] Was the inciter the son of Setada? But surely we know that he was the son of Pandera! Rav Hisda said: The husband of the inciter's mother was named Setada, and so the inciter was known as the son of Setada. But her lover who was in fact the inciter's father was named Pandera, and so the inciter was also known as the son of Pandera. The husband was Pappos the son of Yehuda! Rather, his mother was Setada. His mother was Miriam [*Miryam M'gadla*] the woman's hairdresser! As they say in Pumbedita: That one strayed from her husband."

This passage has been omitted from many editions of the Talmud, including the Vilna edition. In his commentary on the Talmud, R. Adin Steinsaltz, Vol XVIII, Tractate *Ṣanhedrin*, Part IV, (New York: Random House, 1998), 226, notes that Christian authorities censored the passage, most probably at the time of the Inquisition. The censors identified the idolator, son of Setada /Pandera, as Jesus of Nazareth. The references to the eve of Passover and Miriam Magdeline are cited in this context. R. Steinsaltz adds that Pandera was a common name amongst Roman soldiers, being derived from the Greek word Pandaros meaning a panther. R. Steinsaltz records that another passage mentioning the death of Jesus [*Yeshu HaNotsri*] has been excised from the text at TB *Ṣanhedrin* 43a.

34 *Deuteronomy* 13:9.

> around you, those near to you or those far from you, from one end of the earth to the other end of the earth — you shall not accede to him and you shall not listen to him; your eye shall not take pity on him, you shall not be compassionate and you shall not conceal him. Rather, you shall surely kill him; your hand shall be the first against him to kill him, and the hand of the entire people afterwards. You shall pelt him with stones and he shall die, for he sought to make you stray from the near G-d, your G-d, who took you out of Egypt, from the house of slavery. All Israel shall hear and see, and they shall not again do such an evil thing in your presence.

The Biblical language is very strong. Various different responses to the instigator are identified — (i) You shall not accede to him, (ii) You shall not hearken to him, (iii) You shall not pity him, (iv) You shall not be compassionate to him, and (v) You shall not conceal him. Rather, the Bible commands that the person who is the subject of the incitement to idolatry must kill him, and what is more, that person must take the initiative in killing him. *Rashi* stresses that it is a positive religious obligation for a person to kill an instigator who has sought to incite him to idolatry.

A question arises concerning how these Biblical verses are to be given practical effect. Relying on the injunction neither to pity the instigator nor to spare him, Maimonides[35] expounds six negative commandments in the *Mishneh Torah*.[36] Maimonides explains that it is a divine commandment for a layman to kill an instigator who sought to entice him to idolatry,[37] and where an instigator is placed on trial, a person is prohibited from saying anything in his favour. According to Biblical law, a person is absolutely forbidden from "covering up" for an instigator who has incited idolatry. As Maimonides explains:

> If you know something tending to incriminate him, you may not remain silent.[38]

The Mosaic injunction condemning inactivity when confronted with the activities of an instigator inciting idolatry was re-iterated in similar terms in

35 R. Moshe ben Maimon (the *Rambam*), 1135-1204, leading Spanish commentator.

36 Maimonides, MT Negative Commandments, 16 to 21.

37 *Rashi* explains this commandment by reference to the principle of "measure for measure." Since the instigator tried to lure his friend into idolatry, his friend is entitled, indeed obligated, to lure the instigator into transgression for the purpose of securing his conviction and sentence.

38 Maimonides, MT Negative Commandment, 21.

the *Ṣefer HaḤinukh.*[39] After summarising the terms of TB *Ṣanhedrin* 67a, the *Ṣefer HaḤinukh* states:[40]

> The Sages of blessed memory taught further that if the man did not wish to entice two, it is a religious duty to conceal witnesses [*lehakhmeen*] for him. The meaning is that witnesses are hidden in a place where they can see the enticer ...

It is interesting to focus upon how the *Ṣefer HaḤinukh* transmutes the Biblical commandments in Deuteronomy 13:7-12 into a religious obligation to conceal witnesses to entrap a person who incites idolatry. The Hebrew word "*lehakhmeen,*" meaning "to entrap", is the same word used in the Mishnah and the Gemara [*makhmeenin*], sharing its root with the words "*Meekhmun,*" meaning "a hidden store," "*Meekhmus,*" meaning "a hiding place,"[41] and "*Meekhmur,*" meaning "a net or a snare."[42] The etymology of these words is Aramaic, derived from the word "*Kmun,*" meaning "to lie in wait" or "to lie in ambush." "*Kamana*" in Arabic means "to hide or conceal," and "*Kmur*" is used when referring to "hiding fruit in the ground" when making it ripe.[43]

In point of fact, it is possible to argue that the Biblical licence to entrap an instigator inciting idolatry is not quite as strong as first appears. There is no reference to the notion of entrapment, in the sense of *lahakhmeen* or *makhmeenin*, in the verses set out in Deuteronomy 13:7-12, nor for that matter, in any other passage of the Mosaic Code.[44] A comment contained in the *Ṣifrei*[45] is particularly pertinent in this context. Focussing upon the opening words of these verses ("If your brother, the son of your mother, or

39 Attributed to R. Aharon HaLevi, a 13th century commentator in Barcelona.

40 At 464.

41 *Daniel* 11:43, where there is reference to hidden treasures of gold and silver [*b'mikhmanai hazahav v'hakeṣef*].

42 *Isaiah* 51:20, where the impact of desolation experienced by Israel's sons is likened to a wild bull in a net [*kto mikhmar*].

43 See E. Klein, *Etymological Dictionary of the Hebrew Language* (New York: Macmillan, 1987).

44 The serpent's conduct when inducing Eve to eat of the tree of Knowledge in *Genesis* 3:1-7 is sometimes cited as the earliest example of entrapment (see, for example, Strusman J. *in State of Israel* v. *Shnerer* [1986] 3 PM 82 at 86-7, and TB *Ṣanhedrin* 29a, *supra*, section 3 B(ii)). Jezebel's conduct in tricking Navot into scorning her husband Ahab (*I Kings* 21:1-29) has also been identified as an example of entrapment. However, there is no reference to the notion of *lehakhmeen* or *makhmeenin* in either case.

45 Biblical commentators at the time of the 2nd Temple.

your son or your daughter, or the wife of your bosom, or your friend who is like your own soul will entice you secretly"), the *Ṣifrei* explains[46] that further witnesses are necessary in the case of an instigator because the witnesses who heard the incitement are not competent to give evidence against the inciter by virtue of their relationship to him.[47] The force of these verses, according to the *Ṣifrei*, is not to justify the use of entrapment in a case of inciting idolatry but rather to emphasise that the requirement for independent witnesses cannot be suspended in a difficult case.

Whether support for the use of entrapment in the Mosaic Code is strong or weak, it is beyond doubt that, in so far as Jewish law is concerned, entrapment is prohibited as an investigative device in all the but the most limited circumstances.

### *Entrapment — Leading Another Astray*

The Biblical and Talmudic reluctance to utilise entrapment as a device to catch offenders is fortified by reference to another important principle in Jewish law prohibiting a person from leading another into committing a transgression. The prohibition is prosaically expressed in Leviticus 19:14 in the following terms:

> ... You shall not place a stumbling block before the blind (*lifnei eever*)...

Although this prohibition is primarily directed against giving bad advice to a person misleading him to his detriment,[48] it has been interpreted more widely to prohibit a person from aiding or abetting another person to bring about a transgression.[49] *Eever* refers not only to a person who is physically blind, but also to one who is spiritually or morally blind. The Gemara relates that a person "places a stumbling block before the blind" if he passes a cup of wine to a Nazarite or gives a limb taken from a living animal to a non-Jewish person, since a Nazarite is prohibited from drinking wine and a non-Jewish person is bound by the Noahide laws not to eat flesh from a

46 *Ṣifrei* on Numbers and Deuteronomy 64.

47 Relatives are not competent to testify in Jewish law for or against a person to whom they are related. See M. Elon, *Principles of Jewish Law* (Jerusalem: Keter Publishing House, 1975), 607.

48 *Ṣefer HaḤinukh*, 232. For a comprehensive examination of this principle in the context of legal ethics, see S. Resnicoff, "Helping a Client Violate Jewish Law," *Jewish Law Association Studies* X (1998), 191.

49 Maimonides, *Ṣefer Hamitzvot*, Negative *Mitzvot*, 299.

living animal.[50] More pertinently, in the context of entrapment, there is a discussion in another tractate of the Gemara[51] about whether Rav Huna acted correctly when testing the moral character of his son by destroying property in his son's presence to see if his son would become angry. The Gemara asks whether this conduct contravened the prohibition against *lifnei eever* because it could have provoked the son into acting disrespectfully towards his father. Rav Huna responded that he had not transgressed this prohibition because he had told his son that he had waived all honour due to him before destroying the property in question.[52] If Rav Huna had not absolved his son before seeking to provoke him into becoming angry, his conduct would have been prohibited by the principle of *lifnei eever.*

The leaning in Jewish law against laying a trap may be supported by reference to a contemporary work[53] where the ability of an employer to test the honesty of a potential employee is discussed. A situation is posited where an employee seeks to test a potential employee's honesty by leaving tempting articles in his path to see if he can restrain his desire to take them. A test of this nature is not permitted, on the basis that it contravenes the prohibition of *lifnei eever*. A person's evil inclination ought not to be encouraged by putting temptation in his path. Even if the contravention of *lifnei eever* is considered doubtful, the test conflicts with an assumption that the employer should make to the effect that every G-d fearing person is to be regarded as a fit and reliable person, in the absence of conduct which would cause the employee to suspect otherwise.[54]

The nearest instance of Jewish law sanctioning conduct testing a person's honesty is found in a discussion contained in *Masekhet Derekh Eretz Rabbah,* chapter 5.[55] It is recorded that Rav Yehoshua invited a guest to stay in his

50 TB *Pesaḥim* 22b; see also TB *Avoda Zara* 15b (selling weapons to a suspected bandit).

51 TB *Ḳiddushin* 32a; see also TB *Moed Ḳaṭan* 17a (father striking a mature son who may retaliate or curse him).

52 See also TB *Avodah Zarah* 14a.

53 Rav Y. Blau, *Pitḥai Ḥoshen, Hilkhot Gneivah* (Jerusalem, 1996), 4(B).

54 R. Blau relies upon the concept of *b'ḥezḳat kesherim* (assuming a person to be reliable) as support for this proposition. This concept is consistent with the Biblical obligation to "judge your neighbour favourably", related in *Leviticus* 19:15, immediately after the prohibition against *lifnei eever*. See in this context TB *Shabbat* 127b.

55 This is a tractate printed at the back of some, but not all, Hebrew editions of TB *Ṣanhedrin*. It was compiled during the Geonic period.

home. After giving the guest food and drink, Rav Yehoshua provided him with a place to sleep in the loft. After the guest went to sleep Rav Yeshoshua removed the ladder from the loft. During the night the guest took items from the room and tried to leave. The ladder from the loft having been removed, the guest fell to the ground and broke his ribs. The discussion justifies Rav Yehoshua's conduct by pointing out that there is no contradiction between, on the one hand, honouring a guest "as if he was Rabban Gamliel"[56] and, on the other hand, being suspicious of him in case he is a robber.[57] The basis of Rav Yehoshua's suspicion is not recorded, but it seems to be related to the fact that the guest came to Rav Yehoshua very early in the morning, at a time when suspicion might be aroused.

Entrapment, in the sense of actively enticing or instigating a person to behave improperly, does not feature in any of these situations. The ability of a person to resist temptation is being tested, but there is no notion of laying a trap. If conduct testing a person's ability to withstand temptation is prohibited by the principle of *lifnei eever*, conduct entrapping a person into offending conduct must surely be prohibited as logical extension of this principle. Rav Yeshoshua's conduct falls into a different category since he neither devises a test for his guest nor lays a trap for him. Rather, Rav Yeshoshua's conduct is merely precautionary. He removes the ladder from the loft in an effort to prevent suffering a loss. The removal of the ladder does not offend the principle of *lifnei eever* because Rav Yeshoshua had good reason to suspect that the guest might be a robber, and he was right!

### *Entrapment in the Mishneh Torah*

Mindful of the Biblical and Talmudic sources, Maimonides expresses his clear understanding in the Mishneh Torah that, with the exception of an instigator inciting idolatry, entrapment is forbidden in Jewish law. The full passage in the Mishneh Torah reads as follows:

> An instigator does not need a warning. If one incites to idolatry a single individual, the latter should tell him: "I have friends who would also be interested in this," and thus he should lure him into inciting idolatry before two people so that the instigator can be executed. If the instigator refuses to incite idolatry before two people, it is an obligation to set a trap for him. *A*

56 A great Talmudic sage.

57 This appears to be a reference to the principle of *kavadho v'ḥashdaho*, whereby a person is obligated to honour another person whilst at the same time being suspicious of him. See *Igrot Moshe, Ḥoshen Mishpaṭ*, 1:47.

> *trap is never set for a person who violates any of the Torah's other prohibitions. This is the only exception.* How is the trap set for him? The person who is the object of the incitement should bring two people and place them in a dark place where they can see the instigator and hear what he is saying without him seeing them. The entrapper tells the instigator: "Repeat what you told me privately." When he does so, the entrapper should reply: "How can we forsake our G-d in Heaven and serve wood and stone?" If the instigator retracts or remains silent, he is not held liable. If the instigator tells the entrapper, "This is our obligation and this is beneficial to us," those who stand far off have him summoned to court and stoned."[58] (*emphasis supplied*)

Maimonides' language is particularly striking since the general rule against the use of entrapment embraces both capital and non-capital prohibitions.

## *Conclusion*

Accordingly, it can be seen that from the earliest times Jewish law has rejected the use of entrapment as an investigative device in the detection of crime except in the unusual case of a person inciting idolatry. Entrapment is an anathema to Jewish law since the whole purpose of Judaism is directed towards the elevation of human conduct[59] rather than its debasement. Even where entrapment is permitted in one exceptional circumstance, Jewish law ensures that its scope is narrowly circumscribed. Although the requirement in Jewish law, for a person entrapping an instigator to act passively, accords with contemporary secular jurisprudence, comparative analysis between Jewish law and modern legal systems reveals more differences than similarities. Most fundamentally, Jewish law requires a person entrapping an

58 MT, *Hilkhot Avodat Kokhavim* 5:3.

59 In this context it is interesting to note that recognition of a person's right to privacy in Jewish law does not sit easily with the use of entrapment. The traditional starting point regarding privacy of the individual in Jewish law is found in *Numbers* 24:2 with the account of Balaam cursing the Jewish people. The Bible describes how Balaam raised his eyes "and saw Israel dwelling according to its tribes." The Gemara (TB *Bava Batra* 60a) explains that Balaam, seeing that the openings of the tents were not aligned opposite each other, appreciated how much the Israelite nation valued the importance of privacy and was prompted to exclaim that the Jewish people were worthy of blessing. The importance of a person's right to privacy is recognised in the Mishnah (*Bava Batra* 3:7), where the prohibition against constructing windows facing each other is noted. See also the discussion in TB *Bava Batra* 59a.

instigator to offer him an opportunity of retracting his conduct. So far as Jewish law is concerned, entrapment is an acceptable method of gathering evidence[60] only where it is utilised to identify a person who is absolutely determined to proceed with his criminal activity. In contrast to the approach taken by contemporary legal systems, Jewish law resists the temptation to permit the use of entrapment more broadly.

60 There is no exclusionary rule in Jewish law against the admission of illegally obtained evidence. In Jewish law, a judge is commanded to render a judgment that is "true to its very truth" (*din emet le-amito*). Commentators have focused on the duality of the expression *emet le-amito* to argue that proper performance of this injunction requires the admission of all credible evidence, even if it is "the fruit of the poisoned tree." The interaction between the application of this principle and the reception of evidence in a case of entrapment by a person who is *a priori* disqualified as a competent witness because of his established willingness to transgress Jewish law is beyond the scope of this paper. For sources on the application of *din emet le-amito*, see TB *Shabbat* 10a; TB *Eruvin* 54b; TB *Megillah* 15b; TB *Ṣanhedrin* 7a and 111b; TB *Bava Batra* 8b; *Moadi* v. *State of Israel* [1984] 38(i) PD 197; *Military Court of Appeals* v. *Vaknin* [1988] 42)(iii) PD 837, and E. Harnon, "The Impact of the Basic Law: Human Dignity and Liberty on the Law of Criminal Procedure and Evidence — Israel", [1999] 33 *Israel Law Review* 678 at 708-713. For a summary of the approach of Jewish law towards disqualified witnesses, see M. Elon, *The Principles of Jewish Law* (Jerusalem: Keter Publishing House, 1975), 606-7.

5

# A FATHER'S VERSUS A HUSBAND'S AUTHORITY TO ANNUL A VOW (*Numbers* 30:4-17)

by

JOSEPH FLEISHMAN*

A vow is a voluntary assumption of an obligation to do something with regard to God (other than a commandment) under the belief that such a deed would please God. From the moment such an obligation is assumed, it has some measure of holiness, as is stated: "If a man makes a vow (נדר) to the Lord or takes an oath (שבעה) imposing an obligation (אסר) on himself, he shall not break his pledge; he must carry out all that has crossed his lips" (*Numbers* 30:3).[1] Generally a person makes a vow as a means of entreating God to fulfill his wish; but at times a vow is a derivative of a person's desire to achieve a higher level of piety and veneration of God.[2]

In *Numbers* 30:4-16, four cases are discussed in which a woman has made a vow to God:

a Senior Lecturer, Department of Bible, Bar-Ilan University, Israel.

1 T. W. Cartledge, *Vows in the Hebrew Bible and the Ancient Near East*, *JSOT* Sup. 147 (Sheffield: Sheffield Academic Press, 1992), 13; J. Licht, *A Commentary on the Book of Numbers* (Jerusalem: Magnes Press, 1995), 103; B.A. Levine, *Numbers 21-36*, The Anchor Bible (New York and London: Doubleday, 2000), 428-434.

This issue is dealt with in, for example, J. Milgrom, *Numbers*, The JPS Torah Commentary (Philadelphia and New York: The Jewish Publication Society, 1990), 488-490.

2 There are commentators who think that all the vows mentioned in the Bible are conditional upon God's granting the request of the one makes the vow. See, for example, Cartledge, *supra* n.1, at 12, 17-18; Levine, *supra* n.1, at 428-434.

For a discussion of vows that shows that although most of them are conditional, some are not, see Licht, *supra* no.1, at 98.

- The case of an unmarried woman who lives in her father's house (vs. 4-6);
- The case of a married woman who had vowed while still living in her father's house, or who made the vow following her engagement (vs. 7-9);
- The case of a vow made by a widow or divorced woman (v. 10); and
- The case of a vow made by a married woman in her husband's house (vs. 11-16).[3]

It is clear from these cases that a woman is permitted to make a vow like a man, and that her obligations correspond to his.[4] However, the Torah gave a father the authority to annul his daughter's vows while she is "in her father's household by reason of her youth,"[5] and bestowed upon a husband the authority to annul his wife's vow.

This study focuses on the question, did the Torah grant the father and husband identical rights to annul a vow made by a daughter or wife, or is there a difference between a father's and a husband's authority to annul a vow?

With regard to the father's authority, it states:[6]

> If a woman makes a vow to the Lord and assumes an obligation while still in her father's household by reason of her youth, and her father learns of her vow or her self-imposed obligation and offers no objection, all her vows shall stand and every self-imposed obligation shall stand. But if her father restrains her on the day he finds out, *none* of her vows or self-imposed obligations shall stand [lit.: *all* her vows or self-imposed obligations *shall not stand*]; and the Lord will forgive her, since her father restrained her (30:4-6).

Regarding the vow of an engaged or married woman, which was made while under the authority of her father, it states:

> If she should marry while her vow or the commitment to which she bound

3 There are commentators who think that vs.11-16 concern a widow or divorcee who had made the vow while married. See for example, R. Abraham ibn Ezra and Abarbanel's commentaries *in situ*; Levin, supra n. 1 at 433.

4 *Ṣifrei, Numbers*, 153.

5 Our Sages limit this to the period after the first signs of adulthood are seen. She is defined as a girl between eleven years, one day and twelve years, one day. Upon examination this girl is found to be aware of the importance of a vow. See *Ṣifrei, Numbers*, 153. When she reaches puberty, her father no longer has authority over her (*Nedarim,* 47b).

6 The translations of the texts from the Torah are taken from the *JPS Torah Commentary*, *supra* n.1, unless otherwise stated.

> herself is still in force, and her husband learns of it and offers no objection on the day he finds out, her vows shall stand and her self-imposed obligations shall stand. But if her husband restrains her on the day that he learns of it, he thereby annuls her vow that was in force or the commitment to which she bound herself; and the Lord will forgive her (30:7-9).

From the language of v.6 one learns that a father can annul *all* of his daughter's vows. On the other hand, in the case of an engaged or married woman who had made a vow while living in her father's house, the verse specifies that the fiancé or husband "annuls her vow which was in force or the commitment to which she bound herself; and the Lord will forgive her." The world "all," used in connection with the father's authority, does not appear here.

In the fourth case, in connection with a wife who made a vow while married, it is written:

> But if her husband does annul them on the day he finds out, then nothing that has crossed her lips shall stand, whether vows or self-imposed obligations. Her husband has annulled them, and the Lord will forgive her. *Every vow and every sworn obligation of self-denial may be upheld by her husband or annulled by her husband* (30:13-14).

Verse 13 seems to permit a husband, like a father, to annul all of his wife's vows; but v.14 specifically diminishes the husband's authority in such a case. It establishes that a husband could annul only a vow of self-denial. One cannot claim that v.14 does not necessarily diminish the instruction in v.13, since in principle it is possible that v.14 refers to another instance, such as a vow or self-imposed obligation of self-denial that a husband can always annul even if not "on the day he learns of it." A careful reading of vs. 12-15, which concern the vows and self-imposed obligations of a married woman, reveals the following structure: v.15 clarifies the instruction of v.12 and diminishes its application; likewise, v.14 clarifies the instruction of v.13, and diminishes its application. One can add that v.15's structure is chiastic.

The verse that concludes the four cases states: "Those are the laws that the Lord enjoined upon Moses as between a man and his wife, and as between a father and his daughter while in her father's household by reason of her youth" (30:17). The question is if this single verse on man-wife and father-daughter is intended simply as a summation to conclude the section on women's vows, or if it is intended to indicate that there is no difference between a father's authority to annul his daughter's vows and a husband's authority to annul his wife's vows?

A clear reply can be found in *Ṣifrei*:

> Scripture states, "Those are the laws that the Lord enjoined upon Moses as between a man and his wife, and as between a father and his daughter" (30:17), teaching that perforce you must link the law of the husband to that of the father. Just as the husband abrogates only vows [that bear upon their relationship and vows] of self-denial, so too the father may abrogate only vows that bear upon their relationship and vows of self-affliction (*Ṣifrei, Numbers*, 155.[7]

This problem is also discussed in the Jerusalem Talmud, and here, too, the conclusion is categorical.

The Mishna states:

> And these are the vows which he[8] annuls: matters of inflicting self-denial ("afflicting the soul" [*Num.* 30:13]): for example, "if I shall wash," or, "if I shall not wash," "if I shall adorn myself," or, "if I shall not adorn myself." Said R. Yosé, "These are not vows of self-denial."

The Gemara explains:

> It is written, "Any vow and any binding oath of self-denial [her husband may establish, or her husband may make void]" (*Num.* 30:13). I know that the abrogation of vows applies only to vows which involve self-punishment. How do I know that the same applies to vows which are between him and her? (Scripture says,) "... as between a man and his wife..." (*Num.* 30:16). Up to this point we have dealt with the husband's [right to annul a vow]. How do I know that the same applies to the father? (Scripture says,) "... between a father and his daughter [while in her youth, within her father's house]" (*Num.* 30:16). (Accordingly,) just as the husband annuls only those vows which involve self-denial and vows between him and her, so the father annuls only those vows which involve self-denial and vows between him and her (Jerusalem Talmud, *Nedarim*, ch. 11, sec. 5).[9]

Thus according to the *Ṣifrei* as well as according to the Jerusalem Talmud, the concluding verse (17) of the section on women's vows instructs us that a father is permitted to annul only a vow that concerns his daughter and himself,[10] or a vow of self-denial made by his daughter; likewise, a husband is permitted to annul only a vow that concerns his wife and himself or a vow

7 The translations of the sources quoted below are mine, unless otherwise stated.

8 "He" — the father or the husband. This was the explanation of *Pnei Moshe* and of *Ḳorban Ha'edah, in situ.*

9 The translation is based on *The Talmud of the Land of Israel* (*Nedarim*), vol.23, tr. J. Neusner (Chicago and London: University of Chicago Press, 1985), 195.

10 In the case of a father and daughter, the reference is to the obligations of a daughter to her father.

of self-denial made by his wife. This conclusion clearly does not agree with the plain interpretation of the Scriptures.

Maimonides ruled differently from the *Ṣifrei* and the Jerusalem Talmud. According to him:

> A father may annul any of his daughter's vows or oaths the day he hears of them, for Scripture says, "But if her father restrains her on the day he finds out, none of her vows or self-imposed obligations shall stand..." (*Num.* 30:6). On the other hand, a husband may revoke only those vows which involve self-denial or affect matters pertaining to their mutual relationship—for example, if she swears or vows not to paint her eyes or not to adorn herself. For Scripture says, "between a man and his wife" (*Num.* 30:17) (*Hilkhot Nedarim*, ch. 12, sec. 1).[11]

Maimonides rules that the authority of a father regarding his daughter and of a husband regarding his wife in connection with annulling a vow are not identical. A husband is permitted to annul only a vow of self-denial or a vow that concerns their mutual relationship; whereas a father is permitted to annul all of his daughter's vows.

The Sages of Lunel questioned him about the matter:

> In *Hilkhot Nedarim* (chapter 12, section 1) it is stated: "A father may abrogate all oaths and vows of his juvenile daughter upon the day that he learns of it", etc. Enlighten us with the light of your Torah! For it states in the *Ṣifrei* (*Maṭot*, 155) that the law of the husband is to be applied to the father. The same is found in tractate *Nedarim* 79b, on the basis of the verse, "as between a father and his daughter, as between a man and his wife" - a husband may annul only vows of self-denial, while the verse is explicated differently concerning a daughter. Would our Rabbi kindly clarify the matter.

Maimonides wrote in response:

> The question posed should concern every Sage, and I dwelled upon it for several days. It is well-known that according to the link established in the *Ṣifrei*, the father may abrogate only vows that the husband may abrogate, as is explicitly written there. But this has disturbed me for a long time. I thought that surely this ruling must be the lone opinion of R. Simeon, who is considered to be the anonymous voice of the *Ṣifrei* (*Ṣanhedrin*, 86a). For if this position were truly the *halakhah*, it is inconceivable that the Gemara would have ignored it completely. You shall not find that linkage (of the law pertaining to the husband and the law pertaining to the father) anywhere in either the Babylonian Talmud or Jerusalem Talmud. Nor is this law expressed

11 The translation is based on *The Code of Maimonides: Book Six, The Book of Asseverations*, trans. B.D. Klien (New Haven and London: Yale University Press, 1962), 106-107.

> in the Tosefta, nor in the Gemara (*Nedarim,* 79b) ...
>
> From all of this it seems to me that the only area of dispute concerning these vows is with regard to the abrogation of vows by a husband. But with regard to a father, the Sages made no such distinctions, as is implicit in the simple meaning of the verse. For no distinction is made with regard to the father; rather, Scripture states: "none of her vows or self-imposed obligations shall stand." Yet, with regard to a husband, a differentiation is made, as it states, "Every vow and every sworn obligation of self-denial." This approach allows me to comprehend the various rulings and deliberations on this topic, and to remain faithful to the literal meaning of the biblical text. And, as I said, the ruling of R. Simeon, linking the case of the father with the case of the husband, is a lone opinion. This is how the matter appears to me, and may the Lord protect us from any error![12]

Maimonides replied that the *Ṣifrei*'s interpretation that the authority of the father and of the husband were the same in connection with a woman's vows, is based on R. Simeon's view, "for whenever no Sage is specified, the view is that of R. Simeon." Now our Talmudic Sages did not draw an analogy between the father and the husband. From this we learn that Maimonides ruled as he did because he thought that our Sages understood the Scriptures as differentiating between the authority of the father and that of the husband.

R. Moshe of Coucy (France, 13th century) agrees with Maimonides in *Ṣefer Mitzvot Gadol*, #242, 73a. He added:

> I was astonished by the ruling mentioned in the *Ṣifrei* on "*Maṭot*": "As between a man and his wife, as between a father and his daughter," the two laws are linked... And the rabbi, R. Jeḥiel interpreted the rule as applying to an engaged woman, that is, if her fiancé dies, the father does not regain his previous privileges. Prior to her engagement, however, he may abrogate any vow she makes.

These words indicate that Rabbi Moshe (like Rabbi Jeḥiel) thought that the *Ṣifrei* spoke of an engaged maiden whose father or fiancé could have the right to annul her vows. In this matter the Scriptures made an analogy, indicating that any vow that a fiancé could not annul, the father was not permitted to annul. Maimonides, on the other hand, speaks of a maiden who is not engaged and is thus completely under the authority of her father, who therefore is the one who can annul all her vows.

Rabbi Ya'akov, son of the Rabeinu Asher (Spain, 1270-1343) (*Ṭur*, *Hilkhot Nedarim*, *Yoreh De'ah*, section 234) ruled like the *Ṣifrei* and the

12 According to Y. Blau, "*Mikitzei Nirdamim,*" *Tshuvot HaRambam* (Jerusalem: Reuven Mass, 1986), qu. 326, 593-595.

Jerusalem Talmud (also like his father who lived in Spain about 1250). Differing with Maimonides, he stated:

> The law concerning a father with regard to his daughter is identical to the law of a husband regarding his wife. The lone exception to this is that a father may release his daughter from her obligation, as could any sage, for relatives may be approached in this regard. Maimonides however, posits that the father may annul all vows of his daughter, a position that is difficult to sustain. R. Jeḥiel [of Paris] (the father of Rabeinu Asher and grandfather of R. Yaacov) offered a differentiation. Prior to engagement, a father could annul any vow made. Yet, if she were engaged and then her husband died and she reverted to her father's protection, he would be permitted to annul only vows of self-denial. My father, Rabeinu Asher of blessed memory, made no such distinction.

R. Jeḥiel's attempt to resolve the conflict created by Maimonides' words is explained by R. Yoel Sirkes (Poland, 1581-1640) in his commentary *Bayit Ḥadash*:

> The rabbi, R. Jeḥiel, attempted to sustain the authority of both [the literal meaning of the Scriptural verse and of the *Ṣifrei*]. The literal meaning of the Scriptural verse concerns a woman prior to engagement. The ruling of the *Ṣifrei*, however, refers to a woman following her engagement... While she is engaged, the father cannot abrogate only vows of self-denial, and this in conjunction with the husband. Yet once the husband dies, and she returns to the father's authority, there is no basis to grant him privileges of abrogation that he did not have previously. For the father now bears the status of the inheritor of the privilege of the husband. This is why we rule in accordance with R. Jeḥiel. R. Moshe of Coucy, in his work *Ṣefer Mitzvot Gadol*, also expressed an opinion in which he tried to square the literal meaning of the verse with the ruling found in the *Ṣifrei*. See his work, "Prohibitions," sec. 242, p. 73b.

R. Joseph Karo (Tsfat, 1488-1575), in *Keṣef Mishneh* asks a number of questions on Maimonides' reply to the Sages of Lunel:

> It is puzzling to reject an explication of the *Ṣifrei* simply because it does not appear in the Talmuds or in the Tosefta. While it is true that the anonymous voice of the *Ṣifrei* is that of R. Simeon, we may assume that this ruling is a unanimous one, as no dissenting opinion is recorded. In fact, there are several instances in which our master (i.e. Maimonides) rules in accordance with the explication and ruling of the *Ṣifrei*, even though no parallel ruling is found in the Talmuds or in the Tosefta. And concerning his argument based on the literal meaning of the verse, one may counter that since Scripture states, "between a man and his wife, and as between a man and his daughter," the two instances are linked in all regards, and that this was the understanding of the *Ṣifrei* .
>
> Moreover, his statement that this ruling is not to be found in either of

> the Talmuds, is in fact erroneous. For in the Jerusalem Talmud we find the following explicitly stated at the outset of the final chapter of Tractate Nedarim: "Just as the husband may abrogate only vows of self-denial and those that bear upon their relationship, so too the father may abrogate only vows of self-denial and those that bear upon their relationship. It may also be shown that the Babylonian Talmud makes reference to this ruling.

It is difficult to understand R. Joseph Karo's comment that Maimonides' statement that the *Ṣifrei*'s ruling is not mentioned in the two Talmuds was written without sufficient care, for the Lunel Sages wrote specifically that Maimonides' ruling disagreed with the words of the *Ṣifrei* and the Talmud in the tractate "Nedarim." Moreover, in his long reply to the Sages of Lunel, Maimonides discusses the words of Talmudic Sages and explains that his reply does not contradict their words, but agrees with them. Therefore, in my opinion, it is reasonable to assume that the explanations of Rabbi Moshe of Coucy and R. Jeḥiel are valid explanations of Maimonides. That is, one must distinguish between the authority of the father to annul the vows of a daughter who was not engaged and his authority to annul her vows after her engagement. Therefore, a father is permitted to annul all of a daughter's vows and self-imposed obligations as long as she is not a *bogeret*, i.e., an adult. On the other hand, a husband is permitted to annul only vows of self-denial and vows that concern their mutual relationship. One can therefore conclude that Maimonides ruled according to the plain meaning of the Scriptural text, namely that the Torah differentiates between the authority of a father over his daughter and that of a husband over his wife.

# 6

## LENDING - NO, INVESTING - YES: DEVELOPMENT OF THE *IṢḲA* LAW FROM THE 12TH TO THE 15TH CENTURIES

by

HILLEL GAMORAN[*]

In a previous article[1] we discussed how the rabbis dealt with partnerships in which one partner profited by providing the funds for a business enterprise. We discovered that Rabbi Abraham ben David of Posquières (*Rabad*), the leading rabbinic authority of Provence in the 12th century, interpreted the law so as to ease the restrictions which the sages had instituted to preserve the law against usury. His rulings made participation in such enterprises more attractive to investors than they had been earlier.

In the present article, we will explore how the rabbis after the time of *Rabad* dealt with these restrictions.

### *Talmud*

The Talmud had a name for a partnership in which one party provided the capital, and the other acted as the working partner. It was called an *iṣḳa*. An *iṣḳa*, as explained in the Talmud,[2] was considered to be half a loan and half a deposit. The working partner suffered the losses or gained the profits from the loan half of the investment, while the investor assumed the losses and the gains from the deposit half.

The authors of the Mishnah were concerned that such a 50/50 partnership

a Jackson School of International Studies, University of Washington, Seattle.

1 Hillel Gamoran, "Investing for Profit: A Study of *Iska* up to the Time of Rabbi Abraham ben David of Posquières", *Hebrew Union College Annual* 70/71 (1999-2000), 153-165.

2 b*Bava Metzia* 104b.

might result in a violation of the law which prohibited lending on interest. The problem was that the managing partner appeared to be working with the deposit half of the investment, which belonged to the investor, in return for the loan half which he received from the investor. The worker's labor in the lender's behalf was considered interest. For this reason the Mishnah ordained that such an arrangement was legal only if the investor paid the working partner a wage for his labor.[3]

The Talmud provided for more than one way for the worker to be compensated for his labor. It established[4] that in lieu of a daily payment to the working partner, the 50/50, profit/loss arrangement could be altered in favor of the working partner. The working partner could be given two-thirds of the profit while still risking only half of any loss, or the working partner could assume only a third of the liability while still taking half of any profit. In either case, the greater percentage of potential gain over possible loss granted to the working partner served as his wage for handling the investor's deposit. Whenever these arrangements were made, no daily wage payment was required. This method of compensating the active partner for working on the investor's portion of the investment was endorsed by the Geonim[5] and by the Rishonim.[6]

### *When Arrangements Were Not Specified*

There was a difference of opinion among the authorities, however, as to what should be done when the profit/loss split was not specified at the start of the partnership. How were the profits or losses then to be divided? An anonymous Gaon ruled,[7] that in a case where advance arrangements for

3 m*Bava Metzia* 5:4.

4 b*Bava Metzia* 68b-69a.

5 For example, R. Saadia Gaon, (A.A. Harkavy, *Zikhron Larishonim Vegam La'Aḥaronim,* Part 1 [Berlin, 1887], #556), R. Sherira Gaon (*Sha'are Tsedek* [Jerusalem: Klal Ufrat, 1971], Part 4, Gate 8, #5) and R. Hai Gaon (Simḥa Assaf, *Ṣefer Hashṭarot Lerav Hai bar Sherira Gaon,* Supplement to *Tarbiz,* 1 [1930], 35).

6 For example, R. Isaac Alfasi (*Bava Metzia*, p. 39b of the *Rif* pages), *Rambam* (*Shiluḥin Veshutafin* 6:3) and *Ṣefer Mitzvot Gadol,* supra n. 14 at 168, column b.

7 *Ṣefer Hadinim*, recorded in *She'elot Uteshuvot Maharam b. R. Barukh*, Prague edition, #895. The Gaon may have been R. Judah haCohen, eleventh century. See translation and comments by Irving Agus in *Urban Civilization*

dividing the profits or the losses were not made, the investor was entitled to half the profit, for had there been a loss, the investor would have had to accept two-thirds of the loss.

However, R. Solomon b. Isaac (*Rashi*) took a different approach.[8] He said that when the details of a *iṣḳa* were not spelled out, the working partner should receive two-thirds of any profit, but should bear only one half of any loss.

R. Moses Maimonides (*Rambam*) made another ruling altogether.[9] He wrote that in a case where no profit/loss split had been laid out in advance, the working partner had to be favored whether the business gained or lost. In order to avoid breaking the law against usury, he said that if there were a profit, the managing partner was entitled to two-thirds of it and if there were a loss, the investor should assume two-thirds of the loss.

But *Rabad* disagreed with all three of the previous rulings. He said that "the *eṣeḳ* belonged to the investor," and that he "always had the upper hand." The investor could wait and see how the enterprise was going before determining the profit/loss arrangements. Thus, if there were a profit, he could receive half of it, saying that were there a loss, he would have accepted two-thirds of it. Furthermore, *Rabad* maintained that if the investor saw that there was a loss, he had the option of paying the worker his wages and accepting only half of the losses. This ruling of *Rabad* was new and remarkable, for it opened up the a way for an investor to pay the working partner for his labor only in the case of a loss and to give him no advantage at all if the business were a success. As long as the partnership contract contained no specifics about the profit and loss divisions, *Rabad* maintained that the investor could craft the arrangements to his own liking.

Now how did the sages after the time of *Rabad* react to his innovation?

In a responsum that dealt with a successful partnership which doubled its worth, R. Meir of Rothenburg (*Maharam*) rejected *Rabad*'s solution.[10] He was responding to a case where, at the end of the partnership period, the investor requested half the profit. The manager replied that the investor was entitled to only a third of the profit because he, the manager, had received no wage for his labor and would have had to pay for 50% of any loss. The

---

*in Pre-Crusade Europe,* Vol. II (New York: Yeshiva University Press, 1965), 284-286, and introduction to volume I, 43-45.

8 *Bava Metzia* 104b, s.v. *Ḥad iṣḳa.*

9 *Mishneh Torah, Shiluḥin Veshutafin* 6:3.

10 R. Meir ben Barukh of Rothenburg, *Sh'elot Ut'shuvot Maharam ben R. Barukh* (Prague Edition) (Budapest, 1895) #895.

*Maharam* ruled in favor of the investor, saying that "since he did not give Simon any wages, had there been a loss, Reuben would have had to accept two-thirds of the loss whether he liked it or not ... Therefore, since Reuben obligated himself in case of a loss, he is entitled to half the profit." This was the same ruling made by the anonymous Gaon centuries earlier.

R. Moses b. Naḥman (*Ramban*), in the 13th century, also turned away from *Rabad*'s solution to the problem of an unspecified *iṣḳa*. He explicitly declared that *Rabad* was wrong and ruled that where no details were mapped out in advance, the investor should bear half of the losses but take only a third of any gains.[11] A ruling similar to that of the *Ramban* was also issued by the 14th century teacher, Rabbenu Nissim.[12] Both sages were echoing Rashi's teaching of the 11th century.

In the 14th century, R. Yom Tov b. Abraham Asevilli (*Ritba*) voiced agreement with the position of the *Rambam*, saying that the investor receives either half of the profit and two-thirds of the loss or half of the loss and one-third of the profit, and "the choice is the manager's ... in order that the manager receive wages for his labor and his food."[13] In other words, according to *Ritba*, whether the enterprise gains or loses, the manager should get some advantage to reward him for his labor.

What is remarkable about the rulings of the sages of the 13th and 14th centuries is that not a single one of them supported the view of *Rabad*.[14] His novel approach, in which he concluded that the investor "always had the upper hand," was decisively rejected by the authorities who followed him.

Up to this point we might be tempted to believe that the *iṣḳa* was upheld by the Rishonim in the same way that it had been established in the Talmud and maintained by the Geonim, that *Rabad*'s decisions promoting liberalization did not have lasting influence.

But before reaching such a conclusion, we need to examine the outcome of *Rabad*'s other rulings on the subject of *iṣḳa*. Did the Rishonim in the

11 *Kol Ḥidushe Haramban*, Part Two (Jerusalem: Or Olam, 1962) *Bava Metzia*, Chapter 9, 155b.

12 Rabbenu Nissim, *Ḥiddushe Haran, Masekhet Bava Metzia* (Jerusalem: Makhon Harry Fishel L'derishat Hatalmud Umishpaṭ Hatorah, 1994), 332.

13 R. Yom Tov b. Abraham Asevilli, *Ḥiddushe Haritba, Masekhet Bava Metzia*, ed. Shilah Raphael (Jerusalem: Mossad Harav Kook, 1992), Column 558.

14 R. Aaron Halevi (*Ra'ah*) of the 13th century also disagreed with *Rabad*. He disputed *Rabad*'s assertion that the investor had the advantage and could thus decide how profits and losses were to be divided. He said that "the recipient had the advantage because he held the money." *Bet Yosef, Yoreh Deah* #177.

period after *Rabad* uphold his other innovations or did they preserve, without amendment, the centuries long rulings of the Amoraim, the Geonim and the early Rishonim?

*Economic Conditions*

Let us keep in mind the needs of the business community in the Middle Ages. Commerce was growing. Better methods of farming created agricultural surpluses. Improvements in ship building meant that more goods could be transported more quickly and more securely, and greater safety on the roads meant that more traders could bring their wares to far-off places. The establishment of weekly markets and annual fairs also had a profound influence on the economy of Europe. People who could produce more than they needed for consumption could sell their surplus goods, and those who wanted materials that they could not make, were able to acquire them. The 12th, 13th and 14th centuries saw startling growth in international trade. Grain, fish, wine, timber, salt, wool and flax were brought to the towns and fairs as well as textiles, metal products and other manufactured goods.[15]

The economic expansion of the Middle Ages was accompanied by the growing use of credit.[16] As one scholar put it, "Unstinting credit was the great lubricant of the Commercial Revolution."[17] Credit developed in many forms between ordinary buyers and sellers and between professional traders. One technique frequently practiced among Christians was called the *commenda*. An investor gave a merchant the funds with which to do business. If there were losses, they were charged to the investor; if there were profits, three-quarters went to the investor and one-quarter to the merchant.[18]

15 N.J.G. Pounds, *An Economic History of Medieval Europe* (London and New York: Longman, 1994), 353-357; Jean Favier, *Gold and Spices, The Rise of Commerce in the Middle Ages* (New York/London: Holmes and Meier, 1998), 31-52; Brian Tierney and Sidney Painter, *Western Europe in the Middle Ages 300-1475* (New York: Alfred Knopf, 1983), 267-273; Michael Postan, "The Trade in Medieval Europe: The North", in M.M. Postan and Edward Miller, eds., *The Cambridge Economic History of Europe*, Vol. II (Cambridge: Cambridge University Press, 1987), 168-178.

16 Favier, *supra* n. 29 at 200-210.

17 Robert Lopez, *The Commercial Revolution of the Middle Ages* (Cambridge: Cambridge University Press, 1976), 72.

18 Carlo Cipolla, *Before the Industrial Revolution* (New York: W.W. Norton,

Jews, of course, did not use the *commenda*, but in order to function in the medieval economy as merchants and as moneylenders to non-Jews, they needed capital. Similarly, potential lenders, or investors, needed agents or managers to handle their merchandise or to lend money to Christians. But the usury ban stood as a barrier, always ready to inhibit their activities.

There were, in particular, two drawbacks to the *iṣḳa* which were imposed upon it by the usury law. One was the requirement to pay the managing partner for his labor; the other was that the investor had to accept half the risk of any loss.

Was there a way to relieve the *iṣḳa* of these burdens and thereby make it more attractive to those with savings to invest?

### *Payment to the Working Partner for His Labor*

Regarding the requirement to pay the working partner for his labor, a debate went back to the time of the Mishnah as to whether the payment should be based on the going rate for merchants or storekeepers, or whether it was it sufficient to make a token payment. A *Baraita*[19] reported a dispute among the *Tannaim* on this matter. How much was the working partner of an *iṣḳa* to be paid? Rabbi Simeon required that the worker be fully compensated for his labor. Rabbi Judah held that only a token payment was necessary, whereas Rabbi Meir taught that he should be paid "much or little." Another version of Rabbi Meir's teaching[20] was that he should be paid as a *po'el baṭel*, an idle worker. The Gemara accepted Rabbi Meir's view,[21] that he should be paid, neither a full wage, nor a token payment, but rather as a *po'el baṭel*, a worker who came to his place of employment but found no work to do.[22]

This position, that the working partner should be paid as an idle worker,

---

1976), 183-185.

19 b*Bava Metzia* 68b.

20 t*Bava Metzia* 4:11.

21 This is evident by the arguments at the top of 68b and at the top of 69a.

22 The meaning of *po'el baṭel* is made clear in *Bava Metzia* 76b. See Gamoran *supra* n.1 at n.14, and Joseph Heinemann, "The Status of the Laborer in Jewish Law and Society in the Talmudic Period", *Hebrew Union College Annual* XXV (1954), 278-283.

in accordance with Rabbi Meir, was sustained by the Geonim,[23] by R. Isaac Alfasi in the 11th century[24] and by R. Moses Maimonides in the 12th century.[25]

But in the 12th century, in Provence, with the tremendous growth in commerce,[26] pressure grew to allow less restrictive business partnerships by minimizing the wages due the working partner of an *iṣḳa*. Early in the 12th century, R. Judah of Barcelona repeated the *Baraita*'s words, "whether much or little," but added that "even a single zuz would be enough."[27] In essence, then, R. Judah abandoned the notion that the wage be tied to the worker's former income and simply interpreted the words, "whether much or little" to mean that the investor could pay the worker any amount at all, as long as it was agreed to by the two of them when the *iṣḳa* was undertaken.

*Rabad*, later in the same century, continued in this manner, downplaying the importance of the payment due the working partner by saying that the investor could stipulate to pay him "a dinar for his labor, even though his labor was worth more than that."[28]

The ruling that a minimum payment was sufficient, was upheld by the rabbinic authorities in the centuries that followed. The 13th century teacher, R. Moses of Coucy, in the *Ṣefer Mitzvot Gadol*,[29] said that a dinar was adequate payment; the 14th century sage, R. Asher ben Yeḥiel (*Rosh*) said that since the required payment to the worker was to avoid only "the dust of interest, the Sages were lenient, and if he gives him a small payment, it does not look like interest,"[30] and his son, R. Ya'aḳov ben Asher, in the *Ṭur*, said that "if he wants to contract with him for ... even only one dinar, he

23 R. Hai Gaon in *Sha'are Tsedeḳ* (Jerusalem: Klal Ufraṭ, 1971), Part 4, Gate 8, #6.

24 *Bava Metzia*, p. 39b of the *Rif* pages.

25 *Shiluḥin Veshutafin* 6:2.

26 See Gamoran, *supra* n.1 at notes 48-56.

27 R. Judah ben Barzilai of Barcelona, *Ṣefer Hashṭarot* (Berlin, 1898, repr. Jerusalem, 1967), #64.

28 Rabenu Avraham ben David, *Teshuvot Ufeṣaḳim*, ed. Joseph Kafah (Jerusalem: Mossad Harav Kook, 1964), #132. This responsum can be found in *Temim De'im* (Warsaw, 1897), #51 and in Betzalel Ashkenazi, *Shiṭa Meḳubetzet*, Bava Metzia 68b.

29 R. Moses of Coucy, *Ṣefer Mitzvot Gadol, Mitzvot Asei, Hilkhot Shutafin* (Venice, 1547, repr. Jerusalem, 1961), 168, column b.

30 R. Asher ben Yeḥiel, *Rabbenu Asher, Bava Metzia* 5:39, 135b.

may do so."[31] In the 15th century, Rabbi Solomon ben Simeon Duran, ruled similarly, that if they agreed "to divide the profit and the loss equally, it was enacted that he could give the worker something small every day as payment for his labor."[32]

It is clear, then, that the amount paid to the working partner of an *iṣḳa*, which the Talmud took pains to protect (explicitly rejecting the view that a token payment was sufficient), and which the Geonim and early Rishonim likewise upheld, was a non issue from the 12th through the 15th century. A study of the rulings, commentaries and responsa of this period shows that not a single rabbinic authority ruled that the manager's daily wage had to be tied to the value of his labor.

We can say then that the views of the 12th century Provencal scholars, R. Judah of Barcelona and *Rabad*, prevailed. From their time and onward the requirement to pay the working partner for his labor was no longer a deterrent to *iṣḳa* investments.

*The Effort to Reduce the Investor's Risk*

But what about the other disincentive to engage in an *iṣḳa* which was faced by investors, the fact that if the enterprise failed, they would lose half of their investment? Persons with capital would surely be more inclined to participate in an *iṣḳa* if they could be sure that their investment was safe. Was there a way to structure an *iṣḳa* so as to make the active partner fully liable for the investment? Could an *iṣḳa* of this nature be allowed with rabbinic approval?

The Talmud had established that an *iṣḳa* was half a loan and half a deposit. The Geonim, in explaining the significance of this division, made it clear that though the active partner was liable for the loan half, the investor was responsible for the deposit half.[33] When it was suggested that the managing partner, as a paid bailee, might be responsible for the deposit half as well, the Geonim responded that the manager of an *iṣḳa,* who used the deposit in behalf of the partnership, should not be considered an ordinary paid

31 R. Jacob ben Asher, *Ṭur, Yoreh De'ah, Hilkhot Ribit,* #177:3.

32 R. Solomon ben Simeon Duran, *Ṣefer Rashbash* (Leghorn, 1742), #496, 94a.

33 *Ṣefer Halakhot Peṣuḳot,* ed. S. Sasoon (Jerusalem: Mekitse Nirdamim, 1950), 49; *Ṣefer Halakhot Gedolot,* ed. E. Hildesheimer, Vol. II (Jerusalem: Mekitse Nirdamim, 1980), 406.

bailee and should not be held liable for loss or theft. The position of the Geonim, then, was that although the worker was entirely responsible for the loan portion of the investment, the investor was liable for the deposit portion.[34]

In the 11th century, R. Hananel[35] and R. Alfasi (*Rif*)[36] supported this position. The working partner of an *iṣḳa* busied himself with the investment; he could not guard it like a normal guardian, burying the deposit in the ground for safekeeping. So if the investment was lost, the working partner was liable only for the loan portion.

*Rambam*, in the 12th century, took a position in the *Mishneh Torah* that was in agreement with the Geonim and with R. Hananel and the *Rif*, that "if the deposit half were stolen or lost the working partner did not have to pay."[37]

But several scholars, R. David b. Saadia[38] in the 11th century, and R. Judah ben Nathan[39] and R. Moses Hacohen[40] in the 12th century, held that the manager was liable for the entire investment if it was lost or stolen. *Rabad* supported this position as well. He criticized the Rambam's statement that the working partner was not liable for loss or theft, saying, "This is not possible. Why shouldn't he be considered a paid bailee for the deposit, for he receives wages as an idle worker."[41]

In the 13th century, R. Isaac of Vienna,[42] R. Jacob Hazan,[43] R. Meir of

34 *Sha'are Tsedeḳ* (Jerusalem: Klal Ufraṭ, 1971), Part 4, Gate 8, #5; Simḥa Asaf, "T'shuvot Merav Sherira (V'rav Hai?) Livne Pas",*Ginze Ḳedem* 5 (1934), 115-117; Simha Asaf, "Keta Meḥiburo shel R. Yehudah Hanasi Albartziloni L'bava Metzia",*Ginze Ḳedem* 5 (1934), 101-102.

35 Ḥananel ben Ḥushiel, *Perush Harav Ḥananel*, Tractate Bava Metzia, ed. Dov Dumov (Jerusalem: Mossad Harav Kook, 1988), 179.

36 R. Isaac Alfasi, *She'elot Uteshuvot Harav Yitzḥaḳ Alfaṣi,* ed. Dov Zvi Rothstein (New York: Makhon Zvi Lemoreshet Gedole Yisrael, 1975), #75.

37 *Shiluḥin Veshutafin* 6:2.

38 Betzalel Ashkenazi, *Shiṭa Meḳubetzet*, Bava Metzia 104b.

39 *Toṣafot*, *Bava Metzia* 70a, D"H D'ka; *Ṭur*, *Hilkhot Ribit* #177.

40 *Shiṭa Meḳubetzet*, *supra* n.30 at *Bava Metzia* 104b.

41 *Hasagot Harabad, Hilkhot Shiluḥin V'shutafin* 6:2.

42 R. Isaac of Vienna, *Or Zarua* , Part 3 (Jerusalem, 1887), *Bava Metzia* #342.

43 R. Jacob Ḥazzan, *Etz Ḥayyim*, Volume 3, ed. Israel Brody (Jerusalem: Mossad Harav Kook, 1967), 152.

Rothenburg[44] and R. Menahem ben Solomon[45] all echoed *Rabad*'s position by indicating their support for the view that the working partner was a paid bailee and was responsible for any loss or theft that befell the deposit portion of the investment.

The issue, however, did not become permanently settled, for in the 15th century, two teachers took positions similar to that of the *Rambam*. The first was R. Solomon Duran[46] who held the investor liable for the deposit half of the principal. He wrote that if the deposit half "is stolen or lost or sinks into the sea, it is the investor's responsibility." The other was R. Joseph Colon who "ruled out the practice of the Lombards[47] who invest their money for profit, and the lender does not accept liability for accidents like theft, robbery, armed robbers and many other accidents except fire and capture, God forbid."[48]

The rabbis who declared the managing partner responsible for loss and theft of the deposit portion had sought to meet investors' needs for security. But, as we have seen, not all of the later authorities were comfortable with this ruling. Four 13th century rabbis accepted it, but two of the 15th century teachers did not. So naming the working partner a paid bailee turned out to be an inadequate remedy for the investment needs of the time. What investors really wanted, after all, was rabbinic approval for profits without taking any risks at all. What they wanted was for the recipients to be fully responsible for the money they received, like borrowers who assumed all of the risks for their loans. But how could investors be granted immunity from loss, like lenders? If the recipients were to assume all of the risks, then wouldn't the investors' profits be considered interest, forbidden by law?

Was there any way to circumvent the anti-usury law and provide investors with guaranteed safety for their investments? Indeed, there was, for *Rabad* proposed a method whereby one could invest, gain a profit and not risk

44 *Sh'elot Ut'shuvot Maharam ben R. Barukh*, *supra* n.22 at #806.

45 Menahem ben Solomon (*Hameiri*), *Bet Habeḥirah al Masekhet Bava Metzia* (Jerusalem: Meḳitze Nirdamim, 1959), 104b, 388.

46 Solomon ben Simeon Duran, *Yakhin U'voaz, Sh'elot Ut'shuvot*, Part 2 (Levorno, 1782; repr. Jerusalem, 1970), #23.

47 The Lombards, from northwestern Italy, were known primarily as moneylenders. Lopez, *supra* n.31 at 77; Favier, *supra* n.29 at 207-208; Thomas Blomquist, "Lombards", in Joseph Strayer, ed., *Dictionary of the Middle Ages* (New York: Charles Scribner's Sons, 1986), Vol. 7, 653-654.

48 R. Joseph Colon, *Sh'elot Ut'shuvot Mahariḳ Hayeshanot* (Jerusalem: Oraysoh, 1988), Shoresh #119.

the principal.

The *iṣḳa* that was established in Talmudic times made the investor liable for the deposit portion. And even if he was protected by some of the Rishonim from loss and theft of the deposit portion, he was still liable for unavoidable accidents. What if a ship wrecked or the government confiscated the goods or any number of other unforeseen mishaps occurred, how could the investor be exempt from loss? *Rabad* suggested a way for the investor to be completely absolved of liability for the deposit half.[49] It was based on a comment in the *Tosafot*[50] which pointed out that if the manager of an *iṣḳa* deviated from the instructions of the investor, then he was completely responsible if the investment was lost. *Rabad* proposed that, at the start of the partnership, the investor instruct the manager to accept only pledges of silver and gold, that they always be buried in the ground, and that if the manager deviates from these instructions, he be deemed totally liable for the deposit portion of the loss. It was clear that merchants or moneylenders who dealt with their money or goods on a continuing basis were unable to keep these instructions. The investor knew it and the recipient knew it. In essence, this was a formula for allowing the investor to make a no risk investment. If the business prospered, the investor could profit, whereas if the business failed, the loss was completely the manager's.

How did the Rishonim who followed *Rabad* react to this novel approach? His ruling was accepted by the major rabbinic authorities throughout the period of the Rishonim. It was included in the writings of the 13th century teachers R. Moses of Coucy,[51] R. Samson of Sens,[52] and R. Meir of Rothenburg,[53] and in the works of the 14th century authorities, the *Rosh*,[54]

49 Rabenu Avraham ben David, *Teshuvot Ufeṣaḳim,* ed. Joseph Kafah (Jerusalem: Mossad Harav Kook, 1964), #140. This responsum can be found in *Temim De'im* (Warsaw, 1897), #60.

50 *Toṣafot, Bava Kamma* 102a, D"H Hanoten. Later authorities credited the statement in the Toṣafot to R. Isaac of Dampierre. See *Ṣefer Mitzvot Gadol, supra* n.13 at 167, column c; *Etz Ḥayyim, supra* n.36 at 150.

51 *Ṣefer Mitzvot Gadol, supra* n.13 at 167, column c.

52 R. Samson of Sens in R. Isaac of Vienna, *Or Zarua, Part 3* (Jerusalem, 1892), *Bava Metzia* 5:200, 29, column a.

53 Meir of Rothenburg, *Ṣefer Sh'elot Ut'shuvot* (Krimona, 1557, repr. Jerusalem, 1986), #12; *Sh'elot Ut'shuvot Maharam ben Barukh* (Prague Edition, Budapest, 1895), #102.

54 *Rabbenu Asher, Bava Metzia* 9:18, 102b.

his son, R. Jacob[55] and R. Nissim.[56]

*R. Israel Isserlein*

Perhaps the clearest expression of granting permission for a partnership agreement which allowed the investor to profit without risking his principal, came from the pen of R. Israel Isserlein of the 15th century. Isserlein was told, in an inquiry, that Reuben wanted to profit by giving money to Simon "while being almost completely certain that he not lose any of his principal." "How," asked the inquirer, "might this be accomplished legally?"[57]

Isserlein began his response by expressing his reservations about answering the question. He said that the questioner's purpose could, indeed, be achieved, "but I am afraid lest by these rules and by seeking strategies to allow business dealings with interest, the words of the Torah will become a laughingstock."

However, in spite of his concern, Isserlein believed that his views were correct, and he proceeded to answer to the question. He referred to the same passage in the *Tosafot* that had been the source for the comments of the 13th and 14th century scholars, that "a person could give money to his fellow on a half profit basis and could contract with him not to lend it except on pledges of silver or gold and to bury them in the ground, and then the liability would be the investor's. But if he lends in others ways, then the recipient will be liable." But Isserlein went beyond his predecessors by saying that it was not forbidden as being near to profit and far from loss "even though everyone knows that it is not at all the intention of the investor or of the recipient that the stipulation be fulfilled, that is, that he will lend only on silver and gold and will bury it in the ground, but rather, he will lend on debts without any pledges at all, or on pledges which are not silver or gold, or if they are silver or gold, he will surely not bury them in the ground. Nevertheless it is allowed."

The unique feature of Isserlein's response was his open admission that the contract was a subterfuge, and that the parties were well aware that the working partner would not live up to the stipulations. The stipulations were

55 Jacob ben Asher, *Ṭur, Yoreh De'ah* #177:5.

56 *Sh'elot Ut'shuvot Ha-Ran*, Aryeh Feldman, ed. (Jerusalem: Institute Schalem Ṣefunot Kadmonim, 1984), #73, 329.

57 R. Israel Isserlein, *Terumat Hadeshen*, ed. Samuel Avitan (Jerusalem, 1991), #302.

inserted with a wink and a nod by all concerned, knowing that they were simply a way of allowing the investor to place all of the risk on the recipient. Surely the fictitious nature of this undertaking was understood by the Rishonim of the 12th, 13th and 14th centuries, but it was not openly stated by them, perhaps for fear of "making the Torah a laughingstock." In any case, Isserlein's admission of what was going on was new and refreshing.

Isserlein's responsum was unique in one more way. He provided yet another method whereby the investor could place the entire liability onto the shoulders of the manager. This is how it worked: The contract would state that Simon, the working partner, accepts liability for gross negligence,

> and he also accepts upon himself that he is not to be believed even with an oath on the Torah, and even with witnesses, and even if there are a hundred who testify that he was not greatly negligent. Only if the rabbi and the cantor and similar people who are residents of the city and are familiar with the business dealings in the city will testify, will they be believed if they testify with proof and complete knowledge.
>
> And in this way will his principal be secure as he always wishes. For if it is lost, Reuben [the investor] may claim that it was lost intentionally, and Simon will be able to uphold his claim only with the testimony of the rabbi and the cantor. And it is almost entirely certain that they will not know all [of the details regarding] the liability.
>
> And it is permitted to stipulate as has been said ... even though surely neither of them believe that the conditions will be fulfilled, and they make these stipulations only in order to take interest in a legal way.

Perhaps we should not be surprised that the rabbis devised a legal way to allow profitable investments in partnerships. The Muslim jurists, in their day, found a way for its faithful to pursue their business activities without hindrance from their laws against usury,[58] and Christian theologians provided ways for bankers to lend on interest with the Church's blessing.[59] Why shouldn't the rabbis have devised a means to allow the economic activity of their day to proceed within the framework of the *halakhah*?

58 N.J. Coulson, *A History of Islamic Law* (Urdu Bazar-Lahore: Lahore Law Times Publications, 1979), 72-73; R.M. Savory, "Law and Traditional Society", in *Introduction to Islamic Civilization* (Cambridge: Cambridge University Press, 1976), 59. See also Ziaul Haque, *Riba: The Moral Economy of Usury, Interest and Profit* (Kuala Lumpur: S. Abdul Majeed, 1995), 83-106.

59 "Canonists became increasingly broad in their interpretations of the canons as the need for credit grew." Pounds, *supra* n.29 at 410; Jean Favier, *supra* n.29 at 195-197.

The period in which Isserlein lived was one of heavy trade and commerce. In the 15th century, South Germany and Austria were at the center of powerful economic activity.[60] Isserlein's responsa show evidence of the numerous economic activities in which Jews were engaged and of the demands for accomodation which came before him.[61]

As a rule, Isserlein sought to find ways to allow his coreligionists to carry on their business enterprises successfully.[62] In one revealing responsum[63] Isserlein was asked about the case of a man who was owed money by some non-Jews. The lender was engaged in a lengthy discussion with his debtors which included drinking. He had to consider and respond to a number of proposals. He could not cut the conversation short without suffering a loss on the debt. He missed the time for the afternoon prayers and wanted to know if he was allowed to say the evening prayers twice in order to make up for what he had missed.

In responding to this query, Isserlein was faced with the decisions of previous authorities[64] who had ruled that when a person is engaged in an activity in which he is fully aware that he is missing the time for prayers, he may not make up for what he has missed. Isserlein overcame this ruling by stating that the case under discussion, rather than being in the catagory of full awareness, should be considered one of duress. He pointed to a statement in the Talmud[65] which says that a person who loses something is considered under duress when he has to drop other matters in order to go and look for his lost object, and concluded from this that "in all cases where one misses the performance of a mitzvah in order to avoid financial loss, it is considered

60 Pounds, *supra* n.29 at 362; Jacques Bernard, "Trade and Finance in the Middle Ages 900-1500", in C.M. Cipolla, ed., *The Fontana Economic History of Europe, The Middle Ages* (London and Glasgow: Collins/Fontana Books, 1973), 298; Jean Berenger, *A History of the Habsburg Empire 1273-1700* (London and New York: Longman, 1994), 78-82; Robert Lopez, "The Trade Of Medieval Europe: The South", in M. Postan and E.E. Rich, eds., *The Cambridge Economic History of Europe* (Cambridge: Cambridge University Press, 1952), 349.

61 Shlomo Eidelberg, *Jewish Life in Austria in the XVth Century* (Philadelphia: The Dropsie College for Hebrew and Cognate Learning, 1962), 45-47, 106-111.

62 Eidelberg, *supra* n.61 at 45.

63 *Terumat Hadeshen*, *supra* n.57 at #5.

64 Moses Maimonides, *Mishneh Torah, Tefilla* 3:8, R. Jacob ben Asher, *Ṭur*, 108:67.

65 *Mo'ed Ḳaṭan*, 14a.

duress."

Isserlein, as one who was known to be independent minded,[66] who, when the occasion arose was willing to rule on the side of leniency,[67] who had a wide knowledge of business and money matters[68] and demonstrated an understanding of the problems faced by those who earned their living in the business world, frequently interpreted the law in a manner which conformed to the the economic realities of his time.[69]

*Conclusions*

As the time period of the Rishonim drew to a close, investors had within their grasp a means of profiting from their investments without risking the loss of their principal. Just as in the case of a loan where the borrower was completely responsible for any loss, so in the case of an *iṣḳa*, if the proper stipulations were included in the contract, the manager could be held completely responsible for the investment. But whereas any profit from a loan was forbidden as usury, profit from an *iṣḳa* was deemed to be a legitimate business gain.

What the business community achieved, then, was rabbinic sanction for persons of means to earn money with their money. The arrangement was called an *iṣḳa* rather than a loan, but from a practical standpoint, it provided the investor with the benefits of a loan.

66 Eidelberg, *supra* n.61 at 45 and 56.

67 *Terumat Hadeshen*, *supra* n.57 at nn. 1 (re reciting evening prayers early in the day), 16 (re handling bodily needs at prayer time), 64 (re retrieving a stuck knife on the Sabbath) and 114 (re putting out a fire on the Sabbath).

68 Eidelberg, *supra* n.61 at 106-111.

69 Eidelberg, *supra* n.61 at 59.

# 7

## SOME ASPECTS OF THEODICY: THE FLOOD AND THE HOLOCAUST

by

MOSHE ISH-HOROWICZ*

Injustice, suffering and cruelty, as exemplified by the biblical flood and by the Holocaust, are incompatible with God's attributes of righteousness (*tzedeḳ*) and majesty. In particular, why do the righteous suffer and the wicked prosper? Rabbis in all generations have tried to justify God for the sake of his perfection and righteousness. This is theodicy.

In fact God Himself welcomes and accepts criticism in various tragic circumstances. God relented to Abraham's protestations against destroying Sodom and Gomorrah with all its inhabitants, providing He could find there a mere ten righteous persons, a *minyan*. Moses appears to have changed God's intentions, twice: firstly, He forgave the children of Israel for the idolatry of the golden calf. Moreover, in the "affront of the spies," Moses dared to reject the Divine offer to make his descendants into a great nation instead of the stiff necked Israelites. In both episodes this exemplary leader preferred to die with his people in the desert rather than survive and allow them to suffer God's wrath.[1]

Paradoxically, all rabbis preferred the acts of defiance of Abraham and of Moses to the silent total submissiveness of selfish Noah who, according to the Bible, failed to say even a minimal prayer to save others.

Actually, in the words of Micah, God wants to be challenged, as it is said: "O, My people what have I done to you and wherein have I wearied you? Testify against me!"[2] Indeed, our sages even postulate that defiance and criticism emanating from distress brought about by alleged Divine

* London and Tel Aviv. This paper is based on abbreviated extracts from my Ph.D. dissertation presented to the University of Manchester in England, UK.

1 *Numbers* 14:1-20.

2 *Micah* 6:3.

injustice or cruelty are not held against the challenger at the Heavenly Tribunal.[3] Neither would such defiance be punished or condemned by the Heavenly Tribunal if the criticism of God emanated from love, or concern at Israel's suffering persecution and humiliation.[4]

Thence righteous sages and individuals in distress were often successful in their entreaties to the All Merciful for salvation. He usually responded to them either because they deserved it or in order not to shame them by a refusal. For instance, pious 'rainmakers' brought rain to farms stricken by drought. Neither the intercessors nor "He who causes the rain to fall" discriminated between the fields belonging to the righteous and those of the wicked.[5] Rabbi Levi ben Ṣiṣi showed some impudence when, impatiently, he addressed his prayer to the "Master of the Universe who, at His abode on high, showed no mercy on His children." Rain came down, but the rabbi was punished by lameness for his insolence.[6] Ḥoni Hame'agel however was not even rebuked although he was much more impudent and persisting in his demands for immediate rain before he would move out of a circle he had drawn around himself. Because this saintly rabbi was treated in Heaven like a *ben bayit,* a member of the Heavenly Household, the "blessed rains came down."[7]

Zeal and daring beyond the limits of reverence appear also in an interpretation of *Ex.* 15:11 written defectively without a '*yod*' in the biblical text. It is rendered "Who is like you, O Lord, Who keeps silent, though seeing insult heaped upon Your Children [of Israel]."[8] I have not seen a single dissenting voice condemning this *midrash* as blasphemous or offensive. Invariably, the Rabbis showed great sympathy to the protesters. None of them was ever banned or even rebuked. The *midrash* expresses understandable disappointment bordering on despair.

The Torah, the link between God and mankind, explains that, in His goodness and grace, God created human beings in His spiritual image[9] and gave them the earth and its dominion. The ungrateful generations sinned to

3 *Bava Batra* 16b.

4 *Deuteronomy Rabbah* 11:2.

5 *Ta'anit* 23a-26b.

6 *Ibid.*, 25a.

7 *Ibid.*, 23a.

8 *Mekilta de Rabbi Ishmael, Shirta,* translated by J.Z. Lauterbach (Philadelphia: The Jewish Publication Society of America, 1976), II.60.

9 *Genesis* 1:27 and 9:16.

such a degree that God had to exterminate them by the destructive flood.

After Sinai, God expected Israel and mankind to fulfil the Divine purpose to imitate God and pursue righteousness. People were expected to achieve holiness by performing the Divine commands[10] as is expressed in numerous blessings as follows: "Blessed are You Lord our God, King of the Universe Who makes us holy through His *mitzvot* and commands us to [do the particular command, *mitzvah*]." Righteousness provides the ideal and a guide for mankind. Its many facets serve as criteria for evaluating the deeds of human beings.

When God's ways are evaluated and criticised, theodicy steps in to vindicate or defend the Holy One by the same criteria of righteousness. The Holocaust, perpetrated by the Nazis during the Second World War, provides the latest most significant and powerful cause for complaint, accusations and even rebellion. These criticisms and arguments are not new; they are modelled on those of the rabbis and scholars of old in their treatment of the story of the Flood. For example, E. Wiesel's paradoxical stories express profound grief and criticism (*The Gates of the Forest*).[11] He mourns and laments the Holocaust but adheres to his faith like the rabbis did with the flood. E. Berkowitz, in *Faith after the Holocaust,*[12] invokes the concept of *hester panim* (the eclipse of God) just as R. Meir did in *Gen. Rabb.* 36:1, "God hid His face during the calamity,[13] so that He did not know what was happening on earth." R. L. Rubenstein promulgates his rebellious idea of God's death in Auschwitz[14] which is reminiscent of Elisha b. Abuya who became an apostate when he saw the bloody tongue of Ḥutzpit the Interpreter (or Judah the Baker) being dragged into the market by a pig or a dog because they taught the Torah during the Hadrianic persecutions.[15]

The Holocaust manifested man's cruelty against man and was attributed to man's free will, the Nazis' choice of their monstrous path of evil. The flood, however, was justified and, as stated in *Gen.* 6:17, God Himself, disappointed, brought the flood on to the earth.[16] Yet He should have stopped the Nazis before they reached extreme wickedness. At the cruel

10 *Numbers* 15:40.

11 New York: Schocken Books, 1995.

12 New York: KTAV Publishing House, 1973.

13 *Job* 34,29.

14 *After Auschwitz* (Baltimore: John Hopkins University Press, 1966).

15 *Ḳiddushin* 29b; *Ruth Rabbah* 6:4 et al; Cf. R. Akiva, *Menaḥot* 29b.

16 *Ibid.*

extermination of the particularly pious and devout East European Jewry, one could reiterate Elisha b. Abuya's outcry of defiance and despair: "Is this the Torah and its reward?"

*Faith and Religious Truth versus Logic and Scientific Truth*

In his *Philosophies of Judaism,* 1973 p. 82f., D. Guttmann refers to the wrestling between the faculties of reason/logic and faith/feeling. He points out how, initially, theodicy employed reason to vindicate providence when it was criticised for failing to comply with the principle of just reward and punishment in this world as promised in Scripture. However, the intellect, instead of confining itself to the defence of God's righteousness, turned against faith in the sense that it started to question the revealed religious truth. Guttman does not dwell on the possible crux of the issue, that, fundamentally, intellect and faith are different means of cognition and perception. Theodicy's intellectual attempt to answer, by logic, the criticism of unfulfilled Biblical promises of reward and punishment, is futile. Reason cannot bridge the gap between the intellectual and religious perceptions of truth. They operate on different levels, namely cognition by reason as opposed to mysticism and emotion. Man is incapable of bridging the dichotomy between rational and intuitive truths, not only in the sphere of faith but also in other facets of his emotional and spiritual life: love, beauty (visual and literary), the arts and music, where logic plays only a minor part, if any. Aesthetics too, like faith, are perceived by feeling rather than logic. Yet reason operates within the domain of both emotion and belief. Scientific ideas and theories can also be arrived at by intuition and not by the intellect. They too may be logically irreconcilable; for instance, the intrinsically impossible irrational complex number, the square root of minus one, $\sqrt{-1}$, whatever its graphical presentation. Also logically incongruous are the two discontinuous quantum and continuous wave theories of light as shown in reality. The whole truth is known to God alone.

Moreover, the explanation that man's intellect is imperfect applies equally to his world of irrational intuition and feeling. Also, recognition of such fallibility reduces the reliability of his perception of religious truth. Yet, however imperfect and questionable are human perceptions, man, in his search for truth, has no alternative but to use and depend upon the faculties with which he has been endowed. Thus Job submitted to his religious and spiritual need to long for the Divine even when God gave Job no explanation for his unjust sufferings. How could God submit to Satan? In contrast

Elisha b. Abuya followed his reason and ceased to believe in reward for the righteous and resurrection of the dead and abandoned his faith because the martyr, Judah the Baker, instead of being rewarded for toiling in the Torah, died a cruel death at the hands of the Romans.[17]

*Divine Knowledge and Power versus Human Limitations and Fallibility*

In deeply religious persons like Job, there can be no conflict between religious and intellectual truth because of their conviction that human intellect cannot conceive the ways and thoughts of an always righteous, perfect, omnipotent, infallible Deity who is both merciful and just. In the words of *Deut.* 32:4,

> The rock, His work is perfect;
> For all His ways are justice,
> A God of faithfulness and without iniquity,
> Righteous and upright is He.

Human endeavours to understand God's ways and decisions are futile. God has created an imperfect world and in order to "mend" us humans, we must follow the wisdom and laws taught in the Torah.

The stark polarity between man's limitations and God's infinity forms the ultimate argument of a religious person against any criticism of Divine providence. This is also the ultimate logical answer of theodicy in its vindication of God. The pot cannot understand the potter who made it. God's thoughts and deeds are higher and deeper than those of man.[18]

The incoherence and injustice attributed to divine thoughts and actions can result from various factors, such as human limitation, flawed reasoning, faulty interpretation and rationalisation. The fact that values, opinions and ideas within the same individual change according to his own education, age, personality and status demonstrate man's fallibility. A human being, therefore, has to acknowledge his or her insignificance and inadequacy to question God's ways and commands.

17 *Ruth Rabbah* 6:4 et al.

18 *Isaiah* 58:8-9.

*Rabbinical Authority*

The Bible[19] and rabbinical references, *Avot* 1:1, *Bava Metzia* 59b, *Menaḥot* 29b and other sources, established rabbinical authority to interpret the law and to legislate: divine revelation gives way to rabbinic decrees taken by majority vote in the competent rabbinical courts. It dared to ignore even the Heavenly Voice, which supported the opinion of a minority headed by R. Eliezer ben Hyrkanos. For "the Torah was not in heaven"[20] any more, since it had been handed down to the Israelites on Mount Sinai. According to a legend, the prophet Elijah told R. Nathan that, "at that time" the Holy one "laughed (amused or with joy)"[21] and conceded: "My sons have defeated me," a remarkable transfer to and assertion of the rabbinical authority. If God has been removed and is no more a legislating authority, then the "defeat" is permanent or, at least, perhaps until Messiah. Most of the ideas and concepts considered above relate to theodicy and some can only briefly be discussed in the limited space in the paper.

*Change and Immutability*

An extract in *Men.* 29b indicates the flexibility and adaptability of the Torah to the changes that occurred during the interval separating Moses from the age of R. Akiva. The extent of these changes was such that Moses could not understand R. Akiva's interpretations and rulings. The text also evidences the dynamism of the *halakhah*, its pliability and mutability as long as the developments and changes conform with the spirit, righteousness and tradition of the law given to "Moses at Sinai." Continuous rabbinical exegesis of Scripture and the interpretation of older oral traditions entailed development, change and adaptation to the contemporary conditions of the rabbis.

The transition from the cruelty of the Flood, which ended the universal collective retributions and strict justice, to the post-diluvial divine pledges and covenant, teaches compassion and lenience. Mercy, assuaging the rigidity and severity of the law, has always permeated rabbinic decision-making. This is evidenced by the fact that the *halakhah* on the whole followed the academy of the "considerate and kind" Hillel and not that of the

19 *Deuteronomy* 17:8-11.

20 *Deuteronomy* 30:12.

21 *Bava Metzia* 59b.

strict "chief justice" Shammai.[22] Excessive strictness and rigidity are deprecated in the spirit of the rule *lifnim mi'shurat ha-din*, the encouragement to go "beyond the letter of the law." Jerusalem was destroyed because of her adherence to the strict letter of the law.[23]

### *The World to Come*

Theodicy was boosted by the introduction into Judaism of the concept of the immortality of soul and of posthumous and eschatological ideas. Compensation in the world to come will be given, as promised and, according to their deserts, to the righteous and innocent who suffered in this world. This solution offered by theodicy is the final answer to all criticisms and complaints, a kingdom of God. However, in *Berakhot* 5b, R. Hiyya b. Abba, R. Eleazar and R. Johanan neither wanted the suffering nor the reward in the world to come. Associated with the eventual bliss in the world to come are the themes of paradise, the messianic era, resurrection of dead and bliss in the terrestrial world to come, as promised in the Bible.

Rabbi Jacob who developed the above solution considered this world to be like a vestibule in which to become worthy to enter the banqueting hall of the world to come.[24] He was a grandchild of Elisha b. Abuya and the rabbis said that if the grandfather had heard his theory, Elisha would not have become an apostate.

22 *Eruvin* 13b.

23 *Bava Metzia* 30b.

24 *Avot* 4:16.

8

# *MOREDET*: PROBLEMS OF HISTORY AND AUTHORITY

by

BERNARD S. JACKSON*

The problem of the *agunah* has become a touchstone of the acceptability of the *halakhah* in wide sections of the Jewish community. Finding a solution to it is no mere academic exercise, nor is its importance confined to the alleviation of the personal suffering which the current application of the law entails. Any analysis of the problem necessarily has implications for action: indeed, the very act of addressing the problem in public has a "political" significance.

I am increasingly persuaded that the academic community has both a responsibility and a role in this. We do not, of course, claim to speak as "halakhic authorities". Our role, I would suggest, is twofold, first, to contribute our own creative analyses of the problem for the consideration of those who have authority in the matter, secondly, to inform the wider Jewish public of the issues and possibilities involved.

Some may say that such considerations exclude entirely from the debate those whose religious credentials would not be regarded as sufficiently *kosher* by the halakhic authorities. But that is itself a simplification. Good arguments can be taken up by intermediaries. But what is a "good argument" for these purposes? A good argument has to be one which assumes the basic presuppositions of the audience to which it is directed. There is no point in seeking to appeal to Orthodox authorities on the basis of non-Orthodox premises. But one does not have to be Orthodox to advance an Orthodox argument. We need, in this debate, to apply Grice's "co-operative principle":

* Centre for Jewish Studies, University of Manchester; I am grateful to Professors J. David Bleich and Steven Resnicoff for comments on parts of an earlier draft of this paper from which I have profited even where I have not found myself in agreement. Naturally, this is not to imply their endorsement of anything in the present text.

each side of the conversation must assume that the other is speaking co-operatively, in good faith, that it is genuinely interested in seeking a solution, and a solution *within* the *halakhah*.

On a very general level, we might distinguish between "dogmatic" (in the legal sense) and "historical" arguments. The former insists on judging the validity of halakhic propositions (including propositions regarding halakhic history) *ex auctoritate*, the authority of the *poṣkim* and the sources they use.[1] An "historical" argument, in this context, is one which is willing to draw (normative) conclusions form the facts of halakhic history established by (independent) historical research. It might take the following form: the law at an earlier period of our history was different, so why not revert to it? For example, it has been argued that the procedure mentioned in Deuteronomy 14:1-4 was merely the expression of a custom, and "there is no biblical injunction mandating the giving or receiving of a get."[2] There is indeed an oral "*formula contraria*" in Hosea 2:4, "she is not my wife, nor am I her husband" (היא לא אשתי ואנכי לא אישה), which Ze'ev Falk[3]

1 This is a major theme of the debate in B.S. Jackson, ed., *Modern Research in Jewish Law* (Leiden: E. J. Brill, 1980; The Jewish Law Annual, Supplement I); see, esp., I. Englard, "Research in Jewish Law, Its Nature and Function", *ibid.*, at 27-29. See also my "History, Dogmatics and Halakhah", in *Jewish Law in Legal History and the Modern World,* ed. B.S. Jackson (Leiden: E. J. Brill, 1980; The Jewish Law Annual, Supplement II), 1-26.

2 M.D.A. Freeman, "The Jewish Law of Divorce", *International Family Law* (May 2000), 58-62, at 58. The *ṣefer keritut*, however, does appear to be presupposed as the normal procedure by *Isa.* 50:1, cf. *Jer.* 3:8. Steven Resnicoff comments to me that the same issue of voluntariness might apply even at a stage when the procedure was oral. Indeed, that oral stage, viewed historically, was one which preceded *any* role for the *bet din.* By definition, then, oral divorce was voluntary. This model would assist the wife only if she equally had the right unilaterally to divorce her husband by oral formula. The only hint of such a possibility in biblical times occurs in a marriage contract (C5) from the Aramaic papyri of Elephantine, where there are provisions in case "[Miv]taḥiah should stand up in the congregation and say, 'I divorce Asḥor my husband ...". See the discussion in R. Yaron, *Introduction to the Law of the Aramaic Papyri* (Oxford: The Clarendon Press, 1961), 53-64. Yaron notes that there is no indication of the use of a written document at Elephantine, and sees the role of the congregation as purely evidentiary rather than judicial. He views the equality of husband and wife in divorce at Elephantine as "probably due to the Egyptian environment" (at 53). See also Y. Zakovitch, "The Woman's Rights in the Biblical Law of Divorce", *The Jewish Law Annual* IV (1981), 28-46, esp. 43.

3 *Hebrew Law in Biblical Times* (Jerusalem: Wahrmann Books, 1964), 154.

and others think may reflect a stage of oral divorce preceding the introduction of the written document. Such an argument, however, ignores the authority of rabbinic interpretation, which takes no account of the possibility of such an anterior, oral stage, but rather (a) views the procedure of *ṣefer keritut* as mandatory, (b) classifies the procedure as a matter of prohibition (*iṣura*)[4] (since a woman not so divorced is forbidden to any other man) and (c) regards this prohibition as of *de'orayta* status. It is this combination which makes change particularly difficult. For though we might cite Hillel's *prosbul* as an example of rabbinic circumvention of a clearly biblical prohibition,[5] — indeed as one which might prove particularly suggestive (in making the court the agent of the creditor[6]) in the context of our problem[7] — *prosbul*

4 Thus, arguments based upon the capacity of Rabbenu Gershom to ban polygamy also miss the point. What R. Gershom did was (merely) to remove a permission (*heter*) to take more than a single wife. Polygamy was never mandatory nor was monogamy ever prohibited. Indeed, as Professor Resnicoff reminds me, if despite R. Gershom's decree a man took a second wife, the marriage was valid under Jewish law and the second wife was biblically forbidden to any other man. On the classification in this context, see further *infra,* n.8.

5 *Deut.* 15:2: "he shall not exact it (לא יגש) of his neighbor, his brother, because the LORD's release has been proclaimed." The distinction between historical and dogmatic approaches is exemplified here. The proposition in the text is an historical one (in the sense defined in the text above). If, however, we take the Talmud as our authoritative source for earlier halakhic history, then it may be argued that Hillel's *prosbul* was directed against a rabbinic version of the release law, one based upon *hefḳer bet din hefḳer:* see *Giṭin* 35b-36a, to which Rabbi Bleich rightly draws my attention. From a dogmatic point of view, the judgment whether a rule is *de'orayta* or *derabbanan* is not merely an historical proposition; it is a judgment which affects the weight of that proposition as a dogmatic source, and therefore is itself to be made on dogmatic grounds.

6 In fact, the *prosbul* — agency of the court — was not the only means used to circumvent this *lav*: Z.W. Falk, *Introduction to Jewish Law of the Second Commonwealth* (Leiden: E.J. Brill, 1972-78), II.207, pointed to *tena'im* excluding *shemiṭah* found in documents at Murabba'at (DJD II.18), and noted that before the time of R. Meir, a "stipulation made contrary to what is written in the Torah is valid", citing M.B.M. 7:11, *Makk.* 3b. *Aliter,* M. Elon, *Jewish Law, History, Sources, Principles* (Philadelphia: Jewish Publication Society, 1994), 124.

7 However, an explicit agency constituted at the time of the marriage would be revoked by the subsequent marital relations between the parties: Maimonides, *Hilkhot Gerushin* 9:25; on "constructive agency", see Bleich's paper delivered at the Zutphen conference, *supra,* at 7-36.

addresses a problem within *dinei mamonot,* rather than *iṣur veheter,* which traditionally have been regarded as most entrenched against change.[8]

A second type of historical argument might be the following: major historical changes have been made in Jewish law (not least, in the areas of marriage and divorce[9]) in the past; why, then, can we not make the necessary changes to meet the problem of *agunah* today? Against this, the dogmatician might reply: it is not a question of history, but rather of authority. The mere fact that changes were made in the past does not in itself entail the view that we have authority to make such changes today.[10] Indeed, the long history of

8 On the distinction in general, see Elon, *Jewish Law, supra* n.6 at I.123 on M. *Eduyot* 1:12, *Yevamot* 15:3, and 137-140 for the greater capacity of *mamonot* for legal argument and development. On the classification of the constitution of marriage/divorce as *iṣura* rather than *mamona,* see, e.g. Asheri, *Resp.* 35:2, at Elon, *Jewish Law, supra* n.6 at II.851. In his survey of legislation from the tenth century to the present, Elon observes (II.835) that in the area of family law and the law of succession: "On the one hand, the authority to legislate was fully exercised in regard to the financial relationships of family members and the financial aspects of the law of succession, even when a particular enactment overrode previously existing law. On the other hand, legislative enactments avoiding otherwise valid marriages gradually disappeared."

9 Thus (i) the introduction of financial security for the wife through the *ketubah* and its being secured on the husband's property: he forfeits the *mohar* if he unilaterally divorces her without good cause; (ii) a control on unilateral divorce by the husband was imposed via court supervision of the process: a *geṭ* must be authorized by (though it is not issued by) a *bet din.* There is some debate as to when this became mandatory: Freeman, *supra* n.2 at 58, cites I. Haut, *Divorce in Jewish Law and Life* (New York: Sepher-Hermon, 1983), 27-41, and Aiardo in *Albany Law Review* 49 (1984), 131, 138, for the view that it was at the time of R. Gershom that the process of drafting and delivering a *geṭ* was made so complex that supervision by a *bet din* became a practical necessity. However, there is considerable evidence of court involvement from a much earlier period: see Z.W. Falk, *Jewish Matrimonial Law in the Middle Ages* (Oxford: Clarendon Press, 1966), 120-124; (iii) consent of the wife came to be required by Rav Gershom (11th cent., Germany) unless one of a number of serious, defined matrimonial offences was proved; (iv) the ban on polygamy; (v) the rejection of *ḳiddushin* by *biyah*: Elon, *Jewish Law, supra* n.6 at II.851f., quotes Asheri, *Resp.* 35:2: "a marriage is valid only if it conforms to their [that of the halakhic authorities] legislation; even if the marriage is effected by means of intercourse, they have declared the act to be fornication."

10 That, of course, might lead to a converse argument: just as one cannot rely simply upon the fact of historical change as authority for present change in

the *agunah* debate is one in which, as I shall indicate, the very authority for the making of such historical changes was itself challenged by later authorities.

We do, I believe, have to accept as our starting point the premise that changes cannot be made today unless halakhic authority exists to make such changes. The issue then become whether such authority does exist. At this point, the history of the matter re-enters the debate. Careful attention to the history of the development of authority within the *halakhah* is vital to the solution of our problem. For if some of the Rishonim were able to maintain that the *Geonim* were in error in assuming an authority to deviate from talmudic principles,[11] it would appear possible (not least in the light of *hilkheta kebatra'i*[12]) for later generations to take the view that their own predecessors were in error in their more restrictive conception of the degree of authority available within the system. In short, the mere assertion of authority (or its absence) is not conclusive: to assert or to deny authority is itself to make a claim within the halakhic system, which those with the necessary knowledge and authority are entitled to evaluate.

It is worth reviewing the history of the problem of the *moredet*, not so much for the prospects of finding here a universal solution to the problem of the wife refused a *geṭ* by her husband,[13] but rather for the light it casts upon

---

the law, so too one should not rely upon the historical fact of the present reluctance to change (insofar as it reflects a psychological/sociological/ historical attitude, rather than being mandated by the Law itself) as itself being normative.

11 See further *infra,* 119f.

12 *Infra,* n.32.

13 For such a solution to be universal, it would be necessary to establish, despite Rabbenu Tam's rejection of the Geonic approach, (a) that "coercion" remains possible; (b) that it is universally effective (falsified, as regards imprisonment at least, in a notorious case in Israel); and that (c) *either* it still applies to the *moredet* who claims *me'iṣ alai* (since, almost by definition, *any* wife refused a *geṭ* by her husband could make the claim that she is repulsed by him, even if she would have preferred the marriage to continue) *or* that the categories of case where coercion is regarded as (talmudically) permissible are not closed. I do not seek in this article to show that these criteria can be fulfilled. For the view that the categories of permissible coercion are closed, see Moshe Chigier, "Ruminations over the Agunah Problem", in *Women in Chains. A Sourcebook on the Agunah*, ed. J.N. Porter (Northvale, N.J. and London: Jason Aronson Inc., 1995), 73-92, at 77, on *Shulḥan Arukh, Even Ha'ezer* 154 and earlier sources. He argues that, true to the nature of Jewish Law codification, the codes recorded both opinions,

the history of conceptions of authority in Jewish law. This history revolves around two separate, but related, questions: (i) is the *moredet* entitled to a (unilateral) divorce at all on the basis of her claim that she finds her husband repulsive (*me'iṣ alai*)? (ii) if so, will the court go further than merely order the husband to issue a *geṭ*, and *coerce* him to do so if he is recalcitrant?[14]

Both of these issues are beset by the common problems of conciseness of expression in rabbinic (especially talmudic) texts. Very frequently, they are succinct to the extent of being coded:[15] we might very well speak of a rabbinic "restricted code".[16] However, this has not resulted in transparency even *within* the rabbinic circles to which such "restricted code" belongs; the shorthand has left us with doubts in relation to both the remedies contemplated in the Talmud and the means used by the Geonim to make their decrees effective.[17]

The source of much of the classical debate on the *agunah* derives from the ambiguities of the discussion of the position of a *moredet* between Amemar and Mar Zuṭra in *Ket.* 63b. The traditional printed text reads as

---

leaving the matter in dispute to the discretion of the judging court (see Z. Warhaftig, "Coercion to Grant a Divorce in Theory and in Practice" (Heb.), *Shenaton Hamishpaṭ Ha'Ivri* 3-4 (1976-7), 160). If this had remained the position, the court could consider each case on its merits and by a process of deduction could decide whether an order of compulsion was lawful in the particular case, although it was not explicitly mentioned in the earlier lists. However, the later *poṣḳim* have stated that compulsion would be lawful only in the cases distinctly stated by the Talmud. As a result, Chigier argues, the list is now closed.

14 S. Riskin, *Women and Jewish Divorce: The Rebellious Wife, The Agunah and the Right of Women to Initiate Divorce in Jewish Law, A Halakhic Solution* (Hoboken, N.J.: Ktav Publishing House, Inc., 1989), very usefully sets out the sources in (mainly) chronological sequence. Hereafter cited as Riskin, *Women, supra* n.14.

15 Note the frequency of the use of square brackets in the translations of Riskin, *Women, supra* n.14.

16 In the sense of B. Bernstein, *Class, Codes and Control* (London: Routledge & Kegan Paul, 1971), Vol.I, chs. 5-7, esp. pp.108f., 123-137. I have used this concept also in the context of biblical law in "The Original 'Oral Law'", in *Jewish Ways of Reading the Bible*, ed. G.W. Brooke (Oxford: Oxford University Press, 2000; Journal of Semitic Studies Supplement X), 3-19.

17 Indeed, this phenomenon affects also the very definition of *moredet*, and (for those who accept that there are two distinguishable types: *letsa'aro* and *me'iṣ alai*) which one is referred to at particular points in the talmudic argument.

follows:[18]

> What is to be understood by [the term] rebellious wife (*moredet*)? Amemar said: She who says "I wish [to remain married] to him, but I want to cause him pain (ומצערנא);" if she says, however, "He is repulsive to me (מאיס עלי)," she is not forced (לא כייפינן לה) [to resume sexual relations concurrent with the steady reduction of her alimony sum[19]]. Mar Zuṭra said: She is forced (כייפינן לה).

There is a fundamental policy difference between Amemar and Mar Zuṭra: in the case of a wife who is "rebellious" in the sense that she says that she can no longer stand her husband ("He is repulsive to me"), and who (presumably) withdraws sexual relations and wants to terminate the marriage, Amemar sides with the wife and sees this as providing reason to terminate the marriage: the wife, therefore, is not to be pressured into remaining in the marriage. Mar Zuṭra, on the other hand, sides with the husband. He sees this as providing no good reason to terminate the marriage: the wife, therefore, is to be pressured to remain in the marriage. She ought in these circumstances to be disciplined, brought into line.

On the traditional text, Amemar is not explicit as to the means by which the *moredet* claiming *me'iṣ alai* obtains her freedom. There is, however, a variant text, noted by R. Aaron Halevi (Ra'ah) and R. Solomon Adret (*Rashba*), which gives Amemar's conclusion as: "and *he* is not to be forced."[20] The text thus reads:

> What is to be understood by [the term] rebellious wife? Amemar said: She who says "I wish [to remain married] to him, but I want to cause him pain; if she says, however, "He is repulsive to me," he is not forced (לא כייפינן ליה [to divorce her]). Mar Zuṭra said: She is forced (כייפינן לה).

Here, the policy difference between the two views remains: Mar Zuṭra still wants to pressure the wife to remain in the marriage, while Amemar (by implication) is willing for her to be released, but only if her husband is willing to do so. He is not to be coerced. Shlomo Riskin, however, argues correctly that "this other version is not consistent with the Talmud's citation

18 Translations and explanations from Riskin, *supra* n.14 (here, at 40f.) unless otherwise indicated. There are minor differences in translation and explanation in the Soncino Talmud, *Kethuboth,* 383, but none that affect the present issues.

19 *M. Ket.* 5:7, on which the Gemara is here commenting, provides for a weekly reduction of 7 *denarii* in the *ketubah.*

20 See Riskin, *Women, supra* n.14 at 167 n.8, noting that it is cited also by Rabbenu Tam, *Ravad* on the *Rif* and the Responsa of the Sages of Provence.

of Mar Zuṭra, which would then logically have to be: "he is to be forced": (בייפינין ליה), nor is it consistent with the entire content of Amemar's remarks, which seem to contrast the wife who says "He is repulsive to me" with the wife who claims "I wish to remain married [to him], but I want to cause him pain."[21]

The variant noted by the Rishonim is thus sufficient to cast some doubt on the traditional text, but does not provide an entirely satisfactory alternative. The logical oppositions between Amemar and Mar Zuṭra might have been any of the following:

(a) Amemar: "we do not coerce her" v. Mar Zuṭra: "we do coerce her," referring throughout to coercion to remain within the marriage as an obedient wife;
(b) Amemar: "we do coerce him" v. Mar Zuṭra: "we do not coerce him," referring throughout to coercion to give the *geṭ*;
(c) Amemar: "we do coerce him" (to give the *geṭ*) v. Mar Zuṭra "we do coerce her" (to remain within the marriage).
(d) Amemar: "we do not coerce him" (to give the *geṭ*) v. Mar Zuṭra "we do coerce her" (to remain within the marriage).

Of these, (a) is the traditional text and (d) the variant noted by the Rishonim. But (d) differs from all the other possibilities in that the two opinions are distinguished, linguistically, on *two* parameters — both (i) *ley* v. *lah*; and (ii) presence or absence of the negation, *lo* — while both the traditional text and the two alternative reconstructions make them differ only on one linguistic parameter, either *ley* v. *lah* or the presence/absence of the negation. The single parameter opposition is stylistically to be preferred. Hypothetically, we might argue that (b) is to be preferred to (c), in that (b) has both sages refer to the same object of coercion, whereas (c) takes the object of coercion in the two opinions to be different. However, (b) would require us to amend *both* opinions, in comparison with both the traditional text and the variant, while (c) allows the opinion of Mar Zuṭra to remain unaltered. In fact, there is now MS evidence, that of MS Leningrad Firkovitch, which attests (c).[22] Thus, a tradition appears to have existed that

21 *Ibid.*

22 See Elimelech Westreich, "The Rise and Decline of the Law of the Rebellious Wife in Medieval Jewish Law", in this volume, at 209, citing *Maṣoret ha-Shas ha-Shalem* [*The Babylonian Talmud with Variant Readings ... Tractate Kethuboth*], ed. R. Moshe Hershler (Jerusalem: Institute for the Complete

Amemar not only adopted the policy that the wife claiming *me'iṣ alai* ought in principle to be released from the marriage, but that her husband could be coerced to release her, if otherwise reluctant to do so. For here, the text reads:

> What is to be understood by [the term] rebellious wife? Amemar said: She who says "I wish [to remain married] to him, but I want to cause him pain"; if she says, however, "He is repulsive to me," *he* is forced ((כייפינין ליה [to divorce her]). Mar Zuṭra said: *she* is forced (כייפינן לה) [to remain in the marriage as a compliant wife].

After recording this dispute between the Amoraim, the Talmud continues:

> Such an incident once occurred, and Mar Zuṭra forced [the woman to remain married], and R. Ḥananiah of Sura was born [from the continued relationship]. This, however, was not [the proper course of action]. In that case it was the intervention of Providence [which brought about such a satisfactory conclusion].

This, too, speaks against possibility (b) in relation to the position of Mar Zuṭra. It is clear, however, that the Talmud favours the position, in principle, of Amemar, on the policy issue: the woman here ought not to have been forced.[23] The fact that there was a "happy" outcome is taken not to justify the coercion of the woman which was applied in this particular case, but rather is attributed to divine intervention.

As for the final decision of the *Rabbanan Ṣabborai*,[24] the Talmud states:

> Now that it has not been determined, either this way or that way [i.e., the law regarding the dowry garments has not been clarified], if she seized the garments, we do not take them away from her, and if she did not seize them, we do not give them to her. We also make her wait twelve months — a year — for a divorce (אגיטא), and during these twelve months she receives no sustenance from her husband.

This appears to adopt the basic policy of Amemar, in that the wife in such circumstances[25] should ultimately get her freedom: she is to wait "for a

---

Israeli Talmud, 1977), II.88. See also E. Westreich, "The rise and decline of the wife's right to leave her husband in medieval Jewish law" (Heb.), *Shenaton Hamishpaṭ Ha'Ivri* XXI (1998-2000), 126.

23 Whatever measures may or may not be taken in order to secure her release: this, therefore, is consistent with the view of *Rabbanan Ṣabborai*, discussed below.

24 Text and translation at Riskin, *Women, supra* n.14 at 43 (on the case of the daughter-in-law of Rav Zevid); 44 (for the final ruling on the issue).

25 I.e., *me'iṣ alai,* though there is later debate on this point.

divorce" (אגיטא). But the *Rabbanan Ṣabborai* do not make it clear what procedure is here adopted in order to facilitate such freedom. On this, later authorities are divided. Sherira is explicit that the Talmud here implies *kofin*, they coerce him[26] (perhaps aware of the Amemar tradition represented by MS Leningrad Firkovitch) and Alfasi[27] and Maimonides appear to have taken the same view.[28] Rabbenu Tam, on the other hand, is vehement in his denial: "How could a scholar make [such a] mistake as to say that we force a husband to divorce [his wife] when she says 'He is repulsive to me!'?"[29]

This history raises some difficult problems regarding the authority system within Jewish law. Although there is a principle of following the majority view,[30] minority views are preserved in the Talmud itself,[31] and not simply for academic (historical) reasons. Given the principle of *hilkheta kebatra'i*,[32] it is possible for a majority in a later generation to adopt a

26 כופין את הבעל וכותב לו גט: *Otsar HaGeonim*, 8, pp.191-92, quoted and translated in Riskin, *Women, supra* n.14 at 56-59, on which he observes: "It is clear that Rav Sherira Gaon interprets the final statement of the Talmud, "and we make her wait twelve months ...," to mean that the husband is forced to grant his wife a divorce at the end of the twelve-month period, even against his will." See also Elon, *Jewish Law, supra* n.6 at II.660 n.68.

27 Alfasi, *Ket.* 63b; cf. Riskin, *Women, supra* n.14 at 86. But see also Westreich, "The Rise and Decline of the Law of the Rebellious Wife in Medieval Jewish Law", in this volume, at 209f.

28 *Hilkhot Ishut* 14:8-14, esp. 14; cf. Riskin, *Women, supra* n.14 at 87-91; Westreich, "The Rise and Decline of the Law of the Rebellious Wife in Medieval Jewish Law", in this volume, at 210f.

29 *Ṣefer Hayashar LeRabbenu Tam,* quoted by Riskin, *Women, supra* n.14 at 101.

30 The most famous source being the talmudic story of the oven of Akhnai, *B.M.* 59b, which derives this conclusion from the biblical phrase *aḥare rabim lehaṭot, Exod.* 23:2. See further Elon, *Jewish Law, supra* n.6 at I.261-264.

31 Indeed, non-normative views are themselves treated with sanctity: *elu ve'elu divre elohim ḥayyim, Erub.* 13b.

32 *Shulḥan Arukh Ḥoshen Mishpaṭ* 25:8: "Since the later authorities saw the statements of the earlier ones but gave reasons for rejecting them, we assume, as a matter of course, that the earlier authorities would have agreed with the later ones." See Elon, *Jewish Law, supra* n.6 at I.266ff., noting that it applies even to a single individual later in time who disagrees with the views of a number of earlier authorities, and stressing (at 271) that it came to apply only if the later authority refers to and discusses the earlier opinion and shows by proofs acceptable to his contemporaries that, although contrary to the position of the earlier authority, his own view is sound. For an example

minority view of an earlier generation.[33] There is, indeed, a reluctance (at least) to do this if the effect will be to contravene the final decision of the Talmud,[34] but where the latter (as here) is unclear in its effect, the problem becomes one of interpretation of that final decision, and the principle of *hilkheta kebatra'i* may still apply.

In this case, Rabbenu Tam, while not following Mar Zuṭra for the general policy that the *moredet* claiming *me'iṣ alai* should be disciplined back

---

of the use of the principle as recently as the mid-19th century (in the context of *hafḳa'at ḳiddushin* based on *taḳanot haḳahal*), see Elon, *Jewish Law, supra* n.6 at II.874-78, on Isaac Abulafia, *Resp. Pnei Yitsḥaḳ, Even Ha'ezer*, #16 (p. 94d). A quite different account of the history of the rule from that of Elon is offered by I. Ta-Shma, "The Law is in Accord with the Later Authority — *Hilkhata Kebatrai:* Historical Observations on a Legal Rule", in *Authority, Process and Method. Studies in Jewish Law,* ed. H. Ben-Menahem and N.S. Hecht (Amsterdam: Harwood Academic Publishers, 1998), 101-128, translated (with a 1994 Postscript) from *Shenaton Hamishpaṭ Ha'Ivri* 6-7 (1979-80), 405-423. Ta-Shma maintains that the idea that the rule confers authority on the *contemporary poṣeḳ* to reject an earlier precedent (rather than provide him with a rule of preference as between earlier authorities) "is an entirely novel idea of Ashkenazic origin for which I can find no traditional sources" (at 107; see also 114, 125). Rather, "the principle conferring authority upon the current *poṣeḳ* ... originates in an altogether different rule: 'Jephthah in his generation is like Samuel in his generation.'"

33 Elon, *Jewish Law, supra* n.6 at I.259, quotes Samson of Sens, commenting on *M. Eduy.* 1:5 (and relating it to *elu ve'elu ...)*: "Although the minority opinion was not initially accepted, and the majority disagreed with it, yet if in another generation the majority will agree with its reasoning, the Law will follow that view."

34 For the exclusion of "questions that were ... definitively decided in the Talmud as compiled by R. Ashi and Ravina" from the principle of *hilkheta kebatra'i*, see Asheri, *Piṣḳe ha-Rosh,* Sanhedrin, ch.4, #6, quoted by Elon, *Jewish Law, supra* n.6 at I.269, and, in this context, Rabbenu Tam, *Ṣefer Hayashar leRabbenu Tam, Responsa*, ed. Rosenthal, #24 (p.40): "Legislation (*hora'ah*) ended with Ravina and R. Ashi", quoted by Elon, *Jewish Law, supra* n.6 at II.661. However, Elon, *Jewish Law, supra* n.6 at II.665, concludes: "The majority view is that the legislative power of the *geonim* was not limited to monetary matters (as Rabbenu Tam held it was), but was fully effective even with regard to marriage and divorce." Riskin, *Women, supra* n.14, at 108, 176 n.25, also observes that in his view of the authority of the final decision of the Talmud in relation to the constitution of a divorce (specifically, the talmudic view that there must be a twelve-month waiting period even when coercion was permitted), Rabbenu Tam was upholding a minority view.

into the marriage,[35] adopts the then minority view[36] that she could be released only with the consent of her husband, and could not be coerced.[37] We may well ask: if it is possible for the Rishonim to prefer a minority post-talmudic view of what the Talmud decided, is it not possible in the present day (applying *hilkheta kebatra'i*) to review what subsequently became

35 In this event, she may go, but without her *ketubah,* Rabbenu Tam here rejecting what he takes to be the position of Mar Zuṭra in the Talmud (Riskin, *Women,* 104f.: "But if she said 'He is repulsive to me' — we do not force her [to remain married]. That is to say: if she said, 'I do not desire him, neither him nor his alimony; rather, I forfeit everything to him,' this is not considered a forfeiture in error, and we do not force her to remain [in the marriage in the hope that] she will change her mind. If the husband wishes to divorce her without alimony he may divorce her, and he has no alimony obligation, for she has forfeited [it] to him; it is a complete forfeiture. Mar Zuṭra says: we force her; that is, we require her to remain, and perhaps she will change her mind, as with the case of 'I desire him and I am causing him pain,' for it is one case, and they are both considered rebellious [wives]; for since she forfeits on account of rebellion, it is not a complete forfeit, and if the husband wishes to divorce her, he gives her alimony. However, this is not [the law]; rather, as we explained before, [the woman who says] 'He is repulsive to me' is not a rebellious wife." Rabbenu Tam takes the talmudic story of the family of Rav Zevid to exemplify this situation: Riskin, *Women, supra* n.14 at 105.

36 The principal thesis of Riskin's book is that this was a minority view not only in the Talmud itself, but also up to the time of Rabbenu Tam.

37 *Pace* Elon, *Jewish Law, supra* n.6 at II.661f., arguing that Rabbenu Tam objected not to the principle of coercion here, but to the Geonic abolition of the 12-month talmudic waiting period. What is not clear in Rabbenu Tam's position is whether the court should even order the husband to issue a *geṭ* in this situation. He understands Mar Zuṭra's "we coerce her" in the Talmud as *not* applying to the *moredet* claiming *me'iṣ alai.* It is only the *moredet* who wants to stay in the marriage but *letsa'aro* who is "coerced". As regards the *moredet* claiming *me'iṣ alai,* "... anything against her will is called 'forcing,' [including the court] proclaiming against her, causing her to lose her alimony, and isolating her; but [we do] nothing in addition to this [we do not force her to stay with her husband]" (Riskin, *Women, supra* n.14 at 106). This would appear to suggest that pressure (including proclamation in the synagogue and financial sanctions) may be applied to her to persuade her to stay in the marriage, but if this does not succeed, she may go free. Rabbenu Tam has no problem with this if the husband consents. Conversely, he is strongly opposed to coercing the husband to comply with an order to divorce. What is unclear is whether he would approve of a *bet din* even making such an order. There is no indication that he did so, and his overall position would appear to imply opposition to it.

the majority decision of the Rishonim, and prefer the minority view of the Rishonim (which favoured the majority approach of earlier authorities)? To do that, it is not sufficient simply to prefer the outcome of the Geonim and early Rishonim against Rabbenu Tam and his followers. Argument must be advanced that the Geonim were not wrong in their interpretation of the Talmudic passage — in that the latter either stated (Amemar, according to MS Leningrad Firkovitch) or implied the use of coercion against the *moredet* claiming *me'iṣ alai*, or at least that it left the issue open, so that the Geonim did not lack the authority to introduce it — and such argument, Menahem Elon maintains, must be acceptable to the contemporaries of the one propounding it.[38] This latter criterion sounds like a demand for consensus — an issue to which I shall return later.

It is at this point that one's understanding of the relationship between history and authority becomes crucial. There is, as we have observed, an important issue in relation to the text of the Talmud itself. Are we to derive conclusions regarding the authority of views expressed in the Talmud on the basis of what has become the traditional printed text, irrespective of the manuscript tradition behind it (excluding in principle any possibility that the printed text is erroneous)?[39] "What the Talmud said" thus becomes an historical question, upon which issues of authority can clearly depend. How are such historical question is to be decided? Are they themselves to be decided on the basis of authority (we have seen that one variant manuscript tradition was known to some of the Rishonim, who took their own stance on it),[40] or on the basis of scholarly research? What if manuscripts (such as MS

38 See Elon, *Jewish Law*, *supra* n.6 at I.266ff., in n.32, *supra*.

39 The view has, indeed, been expressed to me (in effect) that we should even today adopt a providential view of textual transmission (cf. n.41, *infra,* on the *Ḥazon Ish*): the texts available to earlier authorities were those which God intended to be used for halakhic decision-making. But a providential view might equally be taken of the later discovery of MSS with variant readings! One might, moreover, pose the same question in relation to the now-available forms of electronic searching of the talmudic text, which put the modern generation of talmudic interpreters at a significant advantage compared to earlier generations, notwithstanding the legendary recall and command of the text which some of the latter are reputed to have possessed.

40 Elon, *supra* n.6 at I.259 n.77, quotes *Rashi* on *Ketubot* 57a: "[Whenever there are two versions], we ignore the version according to which two Amoraim are in dispute as to what another said, and we accept the version according to which they themselves differ on the question involved. For when two disagree over what a third authority said ... one of them is making a misstatement of fact; but when two amoraim disagree over a civil or religious

Leningrad Firkovitch) become available which were not available at all to earlier authorities?[41] Would that not qualify, in terms of *hilkheta kebatra'i*, as the basis for a new argument that could not have been known to the earlier authorities, but which, had it been known, would have been accepted by

---

law, each one says what seems to him to be correct and no misstatement is involved. Each one offers his own reasoning: One will show why the matter should be permitted and the other will show why it should be forbidden; one will make one analogy and the other will make a different one. In such a case it can be said that "both are the words of living God" [TB Eruvin 13b, Gittin 6b]. Sometimes, the reasoning of one is apposite and sometimes the reasoning of the other, because [the force of] the reasoning changes with the slightest change in the circumstances of the case ..." The implication would appear to be that *elu ve'elu* does *not* apply to statements of fact; there, we may encounter simple mistakes.

41 This issue has been re-examined at some length by M. Bleich, "The Role of Manuscripts in Halakhic Decision-Making: Hazon Ish, His Precursors and Contemporaries", *Tradition* 27/2 (1993), 22-55, concluding (at 45) that "for halakhic purposes, it is the consensus of contemporary authorities that inordinate weight not be given to newly published material. Even earlier authorities who gave a relatively high degree of credence to newly discovered manuscripts did so within a limited context. Accordingly, formulation of novel halakhic positions and adjudication of halakhic disputes on the basis of such sources can be undertaken only with extreme caution." A more liberal view towards the admissibility of MS evidence was taken, he argues, before the period of "definitive codifications of Halakhah" (and particularly the *Shulḥan Arukh*), e.g. *Rambam*'s overruling a Geonic ruling on the grounds that the talmudic text available to them was at variance with MSS examined by *Rambam* (*Hilkhot Malveh ve-Loveh* 15:2, noted by Bleich, *ibid.*, at 23). However, most of Bleich's argument is directed towards the emergence of MSS evidencing new post-talmudic views (such as might affect our view of what was the majority position at a particular time) rather than new MS evidence as to the text of the Talmud itself. On the latter, see his account at 42 of the view of Rabbi S.Y. Zevin in his Introduction to the first volume of the Talmud Babli of the Makhon HaTalmud HaYisraeli Hashalem (cf. n.22, *supra*), that "a variant talmudic text is significant only when it can be demonstrated that an early-day authority based his ruling upon that version of the text", and the views of *Ḥazon Ish* (quoted at 43-44) stressing divine providence in the transmission of the MS tradition (but not, apparently, in the discovery of new MSS). Rabbi Bleich refers also to an article by Rabbi Z.Y. Lehrer in *Tsefunot* IV/4 (July, 1992), 68-73, which had not become available before he finalised his text. On the history of rabbinic text criticism of the Babylonian Talmud, see also D. Goodblatt, "The Babylonian Talmud", *Aufstieg und Niedergang der römischen Welt* (Berlin: W. de Gruyter, 1979), Bd. II.19.2, 257-336, at 268-70.

them.[42] It has, moreover, been observed that the views of some of the Rishonim as to the basis on which the Geonim enacted their decrees (in particular, whether they saw themselves as following a talmudic view, or as innovating) were formed in the *absence* of texts from the Geonim themselves, which we now have available.[43]

I turn now to the texts of the Geonim themselves. Their basic position was one of sympathy towards the *moredet* who claimed *me'iṣ alai* — or, at least, willingness to accommodate her for fear of what she might do if they did not. They took the view that she should get her freedom, and were willing to take measures in order to secure this. There are some significant variations, however, in the measures they variously contemplated. Rav Yehudai Gaon, for example, employs a ban,[44] which Rabbenu Tam regarded as even more severe than corporal punishment.[45] The fact that the *Rosh* uses the language of *hafḳa'at ḳiddushin*[46] shows that there was an understanding, in some circles, that this freedom was accomplished without the issuance of a *geṭ.* Perhaps, then, we are entitled to see a distinction between the traditional language of *kofin oto* ("they coerce him") and *notnin*[47] ("they give" [her]) or

42 *Shulḥan Arukh Ḥoshen Mishpaṭ* 25:8, quoted *supra* n.32.

43 Riskin, *Women, supra* n.14 at 113, on Naḥmanides, and 118f., on *Rashba.*

44 "When a woman rebels against her husband and desires a divorce, we obligate [the husband] to divorce her, and if he does not do so we place him under the ban until he does it. But in order to bring about peace between husband and wife we make her wait a week or two." See Riskin, *Women, supra* n.14 at 47f.

45 At Riskin, *Women, supra* n.14 at 102.

46 "... For they relied on this dictum: "Everyone who marries, marries in accordance with thc will of the Rabbis" [bKet. 3a] (כל המקדש אדעתה דרבנן מקדש), and they agreed to annul the marriage (והסכימה דעתם להפקיע הקידושין) when a woman rebels against her husband": *Resp.* 43:8, p.40b, quoted by Riskin, *Women, supra* n.14, at 125, 126f., and see Riskin's own comments at 129.

47 The *Iggeret Rav Sherira Gaon* uses the expression: "And after him, Mar Rav Rabba, they decreed in his day to grant an immediate bill of divorce to the woman", לתת אלתר גט לאשה: see Riskin, *Women, supra* n.14, at 59. Rav Shmuel ben Ali, Head of a Babylonian school in the second half of the twelfth century, described by Riskin, *Women, supra* n.14, at 62, as "in effect, a Gaon ... after the conclusion of the Geonic period", writes: "[The court] endeavors to make peace between [husband and wife], but if she refuses to be appeased they grant her an immediate divorce (נותנין לה גט לאלתר), and do not [publicly] proclaim against her for four weeks." See also *Halakhot Gedolot*: "we grant her a bill of divorce immediately (ויהבינן לה גיטא אלתר)", quoted by Riskin, *Women, supra* n.14, at

*kotvin* ("they write [for her]),[48] which might be taken to suggest that it was the court which authorized the writing and delivery of the *geṭ*— even without the participation of the husband. However this may be, the view of the Rishonim appears to have been that the Geonim used physical coercion (*kofin*),[49] and a great debate ensued as to whether they were entitled so to do.

The accounts which the Geonim themselves provide suggest that they were well aware of the evolution of practice in this sphere. Rav Sherira Gaon, in particular, distinguishes a series of stages through which the remedy passed.[50] The Geonim appear to have based themselves upon talmudic authority for the *principle* of applying coercive measures to the husband of a *moredet* who claimed *me'iṣ alai*; however, in abolishing the talmudic waiting period of 12 months and adjusting the rules regarding the disposition of property in a manner such as to relieve the wife of the burden of total loss of the *ketubah*, they self-consciously innovated. There is little doubt that they did so on the basis of *tsorekh hasha'ah*, in particular the fear that the woman

48f.

48 An anonymous 13th-century responsum: "they wrote her an immediate bill of divorce" (וכתבי לה גט לאלתר): Riskin, *Women, supra* n.14, at 52f.

49 A responsum of Rav Ḥananiah ben Yehuda Gaon, the father of Rav Sherira Gaon: "[the court] coerces the husband until he divorces her ..." (וכופין את הבעל עד שיגרש): see Riskin, *Women, supra* n.14, at 55f. Cf. the terminology of the Responsum of Rav Sherira Gaon, quoted at 56f.

50 Riskin, *Women, supra* n.14 at 69, summarizes the development thus: (1) Rav Yehudai Gaon, latter half of the eighth century, provided that the husband of a woman who claims he is repulsive to her is obligated to divorce his wife after a waiting period of merely a week or two. (2) The *Halakhot Gedolot*, probably written in the ninth century, added to the husband's obligation of granting an immediate divorce the wife's right to all her remaining dowry property, whether or not she "seized" them at the time of the divorce. Rav Natronai Gaon endorsed and confirmed this practice. (3) Rav Amram Gaon, who succeeded Rav Natronai in Sura at the end of the ninth century, added that the wife was also entitled to receive a basic alimony sum of either one hundred or two hundred *zuzim*. (4) Rav Sherira Gaon, head of the scholars of Pumbedita in the late tenth century, confirmed all the previous decrees. He clarified the wife's right not only to whatever remained of her dowry (her property which she had brought with her at the time of her marriage), but also to any *nikhṣei tzon barzel* (property which she had brought into the marriage but for which her husband had assumed full responsibility) that was no longer intact. Hence, there appear to be four progressive decrees, each adding some benefits for the *moredet*, and each agreed upon by the two major schools in Babylon: Sura and Pumbedita.

would turn to prostitution[51] if made to wait for 12 months without maintenance, and ultimately would have resort to the Muslim courts if denied her *geṭ*.[52] Such resort was bad enough in itself; worse still if the woman was tempted to convert to Islam in order to facilitate access to the intervention of the Islamic courts.[53]

Such considerations were foreign to Rabbenu Tam, living in a Christian environment where the *moredet* had no possibility of seeking gentile help in order to obtain a divorce,[54] and where, indeed, there was external moral pressure to restrict divorce itself — a factor, as Ze'ev Falk argued many years ago, in the adoption by Rabbenu Gershom of the requirement that (absent specific cause) divorce required the consent of the wife, and could no longer be effected by the husband almost unilaterally.[55] Rabbenu Tam, however, differed from the Geonim in his perception of the process and authority by which the Geonim had effected their reforms. Insofar as the latter purported to be based upon the Talmud, he argued that they were in error, that there was no mention in the Talmud of any coercion of the husband other than in the cases stated already in the Mishnah where the wife was entitled to a unilateral divorce.[56] Insofar as they effected a change in the law as stated in the

51 An anonymous 13th-century responsum, quoted by Riskin, *Women, supra* n.14 at 52f., explains the abolition of the 12-month waiting period on the grounds that the daughters of Israel "went out to "bad ends," either prostitution or apostasy (בין בזנות בין בשמד)".

52 Sherira claimed: "Jewish women were attaching themselves to the gentiles to get divorces from their husbands by force": Riskin, *Women, supra* n.14 at 58.

53 Riskin, *Women, supra* n.14 at 74, sees the threat from Islamic law as consisting in the rule of Islamic law that a woman had a right to obtain a divorce from her husband when (both being non-Moslem) she adopts the Islamic faith and her husband refuses to be converted along with her.

54 Riskin, *Women, supra* n.14 at 110f.; cf. Westreich, "The Rise and Decline of the Law of the Rebellious Wife ...", in this volume, at 218.

55 Z.W. Falk, *Jewish Matrimonial Law in the Middle Ages* (Oxford: Clarendon Press, 1966), ch.IV.

56 Riskin, *Women, supra* n.14 at xiii, 94, 96: "And Rabbenu Tam raised another problem, that in the entire [Talmudic] discussion there is no mention of forcing the husband, only of forcing the wife ..." (*divkhol hashemu'ah eyno mazkir kefiyat haba'al ela kefiyat ha'ishah*, p.94), quoting *Ṣefer Hayashar leRabbenu Tam,* ed. E.Z. Margoliot (New York: Shai Publications, 1959), 39ff., based on *Ṣefer Hayashar leRabbenu Tam, Responsa,* ed. S.F. Rosenthal (Berlin: Itskovski, 1898), *Siman* 24, p.39.

Talmud, the Geonim lacked authority so to do.[57] It is not clear whether Rabbenu Tam acknowledged that the Geonim were purporting to act on the basis of *tsorekh hasha'ah*. That view was taken by some of the Rishonim,[58] but with differences as to whether such "emergency legislation" was and could be effected for more than a single generation.[59] In short, how

57 Riskin, *Women, supra* n.14 at 98f.: "And that which Rabbenu Shmuel [*Rashbam*] wrote — that the Geonim decreed that we do not delay twelve months for a divorce but rather, they force him — far be it from our teacher to increase the number of *mamzerim* in Israel. We hold the halakhic principle that Ravina and Rav Ashi are the last authoritative halakhic decisors, and even were the Geonim able to decree that a woman could collect her alimony from movable property, whether it be on the basis of Talmudic law or their own reasoned judgment, that is only as far as monetary value is concerned. But as for permitting an invalid bill of divorce, we have not had the power to do so from the days of Rav Ashi [nor will we] until the days of the Messiah. And this is an invalid bill of divorce. After all, we learned in the Talmud that [the Sages] did not force [a divorce] until twelve months, and they [the Geonim] advanced the forcing of the divorce before [the time which] the law [allows]." See also Riskin, *Women, supra* n.14 at 106, 107f.

58 The *Ṣefer Ha-Maor* of Rabbenu Zeraḥyah Halevi, written between 1171 and 1186 (identified by Riskin, *Women, supra* n.14 at 86f., as the first source to reject the geonic decrees), explains them in terms of *hora'at sha'ah* (thus accepting that the Geonim had the authority to make them on this basis), but then observes: "But in succeeding generations we make judgments based on Talmudic law." This would appear to mean not that later generations lack the authority to rule on the basis of *hora'at sha'ah* but rather that they may deviate from the Talmud only if circumstances of *hora'at sha'ah* exist (and they are assumed not to have existed from the Geonic period to that of Halevi). This does not mean that they may not exist in future.

59 The *Rosh* also explicitly attributes the change from the geonic decrees to the changed social circumstances and regards it as a temporary measure: "... the Geonim who made this decree made it for that generation [only], for it seemed to them that it was necessary at the time because of Jewish women [who would otherwise rely on Gentiles for divorce but who nonetheless would not divorce their husbands lightly]. And now the matter seems to be reversed: Jewish women in this generation are vain. If a woman will be able to remove herself from under her husband['s rule] by saying 'I don't want him,' not a [single] daughter of Abraham our Father will remain with her husband. They [the women] will cast their eyes upon others and will rebel against their husbands. Therefore it is good to place coercion at a far distance" (Riskin, *Women, supra* n.14 at 127). Contrast Naḥmanides, quoted by Riskin, *Women, supra* n.14 at 112, arguing that *Ṣefer HaMa'or* regards the decree of the *yeshiva* as an emergency and thus temporary ruling (*hora'at sha'ah*), but that from its own words it is obvious that the decree of the Geonim was for

temporary is "temporary"? We may recall, in this context, that the *ḥerem* of Rabbenu Gershom on polygamy was itself conceived as a "temporary" measure, whose duration was limited to a thousand years!

Here, again, important questions regarding the historical foundation on which authoritative views are based arise. Are we entitled to investigate whether Rabbenu Tam conceived the Geonim to be acting on the basis of a general legislative authority, or on the basis of *tsorekh hasha'ah*? If his view was the former, and this turns out to be historically incorrect, does that affect the status of the objections he made to the reforms of the Geonim? And if the basis of the Geonic decrees was indeed *tsorekh hasha'ah,* does such authority continue to exist for later generations, and if so is it restricted to the kinds of *tsorekh* identified by earlier generations?

We may certainly detect in the views of Rabbenu Tam and his successors a reluctance to accept such diversity within divorce practice as appears to have been generated by the different cultural circumstances affecting the Jews of the Middle Ages — broadly, the Sefardim in the Islamic world, the Ashkenazim in Christendom. What was the legal response to such diversity? Maimonides, for one, appears in this matter to have applied the talmudic principle of majority decision (here applied to a majority of communities, rather than scholars), when he rejected the view of the Geonim[60] even though personally reverting to coercion on the basis of what he took to be the talmudic position. Elsewhere, however, Maimonides expresses himself in terms not of majority but rather of consensus,[61] prompting some to see here

[all] generations; Naḥmanides accuses the author of *Ṣefer HaMa'or* of using misleading language, precisely because he wanted to follow the ruling of the Talmud. He comments: "but in truth they decreed for [all] generations. This decree did not move from their midst for five hundred years, and they practiced it into the days of our Rabbi, may his memory be a blessing, as is known from their responsum."

60 In *Hilkhot Ishut* 14:14, he writes that the Geonic decrees were no longer valid because "they did not spread to a *majority* (*berov*) of Israel." That Maimonides seemingly still adheres to a majority view in this context is implied also by the formulation that "many great scholars in most places" disagree with the geonic decrees (*verabim ugedolim ḥolḳim aleyhem berov hameḳomot*).

61 In the Introduction to *Mishneh Torah,* he justifies the binding character of "all matters stated in the Babylonian Talmud" on the grounds that "with respect to all matters stated in the Talmud there is universal agreement [*hiṣkimu aleyhem kol yisrael*] among all Israel."

a reflection of the Islamic doctrine of *ijma*.[62] Another possibility is that consensus emerges in the context of the increasing limitations imposed upon the authority of *taḳanot haḳahal* to impose conditions (such as the presence of a *minyan*) upon the constitution of marriage (breach of which would justify annulment based on כל המקדש אדעתה דרבנן מקדש).[63] However that may be, it has become commonplace nowadays to hear that a proposed solution to the problem of *agunah* cannot be accepted because it lacks consensus. It is a matter of both academic and practical importance to identify the nature of the operation of consensus in Jewish law. It is not listed as a source of Jewish law by Elon in his four-volume *magnum opus*; indeed, "consensus" does not even appear in his subject index! It would appear that "consensus" is not regarded as an independent source of law, but rather as a new and additional condition upon the operation of any established source of law. How did this come about? It is true, of course, that majority decision is no longer as functional as it was when there was a clearly defined institution within whose members a majority could be established or denied. That did not, however, prevent Maimonides from applying it in the context described above. Nor is it inconceivable that a consensus might be achieved as to the composition of an (even informal) "college" of contemporary authorities, within which majority decision could operate.[64]

We have been considering issues of the authority needed for the interpretation, development and change of generally binding rules of law, the *halakhah*. The same considerations do not necessarily apply at the level of adjudication of the individual case. Recent research has addressed the question

62 S.W. Baron, *A Social and Religious History of the Jews* (Philadelphia: Jewish Publication Society of America and New York: Columbia University Press, 1958, 2nd ed.), VI. 100 (I am indebted to Prof. Gerald Blidstein for this reference).

63 Elon, *Jewish Law*, *supra* n.6 at II.856-79. See further B.S. Jackson, "*Mishpat Ivri, Halakhah* and Legal Philosophy: *Agunah* and the Theory of "Legal Sources"", *JSIJ — Jewish Studies, an Internet Journal,* §4.3.3, at http://www.biu.ac.il/JS/JSIJ.

64 Such a college need not have a common physical location. It could operate through modern communications, with its own (private) intranet. When R. Shalom Moses Hai Gagin attacked Abulafia for his use of *hafḳa'at ḳiddushin* (*supra, n.*32), he argued: "It cannot possibly be contended that the world's great scholars ever gathered together and agreed to rule contrary to the saintly Caro even in a single particular" (Elon, *Jewish Law*, *supra* n.6 at II.876). This would appear to imply that a convention of the world's great scholars is indeed capable of making such a ruling.

of Jewish judicial discretion: a case may be made for the proposition that the *bet din* has a residual discretion, deriving from the original conception of the divinely inspired judge, to make decisions not in accordance with the prevailing *halakhah*.[65] In this particular context, we appear to have an example in the writings of the *Rosh*, who, despite following the general approach of Rabbenu Tam, took a more flexible attitude in his responsum on a specific case. Noting that the brother of a woman claiming *me'iṣ alai* had told him that she gave reasonable bases for her 'rebellion', he indicates that the judges must investigate this: "If [her husband's] intent is to "chain" her, it is proper that you rely on your custom at this time to force him to give an immediate divorce" (*ve'im dato le'ignah ra'ui hu shetiṣmokh al minhagkhem ba'et hazot lekofo liten geṭ lizman*).[66] However, reliance upon the application of discretion in the individual case is hardly likely to satisfy the Jewish community in present circumstances.[67] It does not address the symbolic significance widely perceived to attach to this issue; moreover, in a world of global communications, it is arguable that there is a need for a truly global solution.

The focus of this paper has been an attempt to identify the problems of authority which emerge from the history of one particular aspect of the *agunah* problem, albeit one which has exercised a great deal of rabbinic attention throughout the ages. Similar considerations will affect our analysis of other aspects of the problem, and of different solutions to it.

65 See Haninah Ben Menachem, *Judicial Deviation in Talmudic Law* (Chur, etc.: Harwood Academic Press, 1991); see also, more broadly, his "The Judicial Process and the Nature of Jewish Law", in *An Introduction to the History and Sources of Jewish Law*, ed. N. Hecht, B.S. Jackson, D. Piattelli, S.M. Passamaneck and A.M. Rabello (Oxford: The Clarendon Press, 1996), 421-437; B.S. Jackson, "Judaism as a Religious Legal System", in *Religion, Laws and Traditions. Comparative Studies in Religious Law*, ed. A. Huxley (Richmond: Curzon Press, 2001), §3, forthcoming; Italian version: "L'ebraismo come ordinamento giuridico religioso", *Daimon. Annuario di diritto comparato della religioni* 1 (2001), 165-183, at 170-75.

66 Quoted by Riskin, *Women, supra* n.14 at 128.

67 One may compare the fate of the "Brichto proposals" on conversion a decade ago: Rabbi Brichto was prepared to recommend that progressive applicants for conversion submit themselves to the Orthodox *batei din*, in return for a more "flexible" attitude on the part of the latter. However, he was seeking public assurances of such a flexible attitude. For the proposal and reactions to it, see *The Jewish Law Annual* VIII (1989), 247-99. Comparison may now be made with developments in Israel: the reported acceptance by the rabbinic *batei din* of the first "graduates" of the Conversion Institute established in the wake of the Ne'eman Commission.

9

# THE *SHOṬER*

by

STEPHEN M. PASSAMANECK*

Discussions of law enforcement in the halakhah in particular, and the administration of criminal justice in the halakhah in general, have held my rapt attention for the past 20 years.[1] My inquiries have led me in various directions, and the starting point for all those directions, implicitly if not always explicitly, has been the verse from *Deuteronomy* 16:18, *shofeṭim* and *shoṭrim* shall you make yourselves in all your gates which the Lord thy God giveth thee ...", which provides us with the term *shoṭer* (plu: *shoṭrim),* as an official in the context of the biblical justice system, which term after centuries of use comes to mean a law enforcement officer, a police officer.[2]

* Professor of Rabbinic Literature, Hebrew Union College - Jewish Institute of Religion, Los Angeles.

1 My inquiries have resulted in the following publications, among others: "The Use of Excessive Force by a Police Officer — One Halakhic Opinion," *Jewish Law Association Studies* I (1985), 79-91; "The *Berure Averot* and the Administration of Justice in XIII and XIV Century Spain," *Jewish Law Association Studies* VI (1992), 95-106. I am indebted to my colleagues Prof. David Ellenson and Prof. Reuven Firestone who gave me valuable critical comment on this essay.

2 Although the ancient Semitic linguistic background of the term *shoṭer* is not really part of this present inquiry, it is well known that the work traces from the Akkadian *mataro*, a term for writing. It also gives us the Hebrew-Aramaic word *shṭar* — a document. The roots *hrt, srt* meean to carve, to mark with a stylus, thus suggesting that the *shoṭer* was originally some sort of clerk, or scribe, perhaps the court scribe who worked beside the *shofeṭ*. It would seem that in the course of time the *shoṭer* performed clerkly duties in various civil and military contexts. Perhaps the *shoṭer*, the officer of the court, was eventually charged with other sorts of duties and, at length, he became the enforcer as well as the writer of official documents. Clearly the *shoṭer* finally lost his clerical responsibilities and became identified with law enforcement. The standard meaning for the root given by M. Jastrow, *A Dictionary of the*

The *shoṭrim* appear in Scripture long before the deuteronomic command. We meet *shoṭrim* as officers, clearly under-officers, in charge of work gangs during the period of Egyptian slavery. Tradition holds that each taskmaster exercised command over ten Jewish *shoṭrim,* each *shoṭer* having charge of ten worker slaves. The *shoṭrim* were, so to speak, foremen or monitors or crew chiefs. When Pharaoh refused to provide straw for the brickmaking the taskmasters demanded the maintenance of the production quota. But the production fell short of the quota, and the *shoṭrim* were beaten because of that shortfall.[3]

The terms *shoṭer* and *shoṭrim* occur in various forms 25 times in the Hebrew Bible. Probably the best known of these is the verse from Deuteronomy cited above. Indeed the Jews have continued to appoint their judges; but *shoṭrim* are another matter as we shall see. In some sense the rabbis and *dayyanim* of later epochs succeeded to the office of the *shofeṭ,* the judge. Moreover, the rabbinical courts assumed the burden of the justice system of the Jewish people when their temporal sovereignty ceased, and Roman power enveloped the land. Strictly religious and ritual law remained their purview as did matters of matrimonial regimen and some aspects of commercial and personal injury law. While rabbinic jurists have exercised judicial functions, doubtless carrying on in spirit if not in name the function of the *shofeṭim* in Deuteronomy, no similar successors to the *shoṭrim* appear to have emerged in the organization of the rabbinic courts. This is indeed curious since the rabbinic tradition itself declares that the offices of *shofeṭ* and *shoṭer* are interdependent.[4] One cannot exist or properly exercise his duties without the other; if there is no *shofeṭ* there is no *shoṭer,* and vice versa, since the *shoṭer* has the duty of executing the orders of the *shofeṭ.* This brief paper looks at the question of what happened to the *shoṭrim,* and why they virtually disappeared as Jewish law officers for centuries until they reappeared as police officers in the modern State of Israel.

Centuries after the biblical events, the Rabbis, in their reading of the ancient past, coupled the report of the beating with the divine instruction to

---

*Targumim*, etc., is "to draw lines, to arrange": 1555, col.b. See also F. Brown, S.R. Driver, and C.A. Briggs, *A Hebrew and English Lexicon of the Old Testament* (Oxford: Clarendon Press: 1957), 109.

In any event, the philological background of the term is not in point here, only its use in rabbinic literature, both early and late, where it came to mean "officer" and especially a "law enforcement officer".

3 *Exodus* 5:14f.; *Bemidbar Rabbah*, ed. Wilna, sec.15.

4 *Midrash Tanḥuma, Shofeṭim*, sec. 2.

Moses to gather 70 men who were known as elders-and as officers, *shoṭrim*. While this midrash certainly does not represent a reliable historical source for the biblical period, it clearly does believe that in the development of offices in biblical Judaism the office of *shoṭer* represented a post of responsibility and indeed was also conceived as a stepping stone towards an ever higher level of public service. Because the *shoṭrim* had suffered the beating on behalf of the people, they became the elders who shared the divine spirit and the tasks of governance and justice (cp. *Numbers* 11:16 f). One may also imagine that the Rabbis, in their view of biblical history, would have posited that the *shoṭrim* who became the body of elders were replaced by others to act as *shoṭrim* in service to the *shofeṭim* of *Deut.* 16:18, since we hear in *Deut.* 29:9 of heads, tribes, elders, and *shoṭrim* ... all standing before God. And again in *Joshua* 8:33 we have the elders and *shoṭrim* along with *shofeṭim* and indeed all Israel standing on either side of the ark, opposite the priests and levites who carried the ark.

The *shoṭrim* also discharged military duties. According to *Deuteronomy* 20, the *shoṭrim* addressed the Israelite army directly after the war priest had spoken. They presented the criteria for claiming combat deferment, and acted as military wardens of some sort. The Rabbis of the Mishnah, *Ṣoṭah* 8:1-6, in their era, understood the biblical passage in this sense, though obviously the rabbinical authorities were not witnesses to the activity recorded in Scripture.

Apparently the *shoṭrim* functioned as marshals for the invasion of Canaan. Joshua charges them to give the orders to prepare the invasion in *Joshua* 1:10, and in 3:2 the *shoṭrim* give the people their marching orders for crossing the Jordan. One imagines that the *shoṭrim* had sufficient authority to enforce their orders.

In both *Joshua* 23:2 and 24:1, Joshua addresses the elders, heads, judges, and officers *(shoṭrim)* of the Jewish people. This grouping of officials is most interesting. The aged Joshua reviews the past to an audience which specifically includes the civil officers, the senior governance, the magistracy. The sacerdotal officers are not mentioned. Joshua speaks, as it were, to the lords and officers temporal, as distinct from the lords and functionaries spiritual.

The spiritual and sacerdotal officers came from the tribe of Levi and the House of Aaron. The classic biblical configuration of power places the official cult in their care. Other persons from other tribes perform the workaday tasks of governance and justice. While of course the king played a sacerdotal role, and the function of prophets and prophecy transcends the neat division of temporal and spiritual, nonetheless, the cult *per se* was in the hands of priests and levites, while governance was in the hands of elders, judges, and officers. The broad distinction is serviceable if we recall that exceptions and anomalies occasionally intrude into the scheme.

The *shoṭrim* fade from the pages of Scripture after the days of Joshua. We find them again, after many years, in the Books of Chronicles.

In First Chronicles, with its lists and its plethora of organizational detail, David took the census of the levites, of whom 6,000 , so it turned out, functioned as officers *(shoṭrim)* and judges. From the context we learn that levitical duties fell into various categories: the majority oversaw the work of the Temple; there were the officers and judges; then there were 4,000 doorkeepers and 4,000 musicians. Just because a person was born a levite did not mean he was a skilled musician; there was plenty of other work to occupy the landless tribe (*I Chron.* 23:4,5, cp. *I Chron.* ch. 25). The Chronicler refines the lists: in *I Chron.* 26:29 a certain levitical clan was assigned the duties of officers and judges with respect to the "external" work, which medieval commentary identifies as the duties and labors involved in the fields, orchards, forests and quarries that belonged to the Temple, all of which was "external" to Jerusalem (thus *Rashi*, France, d. 1105 and *Radak*, R. David Kimhi, Southern France, 1160-1235, *ad loc.*) The medieval rabbinic comment does not of course purport to be a contemporaneous witness or confirmation of the Chronicler, only a devout attempt to understand the ancient notion of *melakhah hitzonah.* The officers were presumably foremen of work gangs and marshals for the laborers - as the *shoṭrim* of Egyptian slavery had been. Again the *shoṭrim* might have been levites but their duties were certainly not cultic.

The same biblical book records data on the twelve monthly rotations of military officers for royal service, among whom were *shoṭrim*: captains of thousands, captains of hundreds, and their *shoṭrim*, *I Chron.* 27:1. The rank appears to be some sort of a junior officer, perhaps similar in rank and duty to the marshal or the warden for the civilian work crews working for the Temple, or maybe they were something like sergeants. In any event, we have *shoṭrim* rotating in and out of royal service on a monthly schedule. These men were clearly involved with secular tasks.

Second Chronicles also mentions that there were scribes, doorkeepers, and officers of the levites, *II Chron.* 34:13. The officers appear associated with the more mundane tasks under levitical superintendence.

The Chronicles' account of King Jehoshaphat's judicial reforms mentions levitical *shoṭrim* who served in the reorganized courts of Jerusalem,

*II Chron.* 19:11. The *shoṭrim* appear to be officers of the court who may serve either Amariah who was the magistrate for all ecclesiastical suits or Zebadiah, son of Ishmael, the chief magistrate for all cases under royal jurisdiction. No matter which court they served, there is no reason to believe that the *shoṭrim* were any more than enforcement officers. Just because the *shoṭrim* were levites, doubtless a demographically dominant group in Jerusalem, does not mean they had anything to do with matters sacred; they apparently did the mundane work of the ecclesiastical court at the behest of its judges.

Finally, we find a *shoṭer* by name of Ma'aseyahu, who assisted the scribe Jeiel to prepare the muster roll of King Uzziah's army, under the orders of a royal captain, named Ḥananyahu (*II Chron.* 26:11), The task of preparing a military muster roll, while extremely important, is just the sort of assignment that would routinely get kicked downstairs to a military secretary and a junior, or inferior, officer. The *shoṭer* helped with the boring routine of military life.

The term appears once in Scripture in figurative language (*Prov.* 6:6f). One is advised to observe the industrious ant, which works diligently without the presence of any chief or *shoṭer* or ruler. The notion that a *shoṭer, inter alia*, was a sort of foreman or crew chief is quite clear from this ancient advisory.

The *shoṭer* seems to have been a person of a certain rank, lower rank to be sure, but recognized nonetheless. He was apparently a junior officer, a crew chief, warden, or possibly an enforcement official when he served in a court of law. His duties were of a uniformly non- sacerdotal nature, when mentioned in the context of levitcal duties, and certainly of a secular nature when he served the king, the army, or the royal courts. In brief, the *shoṭer* was a secular officer, or as near as one can come to such a status in a government and society that were very much theocratic.

Parenthetically, it is also noteworthy that the term *shofeṭ*, with which *shoṭer* is classically coupled, connotes both judge and secular leader. The *shofeṭim*, Jeptha and Samson for instance, were hardly ecclesiastical or religious figures, but they were leaders of the people. The *shofeṭ* was clearly a magistrate, but a magistrate whose jurisdiction went far beyond ecclesiastical matters. The term *shofeṭ* clearly has some general and secular, or at least non-sacerdotal, sense. The *shofeṭ*, moreover, existed and functioned, or was perceived to do so in rabbinic tradition, when the Judean State enjoyed political independence or a significant degree of it. When such independence was compromised or absent, we no longer find the *shofeṭ*. By the Second Commonwealth period, and certainly from the Roman period onwards, political independence no longer obtained, and the magistrate no longer bears the title of *shofeṭ*. He is a rabbi or a *dayyan*. The restoration of political sovereignty in the twentieth century was the occasion for the reappearance of the *shofeṭ*, a magistrate with a secular charge and duty, as contrasted to the rabbi and *dayyan* whose brief involves the broad spectrum of religious and ecclesiastical matters and the assessment of secular phenomena as they affect religious life.

To return then to the matter of the *shoṭer* - the Mishnah and the Tosefta know virtually nothing of that officer.

The Mishnah mentions *shoṭrim* in only two contexts: the amplification of the military deferments of *Deuteronomy* 20, *M. Ṣoṭah* 8:1-6 (see above, p.127) and the purity of their lineage.

The idea that the Israelite host as drawn up for battle implies a condition of political sovereignty. The *Ṣoṭah* material harks back to an earlier period; the Rabbis are reconstructing ancient history, imagining it as best they could.

In *M. Ḳiddushin* 4:5 we are advised that anyone whose father served as a *shoṭer*, translated often as "public officer" can marry into the priestly ranks. Such lineage is deemed untainted. The Mishnah here however gives no inkling of the duties of such officers.

The Tosefta similarly appears to contemplate a period of independence in its rare mentions of *shoṭrim*. The term occurs in Tractate *Ṣanhedrin*, where the rabbis are discussing the composition of the *Ṣanhedrin* and the people requisite to its proper function. We find reference to the *shoṭre dayyanim*, officers of the judges-note *dayyanim* and not *shofeṭim*, *T. Ṣanh.* 3:9. The *shoṭre rabbim*, public officers, appear in *T. Ṣanh.* 8:2, the context of describing the physical configuration of the Ṣanhedrin during the period of Rabban Gamaliel, late first century, early second century C.E., when the Palestinian community no longer enjoyed political independence and the Roman government was alert to any signs of Jewish insurrection that might attempt to revive Jewish sovereignty. The period did not allow for significant Jewish authority in the secular, governmental area. The mention of *shoṭrim* gives no indication at all of what they did or how they did it. Internal Jewish law enforcement capacity was probably at a low ebb at this period of Roman domination and sensitivity to the least signs of rebellion. R. Elazar b. Simon, after all, acted at the behest of the Romans, and he was criticized severely for what he did, *B. Bava Mezia* 83b.

If *shoṭrim* functioned in the rabbinic legal systems which the Mishnah and Tosefta represent, the logical places to expect them are in discussions of stolen or embezzled property where *shoṭrim* might be detailed to assist in retrieving it and in the descriptions of the various modes of execution for capital offenses or of flogging, where again *shoṭrim* might be detailed to assist in the process. With respect to stolen property and death penalties, the texts are silent about assisting officers; we hear only of the role of witnesses in capital executions. With respect to flogging, *M. Makkoth* 3:12, 14, we read only of the *ṣegan hakeneṣet*, no one else. Since capital jurisdiction implies a fair degree of autonomy or at least self-determination, it is all the more curious that *shoṭrim*, officers with secular duties, apparently play no explicit role in capital proceedings and executions.

The *aggadic* literature offers little expansion on the nature and duties of the *shoṭrim*. One passage merely identifies them as community leaders and chiefs.[5] Another describes Job as having been both a *shofeṭ* and a *shoṭer* in his generation.

The post-Talmudic *halakhic* literature presents two provisions or laws which establish the office of *shoṭer* as the enforcement arm of the rabbinical court and to a degree describe the powers and duties of those officers. Even though the classic statement of the two provisions appears in the twelfth century *Mishneh Torah* of Maimonides, they probably express ideas of a much earlier period.

The first provision appears in *Hilkhot Ṣanhedrin* 1:1 where the *shoṭrim* are described as the armed judicial police who patrol public areas, and especially the market place as market inspectors, and who are to bring before the magistrate all those whom they find breaking the law. The second provision comes in *Hilkhot Yom Ṭov*, 6:21, in which the rabbinical court is charged to appoint *shoṭrim* at festival times to patrol certain locations and prevent men and women from gathering in them, less they feast, drink, and come to sin.

The first law governing *shoṭrim*, which identifies them as the enforcement personnel of the *dayyanim,* suggests by its nature that Jews possess a fair degree of autonomy or self- determination, at least enough to exercise internal police powers. The second law calls for *ad hoc* appointment of officers for a particular task, and this rule also implies that Jews enjoy sufficient autonomy or self-determination to manage their own internal affairs including the free movement of community members without necessary

5 *Midrash Tanḥuma, Shofeṭim*, sec.2., and see *Peṣiḳta Rabbati*, sec. 33 (ed. Ish Shalom).

regard for any external state apparatus. In both cases the *shoṭrim* perform police-like duties, in the second case the secular enforcement of perceived religious requirements. The use of the terms *bet din* and *dayyanim* in the rules indicates that the legal system contemplated rests in he hands of rabbinic jurists who clearly administer and enforce a Jewish law, which, though ultimately revealed and divine in toto, exhibits aspects that are, for practical purposes, both non-sacerdotal, e.g., battery, theft, commercial transactions, and manifestly religious, ecclesiastical, e.g., dietary laws, liturgy, and much personal status law.

The *shoṭer* as contemplated in these two passage was a Jewish official under the orders of the rabbinical courts. It is therefore quite striking that the medieval responsa literature which provides enormous detail on all facets of Jewish life simply does not reflect the existence or activity of such *shoṭrim* serving the *dayyanim* or any other Jewish body. The responsa occasionally mention the *shaliaḥ bet din,*[6] the agent of the court, who apparently enjoyed a degree of power and authority, but who is nowhere identified as a *shoṭer.* The *shaliaḥ bet din* seems to have acted as a sort of bailiff or marshal who produced accused or summoned persons before the magistrate and was permitted to use necessary force to effect this duty. He was also free from liability if he damaged property or caused injury in the discharge of his duties. The community was enjoined to treat this officer with respect, and the *shaliaḥ's* word that he had been treated disrespectfully was sufficient ground for the court to issue a 30-day ban against the offender, and perhaps administer a flogging to him.[7]

The responsa literature is not however altogether mute on the matter of *shoṭrim.* The terms *shoṭer* and *shoṭrim* occasionally appear in the responsa literature, from the eleventh century to the present. That literature provides us with various contexts for the terms, and those contexts provide the clearest

6 See M. Slae, "The Image of the Police Officer" (Hebrew), *Teḥumin* I (5740), 385-96, which mentions the *shaliaḥ bet din* in various contexts presented in responsa and considers those officers to be police or peace officers of some sort. Whether or not they actually did discharge peace officer duties as a regular part of their commission or as an occasional assignment is not at all clear. In the sources, their enforcement authority never approaches what the *shoṭrim* were empowered to do. The *shaliaḥ bet din* may have served the court, but the responsa do not really demonstrate that he was generally a peace officer.

7 *B. Ḳiddushin* 12b, cp. also *B. Mo'ed Ḳaṭan* 16b; *Hilkhot Ṣanhedrin* 25:5,6 and *Shulḥan Arukh Ḥoshen Mishpaṭ* 8:5, gloss and all commentators to the sections in *Hilkhot Ṣanhedrin* and *Shulḥan Arukh Ḥoshen Mishpaṭ.*

evidence of what the terms meant in the actual professional world of rabbinic jurists. In context, both *shoṭer* and *shoṭrim* refer to a gentile official, either a law enforcement officer as such, or an official acting under the orders of a gentile court or sovereign. Sometimes the activity of the *shoṭer* is benign, sometimes not; sometimes the officer assists one Jew against another; sometimes the officer acts against a Jew in the name of the government; and finally, occasionally, the role of the officer appears to be neutral. In the period up to the sixteenth century, the term is rather rare. Only R. Isaac Alfasi, R. Solomon b. Adret, R. Isaac b. Sheshet, and R. Jacob Weil found occasion to use it. R. Isaac Alfasi (eleventh century, Fez) informs us that one Jew who had became a surety for another Jew received a visit, presumably by the creditors, who were accompanied by "officers of the judge."[8] The creditor was suing the surety under gentile law, and the officers were there as officers of the gentile court to assist the creditor in putting the surety under oath. There is no reason to believe that the officers of the gentile court were not themselves gentiles. In the event, witnesses attest that the surety was under some duress because the officers used some verbal persuasion on him, "either swear or give (what is demanded)." R. Alfasi denies the officers put the man under duress; they had only urged and persuaded him.

R. Solomon b. Adret (thirteenth, early fourteenth centuries, Spain) while interpreting a community ordinance, mentions the *shoṭer* as an officer whose power derives from the Crown, and in context of course this means the gentile government.[9] R. Isaac b. Sheshet (fourteenth century, Spain and North Africa) relates a frightening tale of violence and intimidation in the Jewish community; three Jewish gentlemen who were in fear of their lives could not leave their homes without two armed guards — servants of the "officers of the city."[10] This is clearly a reference to some sort of police protection furnished by the gentile authorities. There is no indication that such a guard could or would be furnished by Jewish court authority. At any rate, the officers are aiding one group of Jews who are in fear of their lives from some of their Jewish brethren.

R. Jacob Weil (fifteenth century, Germany) relates the unpleasant case of a group of Jews who willfully split off from their community, even though the community had formally agreed to act as one body with respect to the

8 *Responsa of Isaac of Fez,* Makhon Rambam (Pittsburgh: 1954), no. 156.

9 *Responsa of R. Solomon b. Adret,* ed. Lemberg, 1812, vol.3, no.385.

10 *Responsa of R. Isaac b. Sheshet*, ed. Lemberg, 1805, no.266.

gentile community.[11] This breakaway group brought the town officer (policeman ? constable?) to the synagogue on Rosh Hashanah and had the officer push and shove a community leader from the bimah when he stood to lead the worship. Again, the officer could not have been in any sense an enforcement agent of any Jewish court.

The sixteenth century Ottoman authority, R. David ibn Abu Zimra, received a question about a member of a community whom, so witnesses declared, the community forced to sign a certain document on pain of being remanded to gentile authorities as an informer and slanderer.[12] When the communal officials presented him with the document, they brought with them *shoṭrim* who would arrest him if he did not sign; doubtless those officers were the gentile representatives of gentile authority. Jews hardly wielded the power of arrest. R. Samuel Di Medina, a contemporaneous authority, apparently presents another version of this most bizarre and unseemly incident; in his statement of the facts, a Jewish communal official, not identified as a *shoṭer*, solemnly swore that no "officer" - i.e., gentile officer-was present at the signing.[13]

A sixteenth century Ottoman authority, Joseph ibn Lev, restated the facts of a tragic case of homicide and the testimony taken to establish the victim's death so that the widow could remarry.[14] The witness before the rabbinical court related how he and the victim had been business partners, and how he had spotted the victim's horse during a business trip and tried to buy it back because he thought the horse had strayed from his master. At that time, a number of gentiles asked him, in the course of ordinary conversation, if he had seen how the victim had been killed. The news of the murder alarmed him. He asked who had done it, and was given two names. The witness then said he brought officers who took the two accused men into custody. The officers were certainly gentiles since Jews did not have capital jurisdiction, much less the capability to effect arrests and place gentile suspects in custody.

In an inheritance case reviewed and analyzed by R. Yom Ṭov Tsaḥalon (1559-1620, Ottoman Empire) there is an incidental mention of a *shoṭer*.[15]

11 *Responsa of R. Jacob Weil,* ed. Hanau, 1610, no.140.

12 *Responsa of David ibn Abu Zimra*, ed. Warsaw, 1882, part 6, no.2145.

13 *Responsa of R. Samuel de Medina,* ed. Salonika, 1797-1798, sec. *Yoreh Deah*, no.74.

14 *Responsa of R. Joseph ibn Lev*, ed. Constantinople, 1560-73, part 1, no.6.

15 *Responsa of R. Yom Ṭov Tsaḥalon,* ed. Venice, 1694, no.131.

When the brother of a deceased man, who stood to be the heir under gentile law, learned that he was going to receive substantially less than he expected owing to an agreement struck by Jewish authorities in favor of two grandchildren, that brother called a royal officer, obviously a gentile.

Other authorities of the period also refer incidentally to a *shoṭer.*[16] In two of the cases the term is used figuratively: in one context, every person, it is said, would need a *shoṭer* in his house or there would be no end to a particular wrongdoing, and in the other context the term appears as a stylistic feature in a statement emphasizing the assertion that no coercion had been involved in a particular situation. In neither of these latter uses of the term does it of course refer to an actual person.

The medieval cities and towns in which Jewish communities, by and large, existed in close proximity to non-Jewish communities were small by modern standards. Jews lived in towns because they required the presence of their co-religionists. They needed the quorum of ten for public worship; they needed one or more ritual slaughterers; they needed each other for the communal support of educational programs for both children and adults, and perhaps for a rabbinical court and other social and religious demands of traditional Jewish life. Jews and gentiles perforce physically lived near each other, even if there was a Jewish quarter, or for that matter a ghetto. The present question is how did these small communities (at least by our standards) police themselves? Modern police agencies did not emerge until the nineteenth century, by which time emancipation had significantly eroded the power of the Jewish communities to maintain internal order.[17] In the absence of hard literary evidence, one is left with a reasonable supposition. Since the communities were small, and even the large ones were small by present measurements, it is reasonable to suppose that everyone knew, or knew of, virtually everyone else in town. Thus public ostracism, not to mention excommunication, were powerful weapons. The Jewish court could no doubt summon the aid of a specific person to call upon a wrongdoer and try to dissuade that person from his dangerous pursuits which could only hurt the community as a whole, particularly if the persons became a thorn in the side of the gentiles among whom the Jews lived and whose good will was

16 *Responsa of R. Betsalel Ashkenzai* ed. Venice 15-95, no.1; and R. Isaac Adarbi, *Divre Rivot,* ed. Sedlikow, 1813, no.67.

17 Historians generally accord the London Metropolitan Police pride of place as the first modern police force. It was founded in 1829. The United States Judiciary Act of 1789, however, established the United States Marshals Service, whose brief from its inception was the enforcement of federal law.

always a desideratum. In a pinch, non-Jewish authority might be enlisted to halt a known criminal. Further, self-help and self-defense were both approved in the halakhah and quite available as means of safeguarding both one's person and one's property. No doubt neighbors could look out for each other in the crowded precincts of medieval towns, where streets were narrow, dwellings close together, and the sounds of anger and conflict would have been easily heard. In effect the members of the community as a whole probably policed each other with a good deal of skill. There is of course no sign of any official who was charged with "police" powers. The *shaliaḥ bet din* is never mentioned as a town watchman or patrolman; it would seem that policing was strictly an *ad hoc* undertaking. In the nineteenth century, which provides the next notable group of responsa, western society as a whole was well on the way to developing new political, social, and commercial institutions which profoundly changed the nature and the power of Jewish communities.

In the nineteenth century, a responsum from the collection *Avne Shaish*[18] relates the complex and larcenous activities of several Jews. The story includes the statement that a *shoṭer* was sent to bring back a certain Yom Ṭov, clearly under arrest. The man was brought back in chains and the King put him in jail. The *shoṭer* was acting under gentile authority and was no doubt a gentile himself.

A case from Czarist Russia informs us of Jews who removed their *yarmulkes* out of fear when they caught sight of the Czar's police officers.[19] A case from Britain states that a Jewish woman whose husband was missing inquired of the police and was shown an official photograph of a corpse which had been retrieved from the river Thames.[20]

The responsa collection *Vayiḳra Avraham* preserves a mention of *shoṭer* in a matter which discusses the validity of a particular statement as testimony. A gentile indicates he has heard certain information from another gentile, an alleged murderer; a hypothetical situation is then presented: even if they would say to him that he should assert what he heard before a *shoṭer* and *moshel* in order that the guilty party he punished, even then he would be testifying as to what he heard from the alleged murderer. The larger context

18 R. Solomon Schein, *Avne Shaish,* ed. Kovno, 1926 (privately published), no.85.

19 R. Solomon Kluger, *Elef Lekha Shelomo*, ed. Bilgoray, 1894 (privately published), *Oraḥ Ḥayyim*, no.145.

20 R. Naftali Zvi Berlin, *Meshiv Davar*, ed. Warsaw, 1894 (privately published) part 4, no.23.

is permission for an alleged widow to remarry. The text is obviously not discussing any officer of a rabbinical court, nor is there a sign of such an official in a responsum from *Yeshuot Malko* that refers to the sealing of business premises by a *shoṭer* of the (gentile) king. Again, the term refers to non-Jews, in the employ of the non-Jewish government.[21]

A responsum from the collection *Yehudah Ya'aleh* merely refers to the rule of *Shulḥan Arukh, Oraḥ Ḥayyim* 529:4 that charges the rabbinical court with the responsibility of appointing *shoṭrim* on festival days to patrol areas in which men and women might come together to feast and drive, to prevent such unseemly, not to mention immoral, gatherings. The reference is clearly not to any actual persons who were in fact acting as officers of the rabbinical court at a particular time and place.[22] Several responsa from the nineteenth century use the term in a figurative or picturesque manner, and the redoubtable *Ḥatam Ṣofer* (Moses Schreiber, Hungary, 19th century) recalls the mishnaic description of the ancient Israelite army, drawn up for battle, which was addressed both by the war priest and the officer.[23]

The return of Jews to Palestine in the nineteenth century and the eventual creation of the State of Israel in 1948 meant among many things the creation of a police force to serve the needs of that burgeoning Jewish community of the twentieth century. Although the terms *shoṭer* and *shoṭrim* apparently had uniformly applied to gentile police authorities for hundreds of years, in the State of Israel the officers, the modern *shoṭrim* of the new nation, were of course predominantly Jewish. The connotation of the term was tailor made for the sense of police officer. The appearance of these Jewish police officers in a Jewish State has left its mark in the halakhah. The officers, however, are an arm of the secular state. They are not under the authority of the rabbinical court system. Nevertheless, the responsa of the Israeli Rabbis refer to *shoṭrim* in several contexts.

The responsa collection *Hekhal Yitsḥaḳ* discusses the validity of a Jewish bill of divorce when the husband has issued the document under

21 R. Abraham Adadi, *Vayiḳra Avraham* (Leghorn: E. Benamozegh and Co., 1865), *Even Haezer*, no.5; Israel of Kutno Responsa, *Yeshuot Malko*, ed. Pietrikow, 1927, *Ḥoshen Mishpaṭ*, no.3.

22 R. Judah Aszod, *Yehudah Ya'aleh,* ed. Lemberg, 1873, part 1, *Oraḥ Ḥayyim*, no.38.

23 Raphael Verdugo (?), *Mishpaṭe Yesharim* (Cracow: J. Fischer, 1891), 1, no.388; Joseph Ḥayyim b. Elijah, *Rav Pelaim* (publication data not given), pt.1, *Yoreh De'ah*, no.57; R. Moses Schreiber, *Responsa of Ḥatam Ṣofer* (Schmidsche: 1859), part 4, *Even Ha'ezer* 2, no.155.

duress, which police officers imposed.[24] The discussion mentions both the possibility of duress by gentile officers and duress inflicted by Jewish police acting at the behest of the gentile court, but the entire discussion of such official duress is really examined at that point in the essay as a theoretical matter with respect to a provision of Maimonides, *M.T. Hilkhot Gerushin* 2:20. The continuous and constant nature of law enforcement naturally occasioned conflicts between the necessary activity of police work and the religious requirements of Sabbath observance on the part of observant officers. A responsum in *Tsits Eliezer* suggests that an Arab officer drive the patrol car on the Sabbath and that officers can remain on the scene of a call for service until the conclusion of the Sabbath. Whether or not these suggestions provide realistic procedures to eliminate conflicts between police duties and religious observance does not form part of the discussion here.[25] Clearly, however the far simpler approach to the needs of observant *shoṭrim* is through scheduling: they are given their day or days off to accommodate religious observance, which is really another way of saying that the Arab officer should drive on the Sabbath. The basic question is not, however, police work as such, but rather the matter of maintaining the greatest degree of Sabbath rest.

R. Ovadia Yosef, in a famous responsum, asserted that the civil government of Israel should enforce the decree of competent rabbinic courts in the State.[26] He paraphrases the *Peṣiḳta Rabbati* to *Parashat Shofṭim*: If there are enforcement officers, there are judges. The roles of judge and officer are interdependent, and the one can not discharge his duties without the services of the other. The point made was simply that the rabbinic court should be able to call upon the civil enforcement power when necessary. The religious affiliation of the officers involved in such enforcement is irrelevant, though one imagines they would be Jewish; they are acting as civil, not religious, officers of the State.

Another modern decision asserts that under Jewish law police officers are competent witnesses as to what they saw and did. This opinion rests in turn

24 R. Issac Herzog, *Hekhal Yitsḥaḳ* (Jerusalem, 1959-60) *Even Ha'ezer* 1, no.1.

25 See my article, "Halakkah, Law Enforcement, and the Modern World", *Jewish Law Association Studies* VIII (1996), 101-128. See also R. Eliezer Waldenberg, *Tsits Eliezer,* Jerusalem (Privately published: 1947-51) Part 4, no.4.

26 R. Ovadiah Yosef, *Yabia Omer* (Jerusalem: *Midrash B'ne Tsion*, 1954-6), part 2, *Ḥoshen Mishpaṭ*, no.2.

upon the British case noted above, in which the police showed a photograph of a dead body to a woman whose husband was missing. A police officer, Jewish or gentile, stands in no inferior halakhic position with respect to the significance of his statement in Jewish law than that of a gentile who speaks in all innocence. Morever, a signed confession given to a police officer, which became part of the police file on the case, constitutes a full confession under the halakkah, not just a statement to one witness.[27] The officer in question here may very well be Jewish, but he or she is a civil, not a religious, official.

The term *shoṭrim* still, of course, remains the usual term for gentile officers outside the Jewish state. The *Responsa Minḥat Yitsḥaḳ* records an incident in which the police found a drowning victim and wrote to a Jew, who had been seeking a lost relative, to come and try to identify a corpse which they had found, from items found on the body.[28]

In the twentieth century responsa literature, just as in the responsa of previous centuries, rabbinic authorities cite the Maimonidean provision, seconded by the *Shulḥan Arukh,* to establish a group of morals police to prevent immoral activity at festive religious occasions. The texts furnish part of the arguments against unrestricted social contact, or indeed any sort of unsanctioned contact, between men and women.[29] Despite the citation of the law, however, there is no hint that such officers ever in fact performed their prescribed duties.

The references to *shoṭrim* in rabbinic legal literature permit a few summary remarks. Even though the rabbinic law perceives the *shoṭer* as an officer of the rabbinical court, there is no[30] evidence that officers with that title really did serve the court at any place or time. The *shaliaḥ bet din* seems to have functioned more along the lines of a bailiff or marshal with the very specific duty of serving summonses and escorting persons so summoned to court. Moreover, the term *shoṭer* as we have seen appears to have an association with, or connotation of, secular authority. When the Jews no longer exercised such authority over their own political destiny, and the Jewish justice system functioned as a religious, or a religion-oriented, system, the Jewish secular enforcement officer no longer had a regular or

27 *Piṣḳe Din Rabbaniyim,* sec.8, p.344.

28 R. Isaac Weiss, *Minḥat Yitsḥaḳ* (London, 1955), part 2, no.63.

29 *Ibid.*, part 3, no.111; R. Zvi Mekovsky, *Yeḥaveh Da'at* (Jerusalem: Zukerman: 1935), part 4, no.46; R. Yeḥiel Weinberg, *Seride Aish* (Jerusalem: Mossad Harav Kook, 1961), part 2, no.8.

clearly defined role in the system, so it seems from the absence of references to such an official. Clearly, no host government from Roman times onward could look benignly on a Jewish State within a State that exercised general law enforcement powers quite independent of the host authority.

The secular connotation of *shoṭer* no doubt made the association of the term with the officers (particularly law enforcement officers) of the secular gentile government rather simple. The *shoṭer* became the term for the gentile government law enforcer, and that is the context we encounter time and again in the responsa literature of the rabbinic court, even into our own time. Not until the reemergence of a Jewish State in the twentieth century does the *shoṭer* begin to refer to a Jewish officer, yet not an officer of the rabbinic court, but rather an officer of Jewish secular authority. Significantly much of the discussion of the *shoṭer* in modern rabbinic legal writing concerns proposed adjustments in police work in order to accommodate the Sabbath observance of the Jewish officers. Such considerations, however, properly fall under the ritual law rubric rather than under police regulations.

Despite the clear mandate that the rabbinical court appoint enforcement officers, this appointment does not, and indeed can not, occur even under Jewish secular authority. Presumably as long as political authority in the State remains a secular entity, there will be no *shoṭrim* to carry out the orders of the *dayyanim* except when secular authority permits them to do so.

The conclusion is nigh inescapable that the rabbinical court has functioned during the greater part of its history, without a *shoṭer,* without *shoṭrim*, and that no other officer, even the *shaliaḥ bet din,* has filled this void. Thus, whatever enforcement procedures the rabbinical court has employed over the years-social pressure, excommunication, ostracism, gentile coercion-Jewish law enforcement personnel as an arm of the court have played no role at all, or such a minor one that no trace of their activity remains.

# 10

# SHOULD TRANSGRESSION DISQUALIFY ONE FROM PUBLIC OFFICE?

by

NAHUM RAKOVER[*]

The subject of our discussion is the status of a leader who transgresses and whether he may return to his position of leadership. We also ask whether it is permitted to *appoint* a person who has transgressed to a position of leadership?

*The Immunity of King and Nasi (President)*

Before we discuss the *qualifications* a person must meet to be worthy of a position of authority and the conditions for *removal* from such a position, it should be noted that, like all citizens, a leader is subject to the rule of law. A cursory reading of the Mishnah would seem to indicate the opposite — that a king enjoys immunity and may not be compelled to stand trial:[1] "The king," we read, "may neither judge nor be judged." The Babylonian Talmud, however, takes this passage as referring specifically to kings of Israel (that is, kings not of the Davidic dynasty), whereas kings from the Davidic dynasty, "may judge and be judged."

The Babylonian Talmud states:[2]

> Rav Yoṣef says that the Mishnah refers only to the kings of Israel, whereas kings from the Davidic dynasty may judge and be judged, as is written,[3] "O House of David, thus saith the Lord, execute justice in the morning." If kings

a The Jewish Legal Heritage Society; Former Deputy Attorney General, Israel; Professor of Law, Bar Ilan University.

1 *M. Ṣanh.* 2:2.

2 *Babylonian Talmud, Ṣanhedrin* 19a.

3 *Jeremiah* 21:12.

> could not be judged, how would they be permitted to judge others — is it not written[4] *"Hitḳosheshu vaḳoshu,"* which Resh Laḳish interpreted to mean adorn *yourself* first and *then* adorn others? Why, then, is it prohibited to judge kings of Israel? Because of an incident that occurred in connection with a slave of King Yannai.

Following this passage, the Talmud recounts the well known story of Shimon ben Sheṭaḥ and King Yannai,[5] which is cited as the origin of the regulation that the king may neither judge nor be judged. Accordingly, the rule formulated by the Mishnah is really an *exception*, relating only to non-Davidic kings of Israel, whereas the general rule is the exact opposite — the king may judge and be judged.

It is relevant to note that the Jerusalem Talmud does *not* take the same approach as the Babylonian Talmud with regard to the king's subordination to the court. The Babylonian Talmud cites the Mishnah's ruling that a king *does not* judge as well as the source for ruling that a king *does* judge. The Jerusalem Talmud, however, does not differentiate between a king of Israel and a king of the Davidic dynasty and concludes, therefore, that no king may judge or be judged. Kings, the Jerusalem Talmud concludes, are judged before God. The Jerusalem Talmud states:

> "And you shall not judge him," as is written:[6] "From before You, my judgment will come forth." Rabbi Yitsḥaḳ said in the name of Rebbe, "The King and the public are judged before Him all the day, as is written,[7] 'That He may judge His servants, the nation of Israel every day.'"

Concerning this same issue, *Midrash Rabbah*[8] asks:

> A king of Israel who transgresses — may he be brought to trial? The Sages teach that a king may neither judge nor be judged. King David wrote, "From before You, will judgment come forth." It is not fitting for one of flesh and blood to judge a king — God will do it.

What is the law regarding one who is not a king but holds a position of

4 *Zeph.* 2:1.

5 *Ṣanh.* 19a-b. A slave of King Yannai had killed a man. The king was ordered to appear in court. He came to the court and sat down. Shimon ben Sheṭaḥ demanded that he stand. The king responded that he would stand only if the members of the court demanded it of him. All of members of the court lowered their eyes; none supported Shimon.

6 *Ps.*17:2.

7 *I Kings* 8:59.

8 *Midrash Rabbah*, on *Judges* 5:8.

authority,[9] such as a president?[10] Here we arrive at our main issue. Even the Jerusalem Talmud, which rules that the judgment of a king is before God alone, is of the opinion that a president must face judgment, be punished, and even be removed from office.

The source for this approach is attributed to Resh Laḳish. In the Babylonian Talmud, Resh Laḳish explained the verse,[11] "*hitḳosheshu vaḳoshu*" to mean "Judge yourself before judging others." In the Jerusalem Talmud,[12] Resh Laḳish states that "a president who transgresses shall be judged by a court of three judges." Following this statement of Resh Laḳish, the Jerusalem Talmud asks whether a president is "returned to his position," to which Rav Ḥaggai responds strongly: "I swear by the name of Moses: Of course we do not return him to his position for fear of killing!"

### *Returning to His Position*

Resh Laḳish, it would appear, expresses an opinion only with regard to *judging* a president and does not discuss the issue of returning him to his former position or what is meant by "fear of killing." Nevertheless, the Jerusalem Talmud continues and brings proof that a leader who behaves improperly should have his authority stripped from him.

The Jerusalem Talmud tells the following story:

> When Rabbi Yehuda Nesia heard Resh Laḳish's statement regarding a president who transgresses, he was very angry with Resh Laḳish. Resh Laḳish escaped to a hidden place. Finally, after Rav Yoḥanan's protests, Rabbi Yehuda Nesia called upon Resh Laḳish and freed him. Resh Laḳish was asked by Rabbi Yehuda Nesia why he said what he had concerning a president who transgresses. Resh Laḳish replied that fear of the president would not

9 The term *president* as used throughout this paper translates the term *nasi* as used in the Mishnah. During the mishnaic period, the *nasi* was the head of the supreme judicial and legislative body (the Ṣanhedrin), represented the Jewish people to foreign authorities, and functioned as chief executive of the Jewish people living in Judea.

10 See *Toṣafot haRosh*, *Ṣanh.* 19:2: "The question arises that from the days of King Yannai and onward, there were no kings from the House of David." He answers that the Talmud means presidents and "Resh Galuta" (the heads of the Babylonian community) who were of the House of David. From his answer we can conclude that presidents who are *not* from the House of David are not judged.

11 *Zeph.* 2:1.

12 Jerusalem Talmud, *Ṣanh.* 2:1.

prevent him from saying words of Torah. As a result, Rav Shmuel bar Yitsḥaḳ interpreted the verse,[13] "Know, my sons, that it is not a good report that I hear," to mean that a president [who transgresses] should be removed from office.

We now return to the words of Rav Ḥaggai and the discussion of whether a president is restored to his position. The Jerusalem Talmud asked: "Do we return him to his position?" To which Rav Ḥaggai answered, "I swear by the name of Moses, of course, we do not return him to his position for fear of killing!"[14]

### *Reasons for Not Returning the President to his Position*

Rav Ḥaggai's statement can be understood to mean that a president is not returned to his position for fear that he might kill or take revenge upon the judges that presided in his case.[15]

In a parallel discussion in the Jerusalem Talmud,[16] we find a different version of the text: Instead of the word "Moses," the Jerusalem Talmud mistakenly uses the word "*muṭav* (it is better)," and continues with, "*dinun maḥzarun leh du ḳaṭlun leh* (better to kill him than return him to his position)." The mistaken word "*muṭav* (it is better)" is the version quoted by R. Yosef Karo in *Keṣef Mishneh*, R. Karo's commentary on Maimonides' *Mishneh Torah*.[17] Using this version, R. Karo explains: "It appears that Maimonides understands the passage as follows: those who return him to his high office would do better to kill him — having held a high position and committed an offense punishable by lashes. An alternate explanation of how Maimonides understands the passage would be that returning a president to

13 *I Sam.* 2:24.

14 Also in *Y. Yoma* 1:1, Rav Ḥaggai uses the terms: "I swear by the name of Moses" and "for fear of killing." There the Jerusalem Talmud questions the Mishnah's assertion that the High Priest should have another priest under him and wonders whether the two may be alone together. Concerning this discussion, Rav Ḥaggai responds, swearing by the name of Moses, that the two may not be left alone "*du ḳṭal leh* (for fear of killing)" — that we are concerned that the High Priest may kill the other Priest out of anger and jealousy.

15 As explained by the *Radbaz* in his commentary on Maimonides, *Mishneh Torah, Hilkhot Ṣanhedrin* 17:8.

16 *Y. Horayot* 3:1.

17 *Keṣef Mishneh, Ṣanhedrin* 17:9.

his high office is equivalent to killing him, as people will relate to him contemptuously."[18]

R. Karo brings additional proof that the president is not returned to his position: The Jerusalem Talmud states that the regulation that a high priest does not lose his priesthood after being convicted of a transgression and being punished is based on a Biblical verse. Given that there is no such verse concerning the president, we may deduce that a president who transgresses is *not* returned to office.

According to R. Karo's explanation that a president who transgresses is not returned to office because "it would be better to kill him," the regulation is rabbinic in origin. According to R. Karo's additional proof, the regulation is based on Scripture.

Novel ideas concerning removal of a president from office are brought by R. David ibn Zimra (the *Radbaz*). In his *Mishneh Torah*, Maimonides states:[19] "A *rosh yeshivah*[20] who transgresses must be removed from his position and may not be returned to that position or to membership in the Sanhedrin ... " Concerning this regulation, *Radbaz* asks:[21] It appears that these statements do not correspond with what Maimonides wrote in his responsum concerning a *ḥazan* about whom rumors are circulating that he sinned.[22] Whereas in his *Mishneh Torah* Maimonides rules that a *rosh yeshivah* who transgresses must be removed from his position and may not be restored to it, in his responsum he writes that "No person — from [a member of] the Great Sanhedrin to the *ḥazan hakneṣet* — may be brought down in holiness [i.e., removed from office] unless he transgresses in public [*befarheṣya*]." *Radbaz* explains the contradiction in the following way: In his responsum, Maimonides relates to positions other than *head* of the Sanhedrin. The head of the Sanhedrin may not be restored to office because every sin he commits is considered a public matter and results, therefore, in *ḥillul hashem* — desecration of God's name. For this reason, the head of the Sanhedrin is treated with unique stringency. His every transgression is considered to have been committed publicly and therefore to cause desecration of God's name.

18 See *Shyarei HaḲorban, Y. Ṣanhedrin, ibid.*, concerning *Keṣef Mishneh.*

19 *Mishneh Torah, Hilkhot Ṣanhedrin, ibid.*

20 Maimonides, *ibid.* 1:3, holds the terms *rosh yeshivah* and *nasi* to be synonymous: "The one who excels in wisdom is appointed head of the tribunal. He is the *rosh yeshivah* and is always designated by the Sages as *nasi*."

21 *Resp. Radbaz,* vol. 6, 2078.

22 *Resp. Rambam,* ed. Blau, 111.

*Radbaz* adds another suggestion using the distinction between the head of the Sanhedrin — who may not be restored to office — and the members of the Sanhedrin who may be restored to office. The head of the Sanhedrin "stands in the place of Moses to guide the nation, as is written '*hitḳosheshu vaḳoshu*'[23] — "judge yourself before judging others." Even when a head of the Sanhedrin accepts his punishment, he is no longer fit to fill a public position because he can no longer serve as a role model for others. His sins have rendered him unable to discharge his responsibilities.

### *Summary of the Reasons and Ramifications*

The main reasons given for the president's not being restored to office are as follows:

(1) The president is likely to take revenge on the judges (Jerusalem Talmud, according to the *Radbaz*).

(2) The president's life will be shortened (Jerusalem Talmud, according to *Keṣef Mishneh*).

3) The president will be humiliated (Jerusalem Talmud, according to the *Keṣef Mishneh*).

4) All transgressions committed by a president are considered to have been committed publicly, thereby causing desecration of God's name (*Radbaz*).

(5) *hitḳosheshu vaḳoshu* – Judge yourself before judging others (*Radbaz*).

The different reasons given for removing a president from office have ramifications for other public offices. Some of the reasons are applicable to any position of public authority or responsibility, whereas other reasons apply only to the President.

Reason (1) The president would take revenge upon those who judged him. This reason is relevant only where he has the ability and means to do so. R. Moses Sofer (the *Ḥatam Ṣofer*) infers from Maimonides' ruling in the *Mishneh Torah* that even a *rosh yeshivah* (who is not able to exact revenge) is not returned to his position.[24] Similarly, it is possible that this reason does not apply if the president did not stand

23 *Zeph.* 2:1.

24 *Resp. Ḥatam Ṣofer, Oraḥ Ḥayyim* 41.

trial. A president who has not been tried has no one upon whom to take revenge.

Reason (2) Returning a president to his position will shorten his life. This reason raises the question as to whether the president is permitted to ignore this danger and return to office in spite of it.

Reason (3) A president who returns to office will face humiliation. Possibly, even if the president is willing to subject himself to the risk of being humiliated and shortening his life, he may not return to his position. It is not his personal honor that is at stake, but rather the honor of the entire community.

Reason (4) The transgressions of the president are considered to have been performed publicly. It may be possible to restrict the applicability of this reason to cases in which the president's transgression has become public knowledge. Accordingly, if a transgression has not actually become public knowledge, it may be that it is not considered as having been performed in public, and the president will not have to be removed from office. Viewed this way, this reason also suggests that *any* official whose transgression becomes public knowledge must be removed from office.

On the other hand, the assertion that *every* transgression committed by a president is considered to have been performed in public might be based on the idea that, owing to his unique position, a transgression performed by a president shows unusual arrogance and hence desecration of God's name. Viewed this way, this reason is not applicable to holders of lesser positions for whom transgression does not necessarily imply a unique level of arrogance and does not, therefore, result in a desecration of God's name.

Reason (5) Judge yourself before judging others. This reason seems to apply only to those who stand in the place of Moses to guide the nation. Other leaders, it appears, would not be subject to such reasoning. According to R. Shalom Mordecai HaCohen Shvadron's (the *Maharsham*) explanation of *Radbaz*, though, the most distinguished rabbi of a city is considered to have the same status as a *rosh yeshivah*, and were such a rabbi to transgress, he would not be restored to his high position.[25]

*The Kingdom of Menashe*

Concerning Menashe, king of Judea, the Bible relates that[26] "he prayed to Him, and He received his entreaty, and heard his supplication and restored him to Jerusalem and his kingdom." In the Mishnah, Rabbi Yehuda asserts that "Menashe has a portion in the world to come."[27] The Sages, however, dispute this statement, arguing on the basis of the verse quoted: "To his *kingdom* he was restored but not to the world to come." Can we learn anything from Menashe's restoration?

It may be possible to distinguish between a king who has been judged and one who has not, and between a king whose repentance is complete and a king who has merely accepted punishment for his transgression without repenting.

*The High Priest and the President*

So far, we have discussed the main reasons for removal of a *president* who transgresses. Before the Jerusalem Talmud discusses the president, however, it discusses a high priest who has transgressed. The Jerusalem Talmud states:

> Rabbi Lazar says, "A high priest who transgresses — give him lashes and return him to his position." Rav Mana cites the verse,[28] "*ki nezer shemen mish'hat alav ani hashem* [for the crown of the anointing oil of his God is upon him]," which is to say, Just as I [God] am holy, Aaron is holy.

The law concerning the high priest is unique. It is based on the high priest's unique level of holiness, which is not suspended. This is learned by the Jerusalem Talmud from the verse quoted. In his commentary on the Mishnah,[29] Maimonides explains the difference between a high priest and a president: "A high priest, even one who develops a blemish or is very

25 *Resp. Maharsham*, vol. 2, 56.

26 *I Chron.* 33:13.

27 *M. Ṣanhedrin* 10:2.

28 *Lev.* 21:12.

29 *M. Horayot* 3:2.

elderly, etc., maintains his holiness, because the oil with which he was anointed is never nullified. A president's authority, however, derives only from the performance of his duties; thus, when these are no longer performed, he is nothing but a layman."

This distinction was discussed in a verdict of the Rabbinic Court of Tel Aviv.[30] The verdict was based on the opinion expressed by Maimonides in his commentary on the Mishnah:

> The distinction between holiness and stature illuminates the law of the high priest, where, it is impossible to decrease his holiness. The president, by contrast, has been granted authority and stature, but no holiness — his removal from office results in complete nullification of his authority.

From this the judges conclude:

> It is clear that, in our time, when we judge a person in a position of authority, his authority is comparable to that of a president, not that of a high priest who embodies holiness. This embodiment of holiness is what enables the high priest to be returned to his position, whereas a person who merely holds the position of *rosh yeshivah* is not returned to office.

### *Positions of Authority and the Position of a Rosh Yeshiva*

So far, we have established a rule and an exception to that rule. The rule is: A president is subject to judgment and may be removed from office. Persons who hold positions of authority today share the status of a president in this regard. The exception to the rule is the high priest, whose position is not comparable to positions of authority today.

A different approach, however, is taken by Rabbi Moshe Feinstein.[31] According to R. Feinstein, a high priest is returned to office, because all persons are returned to office. This law is derived[32] from the phrase "thy brother was dishonored in thine eyes."[33] The special derivation, "Just as I [God] am holy, Aaron is holy" was necessary to demonstrate that the law of the high priest is the same as the law of all persons: so that we not imagine that, once a high priest transgresses, his holiness is nullified and he may not be returned to office. According to R. Feinstein, then, we cannot learn from "Just as I [God] am holy, Aaron is holy" that only a person holding a

30 Rabbinic Court Judgments, vol. 8, p.147.

31 *Diberot Moshe, Giṭṭ.*, Chapter 23, Note 56, p.355ff.

32 *Makk.* 3:15.

33 *Deut.* 25:3.

position of holiness may be returned to office.

Rabbi Feinstein's position is that Maimonides' opinion on the president (whom Maimonides calls "*rosh yeshivah*") should be understood in a narrower sense.

Rabbi Feinstein asserts that, even if, in terms of his power, he has the means to take revenge on those who judged him, the president (and even the king), could be returned to office. But since the president serves also as a spiritual leader (*rosh yeshivah*), he is removed from office. He who teaches Torah to others should be like "the Angel of God Almighty," and therefore it is not proper to accept teaching from one who transgressed intentionally. Rabbi Feinstein writes that the source for Maimonides' decisions was not the Jerusalem Talmud's discussion of revenge being taken but rather the statement in tractate *Moed Ḳaṭan*,[34] that when a *talmid ḥakham* (Torah scholar) transgresses, it is no longer permitted to accept his teaching. Moreover, Rabbi Feinstein holds that, prior to being punished for a transgression, a king is not removed from office. At the time he is punished, the king is indeed removed from office (automatically), by virtue of his being placed in a shameful position totally unsuited to a king. Afterward, however, he is returned to office.

### *The Nullification of a Transgressor's Appointment*

Regarding the rule that a transgressor is unfit to hold a position of public service, we turn to a responsum issued by Rabbi Yisrael Isserlin.[35] Rabbi Isserlin was presented with the following question: "A certain individual admitted to swearing falsely in court and had to pay a fine to the city, the duke, and the judges. May he be reinstated to a position of public leadership, a position that entails making serious decisions concerning the needs of the public? It is clear that this person swore falsely and has not repented." Rabbi Isserlin responded that "it is forbidden to return this man to his position unless his repentance is complete according to one of the esteemed rabbis. As it is clear that this person swore falsely in his desire for monetary gain, he is worse than any thief and is "unfit to preside over the needs of the community."

This responsum of Rabbi Isserlin is cited as law by R. Moses Isserles

34 *M.Ḳaṭ.* 17a.

35 *Terumat HaDeshen, P'ṣaḳim U'khtavim*, 214.

(*Rema*) in his commentary to the *Shulḥan Arukh*.[36] Relying on *Rema*'s ruling, *Ḥatam Ṣofer* canceled the appointment of a rabbi chosen by members of the community bribed to appoint him.[37] This approach was used as the basis for a decision by Judge Yitsḥaḳ Kister of the Israeli Supreme Court, who canceled actions taken by city council members who acted with bias and inappropriate personal involvement.[38]

*The Appointment of a Transgressor and of a Transgressor Who Has Repented*

From the responsum of Rabbi Isserlin we understand that there is a qualification to the prohibition against appointing a transgressor to a position of communal leadership: The prohibition applies only when the transgressor has not repented. If, however, he has repented to the satisfaction of a qualified rabbinic authority, he may be appointed.

The Jerusalem Talmud's reasoning that the president may not be returned to his position owing to the likelihood of his taking revenge leaves room for a transgressor who repents to return to office. The reason for this is that the regulation concerning the president deals with a person who has transgressed and received his punishment. The presumption is that such a person is considered "thy brother".[39] But concerning a person who has not received his punishment, there is no presumption that his transgression has been atoned for. Thus, he may not be restored to his position.

However, we saw previously that there are additional reasons given for not returning a president to his position. Some of these reasons seem to apply even to a president who has repented and to whom atonement has been granted for his misdeeds. These reasons are based on the negative feelings of the public toward the transgressor and the desecration of God's name that results from an important figure's transgression. Therefore, the *Ḥatam Ṣofer* concludes that even if a person repents, he may not be restored to his position. The *Ḥatam Ṣofer* was asked regarding the episode of Herschel Marcus, who presided over the marriage of a man to his uncle's wife: "What is the law regarding one who presides over such a marriage thereby

36 *Rema, Ḥoshen Mishpaṭ* 37:22.

37 *Resp. Ḥatam Ṣofer, Ḥoshen Mishpaṭ* 180.

38 H.C. 311/65, Marciano v. *The Council for General Elections of Ofakim*; H.C. 21/65, *Khatabi* v. *Leebee, Chairman of the Local Council of Kiryat Eḳron.*

39 *M. Makkot* 3:16.

encouraging such things?[40] *Ḥatam Ṣofer* answers:

> Indeed the punishment for the incitement and immorality performed by Herschel Marcus should be severe and bitter. The couple was following their evil desires, but this provocateur, who had the specific intention of violating many prohibitions and increasing the number of bastards in the world, faces much more severe punishment than they do. He should never be permitted in any position of trust or public leadership ever again. If he does eventually choose to repent, it will be extremely difficult. In any event, he must not be placed in any position of authority or responsibility, so as to avoid the situation described in Tractate *Bava Batra* 16:2 when a judge would tell the defendant, "Remove the splinter from between your teeth" (refrain from a minor infraction) and the defendant would respond, "Remove the beam from before your eyes" (refrain from a major transgression). If a judge said, "Your silver is tarnished," the defendant would reply, "Your wine is mixed with water." This concept is very clear and apparent in our holy Torah.

What is the argument against the transgressor being able to fill a position of public leadership? The *Ḥatam Ṣofer*'s examples are based on the Sages' interpretation of the verse[41] "And it was in the days of judgment of the Judges." The Sages explain this verse to mean "a generation that judged its judges." Accordingly, a transgressor cannot be trusted to guide or admonish the community because its members will simply answer by reminding him of his obligation to examine his own deeds first. Regardless of whether members of the community are justified in their response, the transgressor is unfit to be in this position, because his words will not be heeded. Nevertheless, it is possible that, if he performs complete repentance and this is known to the public, then even the *Ḥatam Ṣofer* would agree that he may be restored to his position — given that people will not be able to say to him "examine yourself first."

### *A Transgression before the Assumption of Leadership*

Is there a difference between restoring a leader to his position and appointing a person to a position of leadership that he has not held previously? To answer this question we must return to the reasons offered for not restoring the president to his position. The reason that all the transgressions of a president are considered to have been committed in public (*befarheṣya*), thus causing a desecration of God's name, apparently does not

40 *Resp. Ḥatam Ṣofer,* vol. 4, 49.

41 *Ruth* 1:1.

apply to one who transgressed before being appointed president. Transgressions performed before a president's appointment would not seem to disqualify him. Therefore, a president whose past transgression is publicized only after he assumes office is not removed from his position. Because the transgression did not take place when he was in office, it is not considered to have been committed publicly.

The explanation that a president who transgresses is not restored to office because he stands in the place of Moses to lead and guide the people may well apply to a person who transgressed before being appointed president. This is so because, in the final analysis, the principle "judge yourself before judging others" applies.

### *The Relationship Between the Transgression and the Position*

It is possible to differentiate between a transgression that is *related* to the responsibilities of one's position and one that is *irrelevant* to one's capacity to act effectively in such a position. Rabbi Yosef Albo, author of *Ṣefer HaIḳarim,* makes this distinction with reference to King David, who remained king even after transgressing, and King Saul who lost his throne as a result of his transgression.[42] Rabbi Albo explains that King David's sin with Batsheva was one that could have been performed by any man. David was therefore punished as any citizen would have been. By contrast, Saul's violation of God's command by allowing Agag, king of Amalek, to live, was one that could be performed only by the king — hence his punishment.

Afterward, however, R. Albo brings another explanation similar to the first:

> Another reason has been given for this, namely that Saul transgressed in connection with his calling as king, and it was proper, therefore, that he be removed from that calling. David's sin, on the other hand, had no connection to his calling as king; therefore, David's sin could be forgiven.

The throne was taken from Saul because Saul's sin was related to his duty as king. Therefore, it was proper that the throne be denied him. By contrast, David's sin had no connection to his duty as king. It was, therefore, not proper that he lose his throne.

Rabbi Albo demonstrates his point with a parable:

> There were two scribes, one who forged a document and one who engaged in illicit relations. When the king sentenced the scribe who engaged in illicit

42 *Ṣefer HaIḳarim* 4:26.

> relations he declared that after he had received his punishment he could continue being a scribe, for his sin had nothing to do with his professional performance. After the King had punished the scribe who had forged a document, however, he declared him unfit to serve as a scribe in the future based on his unscrupulousness with regard to his profession. So too, with Saul, whose transgression involved his duties as king.

Although Rabbi Albo speaks of loss of the throne as "punishment," his parable of the scribes leads us to understand his opinion as a response to the loss of confidence caused by the act. Thus he writes that the scribe who produced a forged document will no longer be granted a license to practice his profession.

### *A Person Who Has Killed: Restoration to a Position of Leadership*

In our discussion concerning a leader who transgresses, we turn our attention to what can be learned from the law of one who enters a City of Refuge after killing someone unintentionally — whether such a person may be restored to his position of leadership.

Concerning this question there is a disagreement between Rabbi Meir and Rabbi Yehuda.[43] Rabbi Meir holds that the person may be returned to his position, whereas Rabbi Yehuda holds that the person may not. Several questions arise from this:

(1) What is the law concerning transgressions other than killing?
(2) To what "position" may such a person not be restored?
(3) What is the law with regard to appointing a person who has killed to a position in which he has not served previously?

### *(1) Transgressions Other than Killing*

From the words of Maimonides,[44] it seems that the law is referring only to a person who had killed another human being. R. Yom Ṭov ibn Asevilli (the *Ritva*),[45] however, holds that the law is not limited to a person who has killed another. According to the *Ritva*, the law applies to persons guilty of any serious transgression. Complete repentance can rectify transgressions other than killing, and one who has transgressed and repented can, in addition

43 *M. Makk.* 2:8.

44 *Mishneh Torah, Hilkhot Rotze'aḥ Ushemirat Hanefesh* 7:13-14.

45 *Ritva, Makk.* 13a.

to being restored to his position, even be appointed to a position not previously held.

*(2) What "Position"?*

*Rashi* explains the intentions of Rabbi Meir's statement: The transgressor returns to the authority which he previously possessed, whether as president or *rosh yeshivah.* What about a position of lesser authority? It is possible from *Rashi*'s point of view that Rabbi Yehudah disqualifies the transgressor only from holding the position of president or *rosh yeshivah.* On the other hand, it is possible that Rabbi Yehuda also forbids restoration to lesser positions and *Rashi* seeks to inform us that Rabbi Meir allows the transgressor to be returned even to such positions.

The *Ritva*, who states that a person who caused an unintentional death should not be appointed to any new position, also states, "Even the head of the flour mill," to inform us that one who causes death unintentionally is unfit to hold even a very low position of authority.

*(3) Appointment to a Position Not Previously Held*

Is the disagreement between Rabbi Meir and Rabbi Yehuda limited to the question as to whether one who returns from a city of refuge may *regain* his position, or does it also apply to an *appointment* he has not held previously? The *Ritva* explains that both Rabbi Yehuda and Rabbi Meir agree that such a person may not be appointed to any new position under any circumstances, even to a very minor position. This is applies with even greater force if the killing was committed intentionally, because not only is the killer unworthy of the position, but even if the members of the community want to appoint him, they may not.

On the other hand, Rabbi Yosef Rozin (the "*Rogachover*") claims that it is permitted to appoint one who has killed to a new position. He feels that Rabbi Yehuda is stating that the killer's past does not remain with him and may be disregarded. The community is not obligated to restore him to his former position, and from this we can infer that a new position is permitted.[46]

We see, therefore, that it is often acceptable to appoint or re-appoint a leader who has transgressed. However, when the transgression is a serious

46 *Tzafnat Pa'aneaḥ, Makkot* 13:1.

one, such as the killing of another human being, even unintentionally, holding a position of leadership is out of the question.

*Conclusion*

Our concern is the relationship between the past actions of an individual and his present ability to lead properly. Can one's past criminality prevent him from holding a position of public leadership? What determines the significance of what took place in one's past and the relevance those actions hold at the present time?

One important question in this context is the possible distinction between a transgression performed while in office and one performed previously.

In our introduction, we stated that a person in a position of leadership is not immune to being held responsible for his actions by the law. We have seen, however, that, according to the Jerusalem Talmud, the unique status of the king — who is judged only before God — does indeed grant him immunity to prosecution in worldly courts.

We have raised and examined many questions in order to clarify the differences outlined in the Jerusalem Talmud between the High Priest – who continues his service after receiving lashes for his transgression, and the president of the Sanhedrin who does not remain in office after receiving his lashes.

Several reasons were offered for these regulations; some by the Jerusalem Talmud itself, and some by other authorities. In light of these reasons, we sought to examine the suitability of various types of leaders: leaders with the governmental authority to take revenge upon the judges; leaders meant to dictate norms of behavior, who must serve as fitting examples (as expressed in the dictum "Judge yourself before judging others"); and leaders whose duty it is to teach Torah. An important ruling by Rabbi Yisrael Isserlin states that leaders of the community, when deciding on the needs of the community and the needs of individuals, have the status of judges and may be disqualified on the basis of their transgressions (as any judge is disqualified by a transgression). We also noted that a possible claim of "Remove the beam from between your eyes" against a leader may constitute reason for preventing him from serving in a public capacity — even if such a claim is not justified — because of the contempt that will accrue to the office held by such a leader.

Although it appears that a distinction should be made between a person who has repented and a person who has not repented, we learned that this is not necessarily so. It is true that a person who has received corporal punishment for his transgression might be considered qualified to return to his former office, although there is no proof that he has repented. Nevertheless, even a person of whom it is certain that he has repented, may not be qualified to hold public office. This may be because his holding of a public office may have a negative impact on the public's attitude toward his office or because such an appointment may be interpreted as disregard for the seriousness of his transgression. Serious consideration must also be given to the nature of his transgression and to the relationship between his transgression and the responsibilities of the office for which he is being considered.

Finally, in light of the various reasons for disqualifying a person who has transgressed, we showed that there is room to distinguish between continuing the tenure of an office holder, on the one hand, and appointing a transgressor to a position that he does not currently hold, on the other.

# 11

## JEWISH FRAUDULENT TRANSFER LAW

by

STEVEN H. RESNICOFF[*]

Academic papers addressing Jewish law (*halakhah*) disproportionately focus on its "bottom line" substantive rules, either as they exist now or as they existed in a particular historical period or place. Far too little effort is invested in examining the process through which these halakhic rulings emerge. Often, although certainly not always,[1] they arise directly or indirectly through authoritative exegesis of, and extrapolation from, specific Talmudic texts. This process takes place on at least two levels. First, individual Talmudic authorities engage in their independent analysis of the texts. Second, normative rules develop over time from the frequently conflicting conclusions of these various decisors.

Such development of halakhic rules confronts numerous challenges. Part of the reason why proper interpretation of Talmudic texts is such a formidable enterprise is that its editors intended it to be so. The Talmud focuses on and constitutes part of the "Oral Law" which supplements the written laws of the Pentateuch.[2] Initially, the Oral Law was not supposed to

a Professor, DePaul University College of Law. I thank Dean Teree Foster for her support and the DePaul College of Law for a summer 2000 grant that enabled me to write this chapter and work on other projects. I also thank Rabbi Aaron Small, with whom I studied many of the sources mentioned herein and who made helpful comments on a draft of this chapter.

1 Sometimes, for instance, Jewish law is based on explicitly promulgated rabbinic decrees, Jewish communal legislation, or informally established communal customs unmentioned in the Talmud.

2 The sages explain that the Oral Torah was also given to Moses at Mount Sinai to supplement and explicate the Written Torah. Rabbi Shlomo Yitzḥaḳi (*Rashi*; 1040-1105) explains that the Oral Torah is alluded to in the verse, "These are the decrees, the ordinances, and the teachings ("*Torot*") that HaShem gave ... " (*VaYiḳra* 26:46). He writes, "'and the *Torot*' [note: *Torot*

be studied from a text[3] but, rather, to be transmitted directly from *rebbe* to *talmid*. This process would allow any ambiguity to be immediately and effectively resolved and would prevent those who were unqualified — intellectually, ethically or spiritually — from having access to it.[4] Once a

---

is the plural of the Hebrew word *Torah*]: One written and one oral, to teach us that both of them were given to Moshe at Sinai."

Even without the sages' testimony about the Oral Law, there are a number of reasons why its existence could have been deduced. Without such an Oral Law, many important parts of the Written Law could not have been understood or implemented. For example, although the Written Law forbids Jews to do "work" (*melakhah*) on the Sabbath and, under certain circumstances, makes the doing of such "work" a capital offense, it nowhere explains what constitutes "work." The Oral Law provides the needed definition. Likewise, while the Written Law states that Jews are to slaughter animals "as I [HaShem] commanded you" (*Devarim* 12:21), only the Oral Law describes how the slaughtering is to be done. Similarly, the Written Law's reference to the four species (*arba'ah minim*) that are used in the holiday of *Sukkot* are unclear and ambiguous. For instance, it identifies one of the species as "the fruit of the beautiful tree." It is only the Oral Law that clarifies that this means the *etrog*, a certain type of citron. See, generally, H.C. Schimmel, *The Oral Law* (Jerusalem: Feldheim Publishers, 1996).

3 See, e.g., *T.B. Temurah* 14b:

> Did not R. Abba the son of R. Ḥiyya b. Abba say in the name of R. Yoḥanan, "Those who write the traditional teachings are like those who burn the Torah ... " And R. Yehudah b. Naḥman the translator of Resh Laḳish explained: "One verse says 'Write for yourself these words' and another verse says 'For according to these words [literally, *al pi ha-devarim ha-e'leh*]' This is to teach you that you are not permitted to write down the Oral Torah and you are not permitted to recite the Written Torah without a writing."

Nevertheless, there is a dispute among early authorities as to whether individual scholars would write down notes for themselves even though they would not make these notes available for others to learn from. See, e.g., *Encyclopedia Judaica*, entry, "Mishnah":

> [As to the issue] of the writing down of the Oral Law ... there were divergent views between the *Geonim* and the early authorities. Saadiah Gaon, R. Samuel b. Ḥophni, Rabbenu Nissim, and Maimonides held that each sage committed the Oral Law to writing for himself, as did Rabbi, too, in the case of the Mishnah. However, Rashi and those who followed his view maintained that nothing was written down in early times, and even the Mishnah and the Talmud were not committed to writing until the days of the *Ṣavoraim*.

See also Aryeh Kaplan, *The Handbook of Jewish Thought* (Brooklyn: Moznaim Publishing Corporation, 1979), 9:34-37, 185-187.

4 See, e.g., *ibid.*, 177-187.

teaching is reduced to writing,[5] the unqualified, whether intentionally or unintentionally, may misconstrue it and mislead others. Composition of the Talmud — and of the Mishnah, the Talmud's predecessor — was a concession to persecution that, through the execution of Jewish teachers and other hardships, threatened to effectively end oral transmission of the Law.[6] Nonetheless, wanting to ensure that the Oral Law remained, as much as possible, the domain of Jewish scholars, the sages composed the Talmud in a way that rendered it relatively inaccessible to others.[7]

5 Composition of the Oral Law also facilitated its translation into foreign languages, producing a problem similar to that which arose when the Written Law was first translated. In listing days on which it is appropriate to fast, the *Shulḥan Arukh* states, "On the eighth day of the month of Tevet, the Torah was written into Greek in the days of King Ptolemy, and the world was dark for three days." *Shulḥan Arukh, Oraḥ Ḥayyim* 580:2. R. Moshe Ṣofer (*Ḥatam Ṣofer*; 1762–1839) explains that the Hebrew language is richly textured and layered, allowing various meanings and nuances to be encrypted into each word. Consequently, it was virtually impossible, on the basis of language alone, to defend one textual interpretation over another. While the Torah was written only in Hebrew, those who wanted to learn its true message knew that they were dependent on Torah scholars for guidance. Other languages, the *Ḥatam Ṣofer* writes, are incapable of capturing the ambiguities of the Hebrew original. Thus, the translations resulted in a more precise, literal — and limited — version of the Written Torah. Therefore, those who read these translations often mistakenly believe they do not need the assistance of Torah sages but, instead, can independently plumb the depths of the Talmudic sea. As such persons turned away from the sages, who are conveyors of the Torah's light, the world was plunged in darkness. The statement that the darkness was only temporary — lasting but three days — reflects the fact that the existence of the Oral Law ensured that people would still seek to learn from the sages and to obtain light from them. Composition of the Oral Law and its subsequent translation, of course, have unfortunately decreased dependence on the sages. See R. Eliezer Waldenberg (contemporary), *Tzitz Eliezer* XIV:1 (citing *Ḥatam Ṣofer, Drashot* at 101b).

6 The sages cite sources indicating that it is permitted to write down the Oral Law to prevent it from becoming forgotten. See, e.g., *Rashi, T.B. Gittin* 60b, s.v. *Devarim*. See, generally, Aryeh Kaplan, *The Handbook of Jewish Thought* (Israel: Moznaim Publishing Corporation, 1979), 189 (citing sources); Menachem Elon, *Mishpaṭ Ivri* (Jerusalem: Magnes Press, 1992), at I.199-201.

7 See, e.g., R. Moshe b. Maimon (*Maimonides* or *Rambam*; 1135-1204), *The Guide for the Perplexed,* translated M. Friedlander (New York: Dover Publications, Inc., 2nd ed., 1956), at 108 ("Care having been taken, for the sake of obviating injurious influences, that the Oral Law should not be

A second problem arose, in part, from technological limitations. Early handwritten texts were sometimes difficult to read — or even to preserve — leading to variant versions of Talmudic texts. Nor did the invention of the printing press fully prevent textual corruptions, because there remained room for human error. As a result, it is sometimes unclear which of several texts is "authentic." Moreover, when considering the views of ancient halakhic authorities, it is not always apparent with which text they were working.

Third, the writings of post-Talmudic authorities sometimes appear equivocal and even ostensibly self-contradictory. In some instances, statements made by an authority in one work, such as in his commentary on the Talmud, appear to reflect views different from those expressed in his *responsa,* i.e., his written answers to particular legal questions posed to him. Inasmuch as most of these authors perished long ago, there are limited mechanisms for reconciling these apparent inconsistencies.

This paper provides a "mini" case study of this process by focusing on Jewish law's approach to the ancient and vexing practice of debtors who try to "protect" their property by "transferring" it to friends or relatives. Our purpose is not to render a definitive halakhic ruling on any particular case.[8]

---

recorded in a form accessible to all ... "). Various factors contribute to the somewhat cryptic nature of the text, whether or not all were intended to do so. For example, instead of being strictly arranged by subject matter, the Talmud seems to comprise relatively desultory discussions replete with numerous tangential discourses. In addition, although a matter is addressed in one Talmudic tractate, a more exhaustive and authoritative treatment of the topic may appear in an entirely different tractate. A reader who relies on the former discussion may be entirely mistaken as to the correct legal conclusions to draw. See Nissim b. Yaaḳov ibn Shahin (*Nissim Gaon*; c. 990-1062), *Introduction to the Babylonian Talmud, Tractate Berakhot.* Even a reader who is conversant with all of the various places in which a particular subject is discussed may not know how to determine the Talmud's conclusions. Trained Jewish law authorities employ various rules for this purpose: *ibid.* Often Talmudic concepts are refined not merely by consideration of what is contained in a particular Talmudic passage but by focusing on what is omitted. The Talmud's failure to raise a particular objection or to provide a certain response is considered purposeful, and a proper appreciation of this process refines the reader's understanding of the legal doctrines in question. Unless the reader is well-versed in Talmudic literature, he or she may be ignorant of the various alternative arguments that the Talmud implicitly rejected.

8 If any of the questions addressed by this article actually arises, the reader is encouraged to consult with a competent halakhic authority for a specific ruling based on the details of the particular case.

Rather, our objective is to utilize a limited aspect of this topic to illustrate the first of the two steps in the halakhic process, how Talmudic authorities examine the relevant texts and extrapolate therefrom to novel scenarios. Part I introduces our discussion by setting forth a few important background rules and by describing the specific questions we will consider. Part II presents the most relevant Talmudic passage, explores its ambiguities, and examines how these issues are resolved. Rather than cataloging the positions of as many authorities as possible, we will examine the positions taken by three early decisors, Rav Yaakov ben Meir (Rabbenu Tam, 1100-1171), Rav Shlomo ben Aderet (*Rashba*, 1235-1310) and Rabbenu Asher ben Yeḥiel (*Rosh*, 1250-1327). The views of Rabbenu Tam and *Rosh* are especially significant because they are reflected in the *Shulḥan Arukh*, originally published in 1565, which, in light of the numerous commentaries written thereon over the succeeding centuries, has become the most authoritative code of Jewish law. Although *Rashba's* approach *may* also have influenced the *Shulḥan Arukh*, his position is of more importance to us for other reasons. First, it seems to constitute an interesting hybrid of the interpretations of Rabbenu Tam and *Rosh*. Second, it appears to be predicated upon a particularly imaginative, and counter-intuitive, construction of the relevant Talmudic passage. Part III summarizes the differences among these approaches and their respective implications for debtor-creditor law.

## PART I — INTRODUCTION

In order to understand how, in the hypothetical case we will soon describe, the debtor attempts to protect his property from his creditors, it is important to mention a few halakhic provisions regarding debtor-creditor law. First, if B borrows money from A, A obtains a lien ("*shibud*")[9] — in all of B's property, both personalty ("*meṭalṭelin*") and realty ("*ḳarḳa*").[10] As to

9 For a discussion of possible differences between the halakhic term "*shibud*" and the English legal term "lien," see Isaac Herzog, *The Main Institutions of Jewish Law I* (London: Soncino Press Limited, 1965), 89-91.

10 There is a Talmudic debate between the Amoraim, Ullah and Rabbah, as to whether such a lien is biblically or only rabbinically valid. See *T.B. Bava Batra* 175b. It is unclear, however, whether Ullah and Rabbah differ even about situations in which the liened property is still owned by the debtor or only about some other situations, such as after the debtor has voluntarily alienated the property. Thus, some authorities believe that Ullah and Rabbah agree that, so long as the debtor owns the property, the creditor's lien in the

personalty, however, the lien often ends when B transfers the property to someone else.[11] Even as to realty, if the loan is not evidenced by a written agreement ("*shṭar*"), the lien generally ends when B transfers the realty to another. If, however, the loan is evidenced by a *shṭar*, A's lien in the realty survives B's alienation of ownership.[12] Thus, suppose: (1) B signs a promissory note when he borrows from A; (2) B subsequently transfers some of his real property to C; and (3) B then defaults on his debt to A. If B does not have adequate resources with which to pay A, A is entitled to foreclose on the transferred real property, even though it is now held by C.

Consider the following hypothetical case. B wants to borrow money from A for a relatively risky venture. Before B borrows the money, B transfers his property to C. In this way, when A lends B money, B hopes that A will not acquire a lien in the transferred property.

Among others, the following two questions arise:

1. Suppose B defaults on the loan to A. May A foreclose on any of the property that was transferred to C?
2. Suppose B changes his mind and wants the property back from C. Is B entitled to recover the property?

The answer to these questions, however, may depend on many variables.[13] We will consider two, because these are the ones addressed by

---

property is biblically valid. See, e.g., *Toṣafot*, *ad loc.*, and R. Menaḥem b. Shlomo (*Meiri*; 12th century), *Beit ha-Beḥirah*, *ad loc.* There seems to be no explicit Talmudic debate as to whether the lien in personalty is biblically or only rabbinically valid.

11 If the personalty is transferred as a gift, however, and it is transferred only to prevent a creditor from foreclosing on it, the lien may in certain circumstances survive. According to a number of authorities, the reason why a lien does not ordinarily survive the transfer of personalty is because of "*taḳanot ha-shuḳ*," a rabbinic decree designed to grease the wheels of commerce and encourage people to purchase personalty. Prospective purchasers would be afraid to buy if their purchases would be subject to pre-existing liens. The decree typically applies even to gifts, because it is assumed that even "gifts" are given in exchange for some benefit from the recipient. Nevertheless, if the transfer is clearly made just to prevent a creditor from reaching the property, and not in exchange for some benefit received from the grantee, the rabbinic decree may not apply. See, R. Aryeh Leib ha-Kohen Heller (1745-1813), *Ḳetzot ha-Ḥoshen*, *Ḥoshen Mishpaṭ* 99, *ṣif ḳoṭon* 8; R. Avraham David of Buczacz (19th century), *Keṣef ha-Ḳodshim*, *Shulḥan Arukh*, *Ḥoshen Mishpaṭ* 99.

12 *Shulḥan Arukh*, *Ḥoshen Mishpaṭ* 111:1.

13 Halakhic authorities identify many other relevant variables, such as (1)

the relevant Talmudic passage which we will deal with in Part II:

1. How much of his property did B transfer to C? Did he transfer "all" of his property or only "part" of his property?
2. If B transferred the property by deed, did the language of the deed indicate that B was retaining a right to revoke the transfer and get the property back?

## PART II — TALMUDIC SOURCES

The Talmud does not explicitly address the exact hypothetical case described in Part I. In two places, however, it does address a similar scenario, and Jewish legal scholars use these Talmudic discussions as bases for ruling on the hypothetical case.[14] To comply with the constraints of this forum, we will only discuss the passage that is more extensive and, from the words of the commentators, more directly relevant to our hypothetical case.[15]

To appreciate even this passage, however, it is necessary to review a few rules regarding marital rights. Under Jewish law, when a woman marries, her husband obtains certain rights in her property. Much of the woman's property is designated as *nikhṣei melog,* and the husband is entitled to the use of *nikhṣei melog* and to any income generated by *nikhṣei melog*. Thus, if a woman's *nikhṣei melog* includes an orange orchard, the husband would be entitled to any fruit grown in the orchard. If, at the time of the marriage, the husband does not know that his wife owns certain property, that property does not become *nikhṣei melog* until and unless he learns about it. In

---

whether B actually transferred possession and enjoyment of the property to C; and (2) whether B had reasons for transferring the property in addition to preventing A from foreclosing on the property, and, if so, the relative importance of B's various reasons. See *Shulḥan Arukh, Ḥoshen Mishpaṭ* 99:6, 7 and the commentators thereto. Of course, the analysis could also be very different if the debtor transferred his property after he was already indebted to his creditor. However interesting these issues are, they exceed the scope of this essay.

14 *T.B. Ketubot* 78b-79a, and *Bava Batra* 151a.

15 When mentioning this specific limit on our study, namely, the fact that we will not review the second of the two discussions, it is perhaps opportune to point out another restraint. When Rabbenu Tam, *Rashba* and *Rosh* analyze any particular Talmudic passage, their approaches are often influenced by principles and perspectives that they discerned or developed from analyzing many other passages. Consequently, our mini case study is perforce inherently limited.

addition to the right to the enjoyment of *nikhṣei melog*, a husband is entitled to inherit all of his wife's property in the event that she predeceases him.[16] According to some authorities, the husband's right to inherit his wife is biblical in nature, while according to others this right was rabbinically created.[17]

In tractate *Ketubot,* the Talmud deals with a situation in which a woman does not want her prospective husband to obtain rights in any of her property. For convenience, we will divide the passage into four segments, Texts A, B, C and D.

Text A:

> A certain woman, who wanted to protect her property from the man she intended to marry, deeded the property[18] to her daughter. Thereafter she married and, later, divorced. She went before Rav Naḥman [to have him order her daughter to return the property]. Her daughter produced her deed [and argued that the property now belonged to her]. Rav Naḥman ripped up the deed [and ruled for the mother]. Rav Anon went to Mar Uḳvah and said to him, "Did you see how this boorish Naḥman rips up people's deeds? He [Mar Uḳvah] said to him, "Tell me the precise details of what happened." He [Rav Anon] told him. He [Mar Uḳvah] said to him, "You mean you are talking about a protective deed [*shṭar mavreḥet*]?[19] This is what Rav Ḥanilai said in the name of Shmuel, 'I am an officially authorized judge, and if a protective deed came to my hands, I would tear it up.'"

Text B:

> Rava said to Rav Naḥman: "What is the reason [why Shmuel would tear up a protective deed]? Isn't it because a person would not leave herself penniless

16 *Shulḥan Arukh, Even ha-Ezer* 90:1.

17 The authorities disagree as to whether the husband's general right to inherit is rabbinic or biblical in nature. The *Rambam, Mishneh Torah, Hilkhot Ishut* 12:3, contends that it is rabbinic. Among those that maintain that it is biblical are *Rashba* and R. Avraham b. David of Posquières (*Ravad* III; 1120-1198). See R. Shmuel ben Uri Shraga Phoebus (second half of 17th century), *Beit Shmuel, Shulḥan Arukh, Even ha-Ezer* 90:1.

18 As becomes apparent from Text C, the woman in this case transferred all of her property, as opposed to just some of it.

19 The Soncino Talmud translates the Hebrew phrase as "a deed ... intended as a means of evasion." This translation, while accurate, is awkward given our need to refer to the term frequently and to employ a verbal form of the term. Consequently, we will translate the phrase as "a protective deed" and will translate the verb *mavriaḥ* as "protect."

and give all of her possessions to others? But we only say this regarding gifts to others; but a person may give all of her possessions to her daughter!"

[Rav Naḥman answered]: "We say this even with respect to a gift to a daughter. [In this respect] a person prefers herself even over her daughter."

Text C:

A question is raised regarding Shmuel's ruling from a *Baraita* (i.e., a non-Mishnaic source that nonetheless is authoritative): "If someone wants to protect her property from her husband, what should she do? She should write a deed of trust. These are the words of Rav Shimon ben Gamliel. The Sages say: '[If she wrote a deed of trust], the recipient could "play with her" [and keep the property] unless she wrote [in the deed that the gift was valid] "from today and when I want (*me'ha-yom velikh'she'ertze*)." Rav Zeira says "The *Baraita* is not a problem. Shmuel refers to a case in which someone gives away all of her property; the *Baraita* refers to a case in which someone gave away only part of her property."[20]

20 Halakhic authorities disagree as to what is meant in this context by "all" of one's property and "part" of one's property. *Rosh* explains that the basic issue turns on human psychology. The halakhic presumption mentioned in Text B applies to a case in which a person transfers "all" of his property because it assumes that a person would not leave himself with no means of support other than seeking charity. *Rosh* argues that this presumption applies until and unless the transferor leaves himself with enough money to cover his living expenses. See, e.g., *Shut ha-Rosh, klal* 78, *ṣiman* 3 (the presumption applies unless the transferor keeps for himself enough "for his living"). Some other authorities, however, think that the presumption becomes inapplicable if the transferor retains much less property (a "*kol shehu*"). See *Ḳetzot ha-Ḥoshen, Ḥoshen Mishpaṭ* 99, *ṣif ḳoṭon* 6 (explaining that *Rif* and *Rambam* hold this view). Even according to these authorities, however, it would seem that the transferors could keep *some* property, such as the clothes they are wearing, without rendering the presumption inapplicable. For simplicity, we will merely use the Talmudic categories of "all" of his property and "part" of his property without reaching definitive conclusions as to what these phrases mean.

It should be acknowledged that societal circumstances have surely changed since the times of *Rosh*. In many countries, secular governments provide various welfare services for the indigent. It is possible that people might be more willing to rely on such governmental programs than, in the days of *Rosh*, they were willing to rely on charity. If so, this "change" in human psychology might affect, according to *Rosh* or others, whether a halakhic presumption should or should not arise when someone gives away all of his property. Nevertheless, an evaluation of this question would exceed the purview of this paper.

Text D:

> But if the acquirer ["*loḳeaḥ*"] does not obtain ownership of the property, the husband should acquire it. Abaye says, "The Rabbis ruled that the property should be treated as if it were property which was unknown to the husband at the time of the marriage," and according to Rav Shimon. [According to Rav Shimon, a husband does not acquire rights in such property as long as he does not know about it and, if the wife transfers ownership of the property before the husband finds out about it, the new owner takes the property free of any claims by the husband.]

These segments raise many questions, but we will only address two of them. Interestingly, the ways authorities on Jewish law resolve these two textual questions go a long way toward explaining how they may answer the questions posed by our hypothetical case.

First, according to the sages in Text C, what is the effect of a deed that contains the language "from today and when I want"? There are several difficulties. One is that the Hebrew expression is somewhat ambiguous. The phrase "from today and when I want" (*velikh'she'ertze*) might mean: (1) "from today and *until* when I want,"[21] which might mean "so long as I want"; or (2) "from today and if I should want," which might mean "retroactively from today but only if I later indicate that I definitely want." As we will see, each of these approaches is advanced by some authorities. A second problem is that, as we shall see below, some commentators seem to have had the word *likh'she'ertze* instead of *velikh'she'ertze*. Consequently, the phrase might mean "from today until when I want" rather than "from today and when I want." A third problem, which is exacerbated by the first two, is that the object of the verb "want" is unclear.

There are two basic approaches as to the effect of this deed. The first approach is that the deed immediately transfers title to the recipient, subject to complete divestiture if, at any point in time, the woman says that she wants the property back. This view is adopted by *Rosh*, *Rashba* and others. One of these other commentators, Rabbenu Ḥananel ben Ḥushiel (*Raḥ*)[22] seems to have a text with the word "*likh'she'ertze*" and appears to have interpreted it as "until when I want" or "so long as I want," with the entire

21 The word *u-k'she'ertze* rather than *velikh'she'ertze*, would have been sufficient to denote "and when I want."

22 R. Ḥananel ben Ḥushiel (d. ca. 1055). *Raḥ's* view is reported by Rabbenu Nissim (*Ran:* d. ca. 1380), Commentary on R. Yitzḥaḳ ben Yaaḳov (*Rif:* 1013-1103), *T.B. Ketubot* 37b.

phrase being "from today, so long as I want [but when I no longer want the property to be yours, I can revoke and recover my property]." According to this interpretation, the object of "want" is that the property should belong to the grantee.[23] *Rosh* also uses the word *likh'she'ertze*, rather than *velikh'she'ertze*, when he explains Text C. His reading of the language is somewhat unclear, but he may be saying the same thing as *Raḥ*.[24] He certainly agrees with *Raḥ* that the effect of the language is to effectuate a transfer immediately, subject to divestment whenever the transferor wants.[25] *Rashba* does not seem to try to explain precisely how this result, with which he agrees, is implicit in the words of Text C.[26] There are, of course, other possible ways to understand the text as yielding the same result.[27]

23 Because the text frequently refers to the person alienating the property as the "transferor," one might expect that the recipient would be referred to as the "transferee." Nonetheless, because repeated use of "transferor" and "transferee" might be confusing and might seem stilted, we will use "grantee" instead of "transferee."

24 *Rosh* says that the conditional language means "from now until when I want *(likh'she'ertze)* to establish it, but at any time that I want I have the right to invalidate it." The difference between this and *Raḥ's* reading is *Rosh's* insertion of "to establish it" as an object of the verb "want," similar to the reading of *Rambam* mentioned in the following text. Arguably, this suggests that *Rosh* had in mind the possibility of some future statement by the transferor showing that the transferor wants the transfer to take place. Nevertheless, this suggestion seems wrong for several reasons. For example, it is inconsistent with *Rosh's* clear statements that the transfer in this case is immediately effective without the need for any future approval by the transferor.

25 R. Asher b. Yeḥiel (*Rosh*), *T.B. Ketubot*, chapter 8, *ṣiman* 3. See also R. Natanel Weil (*Ḳorban Netanel*), *ad loc.*, *ṣiman* 50 (so construing *Rosh*), and R. Meir Schiff (*Maharam Schiff*), *ad loc.* (so construing *Rosh*). See also R. Moshe Lima (1605-1658), *Ḥelḳat Meḥoḳeḳ*, *Shulḥan Arukh*, *Even ha-Ezer* 90, *ṣif ḳoṭon* 25 (saying that *Rosh* and *Raḥ* maintain that the language in the deed means that "so long as I am quiet the transfer is valid, and if I want to revoke it, I have the power to do so").

26 *Shut ha-Rashba* II:312. There may certainly be alternatives to *Raḥ's* reading, each with its own strengths and weaknesses. For example, the phrase might be read as "from today and [i.e., but] when I want [I can revoke the transfer and recover the property]."

27 For example, it is possible that the phrase cited by the Talmud is incomplete and that the unstated object of the phrase "when I want" is "to revoke the transfer." See, e.g., R. Betzalel Ashkenazy, *Shiṭah Meḳubetzet* III, 169 (citing the view of unnamed commentators).

The second approach is that the deed does not immediately effectuate a transfer. Rather, the transfer only takes place if and when the woman declares that she wants it to take place. Thus, if the husband attempts to take possession of the property, the woman can announce that she wants the transfer to be effective and it becomes valid retroactively, depriving her husband of any rights in the property. This is the way Maimonides (*Rambam*)[28] and some others interpret Text C.[29] According to them, the phrase seems to mean "from today and when [i.e., but only if and when] I want." The act of "wanting" has to be realized by some future affirmative statement.

There are important differences between these two alternative interpretations. However, many of the differences are only tangential to our purpose and, for this reason, we will not explore them here.[30]

The second question concerns Text D. Texts A and B deal with a transfer of all of one's property *without* any special language in the deed. Text C deals with a transfer of part of one's property *with* special language in the deed. Is the question posed by Text D, "but if the grantee does not acquire the property, the husband should acquire it," asked as to both of these devices or as to only one of them and, if so, to which?

28 This seems apparent from *Rambam's* statement in *Mishneh Torah, Hilkhot Ishut* 22:9. This is how the *Rambam* is interpreted by Rabbenu Nissim (*Ran*), Commentary on *Rif, T.B. Ketubot* 37b.

29 See R. Betzalel Ashkenazy, *Shiṭah Meḳubetzet* III, at 169 (citing the views of Rav Yom Ṭov ben Avraham Asevilli (*Ritva:* d. beg. 14th century), R. Aharon ha-Levi (*Ra'ah:* c. 1230-1300), and others).

30 For example, assume that the woman dies while still married and without either confirming or nullifying the transfer. According to *Rashi* and *Rambam*, the person who has been holding the property (i.e., the grantee in the deed) never became its owner and would not be able to retain it. According to *Rosh* and *Raḥ*, however, the grantee was the owner from the time of the initial transfer and, given that the woman did not cancel the conveyance, he would remain its owner. Similarly, if the woman retracts before she dies, according to *Rashi* and *Rambam*, the grantee would be liable — absent some other Jewish law doctrine — for any income from the property that he had previously consumed. According to *Rosh* and *Raḥ*, however, if the woman's retraction does not operate retroactively, the grantee would not be liable for such income because, at the time he consumed the income, he was the owner of the property. See, e.g., R. Netanel Weil (*Ḳorban Netanel*), *Commentary on Rosh, T.B. Ketubot*, chapter 3, *ṣiman 50*.

*Text D As Applying to Text A & B Transfers of All of One's Property*

Some commentators answer that the initial sentence of text D refers, at least, to the transfers discussed in texts A and B, i.e., where the woman gives away all of her property in anticipation of her marriage and where the deed she uses does not contain any special restrictive language. Accordingly, Text D asks, "But if the grantee does not acquire the property, the husband should acquire it."

According to this interpretation, the first sentence of Text D seems to assume that the grantee of the woman's transfer does not acquire the property. The obvious question, however, is why this assumption is made. After all, a number of commentators, including *Rosh*, believe that when the woman conveys all of her property, the recipient immediately acquires an ownership interest, albeit limited, in the property. Because of this interest, the grantee gets to keep the property if the woman predeceases her husband,[31] notwithstanding the general rule that a husband inherits all of his wife's property. Yet how can one reconcile this view with Text D's apparent assumption that the wife's grantee does not acquire ownership of the property?[32]

One might hope to discover an answer to this question by examining the circumstances in which the grantee's rights may divest. In Text A, Rav Naḥman ruled that a woman who transfers property to her daughter in anticipation of marriage can recover the property in the event that her husband divorces her. This is based on the presumption, mentioned in Text

31 Rav Mordekhai ben Hillel Ashkenazy (*Mordekhai:* 1248-1298), *Ṣefer Mordekhai L'Bava Batra*, *ṣiman* 623, for example, explains:

> And one can explain, as I was taught by my teacher, my relative, ha-Rav Eliezar from Metz, that the statement that a protective deed does not transfer ownership applies [only] if the transferor revokes the transfer ..., but if she does not revoke the transfer, the grantee acquires the property in his hands.

See also *Mordekhai*, *Ṣefer Mordekhai L'Ketubot*, *ṣiman* 208; *Rosh*, *T.B. Ketubot*, chapter 8, *ṣiman* 2. A similar statement is brought in the name of Rav Yeshayah ben Eliyahu (*Ri M'Trani* or *Toṣafot Rid*; 1180-1260), cited in Betzalel Ashkenzy, *Shiṭah Meḳubetzet* III, at 169. But see *Toṣafot Rid*, *T.B. Ketubot* 79a (explaining that he retracted what he had originally stated in *Toṣafot Rid* and now thought that the grantee does not inherit the property even if she, the transferor, dies while married).

32 Indeed, *Ran* states that it is for this reason that the *Rambam* construes Text D's question as applying to the type of transfer discussed in Text C and not the type involved in Texts A and B. See *Ran*, Commentary to *Rif*, *T.B. Ketubot* 37b.

B, that a woman would not want to leave herself penniless. Even at the moment a woman transfers property in anticipation of her marriage, she understands that her marriage may end and she would not want to make a transfer that, in such an event, would leave her penniless. Rav Naḥman dealt with a case of divorce. The commentators make it clear that the same result would be reached if the woman became a widow.[33] Consequently, divorce and widowhood can give rise to divestiture.[34]

The problem, however, is that once a woman is divorced or widowed, her former husband would have no rights in her property. If the grantee's rights are inviolate throughout the woman's marriage, why should Text D assume that the fact that the grantee's rights may be divested upon *termination* of the marriage would somehow allow the husband to defeat the grantee's rights *during* the marriage?

### *Rosh's View*

If we were to proceed on a strictly chronological basis, we would first consider how Rabbenu Tam answers this question and only thereafter take up the approaches of *Rashba* and *Rosh*. Nevertheless, *Rosh* provides the most explicit and detailed explanation of Text D, and, where the various approaches differ, his is arguably the most natural way to understand it. Moreover, once *Rosh's* approach is explained, the alternatives can be effectively introduced by way of comparison and contrast. Consequently, we begin by describing *Rosh's* view.

*Rosh* does not believe that Text D is based on the assumption that the fact that the grantee's rights may be divested upon *termination* of the marriage would allow the husband to defeat the grantee's rights *during* the marriage. Instead, *Rosh* believes that even while she is married, the woman has the right to revoke the deed and recover the property whenever she wants. The existence of this right means that the property never fully "leaves her

33 See, e.g., *Rosh, T.B. Ketubot*, chapter 8, *ṣiman* 2; *Rashi, T.B. Ketubot* 78b, s.v. *Diboya*.

34 It is not entirely clear whether, upon the woman's divorce, the property automatically reverts to her or whether she merely has the right to revoke the transfer. See, e.g., R. Netanel Weil (*Ḳorban Netanel*), *Commentary on Rosh, T.B. Ketubot*, chapter 3, *ṣiman* 50 (arguing that, according to *Rosh*, there is an automatic reversion of the property). Cf. Yehoshua Boaz ben Shimon Barukh (16th century), *Shilṭei Giborim*, Gloss to *Rif, T.B. Ketubot* 37b, *ṣiman* 1.

domain." According to this view, Text D can be understood as assuming that the property remains so much in the woman's domain that her husband should obtain the right to enjoy the income from the property.

*Rosh* explains:

> The passage seems clearly to go as follows: "If the grantee does not become the owner," as Shmuel says that in a case in which the woman conveys all of her property, the grantee does not acquire them, "the husband should acquire [rights in] the property." Because the property is subject to her right to revoke the conveyance (*birishut ha-isha laḥazor bah*) whenever she wants, the property never left her domain, so how could they have been protected from the husband? The husband should acquire [rights in] them.[35]

35 *Rosh*, Commentary to *T.B. Ketubot*, chapter 8, *ṣiman* 3. Similarly, R. Yaaḳov Lorbeerbaum (c. 1760–1832), *Netivot ha-Mishpaṭ*, *Shulḥan Arukh*, *Ḥoshen Mishpaṭ* 99, *ṣif ḳoṭon* 5, explains:

> The basic rule regarding protective deeds is that the grantee acquires complete ownership, but the transferor can revoke the transfer any time he wants, as the *Rosh* explains in *Ketubot* 79. The creditor acquires rights in the property because, since it is within the control of the transferor to revoke, the property never leaves the transferor's domain, as the *Rosh* says ...

Similarly, *Beit Shmuel*, *Shulḥan Arukh*, *Even ha-Ezer* 90, *ṣif ḳoṭon* 31, states:

> It is clear from the *Rosh* and the *Ṭur* [i.e., a work written by R. Ya'aḳov *Ba'al ha-Turim* (1270-1343), the *Rosh's* son] that she [the woman] can revoke the transfer even while her husband is alive and give it to someone else — and so wrote the *Maggid* [R. Vidal Yom Ṭov diTolossa of Spain (*Maggid Mishneh*; 14th century)], *Hilkhot Zekhiyah*, chapter 6, *halakhah* 7, in the name of the *Rashba*, and he must have been referring to the case in which the woman transferred all of her property [i.e., a Text A or B transfer], because if he referred to where she said [i.e., wrote] *me'ha-yom velikh'she'ertze*, it is obvious that she can revoke.

See also R. Yoṣef Ḳaro (1488-1575), *Beit Yoṣef*, *Ḥoshen Mishpaṭ* 99, s.v. *Dinei Kotev Nikhoṣov* (quoting *Rashba* that a person who transfers all of one's property has a right to revoke the transfer whenever the person wants); Avraham Yeshayahu Karelitz (*Ḥazon Ish*; 1878–1953), *Ḥazon Ish*, *Even ha-Ezer-Nashim*, *Hilkhot Ketubot*, *ṣiman* 76(5) (apparently assuming that the woman, while married, could revoke the transfer by selling the property to someone else).

It should be noted, however, that the halakhic presumption mentioned in Text B, namely, that a person would not give away all of his property and leave himself penniless, does not provide support for the contention that the wife retains the right to revoke the transfer while she is married. While human psychology may tell us that a person would not leave herself penniless, forcing her to ask for charity, it does not tell us that a woman would not give away her assets for the duration of her marriage, because during her marriage she may expect her husband to fulfill his halakhic duty to

Of course, one may ask how *Rosh* knows that the woman possesses a right to retract the conveyance whenever she wants, even while she is still married. To answer this, one must consider how the Talmud knows that the woman can recover the property if she is divorced or widowed.[36] After all, in the Text A and B types of transfers, the language employed by the transferor is, on its face, without condition or exception. Talmudic commentators, including *Rosh*, explain that *halakhah* recognizes various principles of human psychology and, consequently, that certain situations give rise to halakhic presumptions (*umdenot*) regarding a person's intentions or motivations.[37] Indeed, Text B provides a clear illustration by stating that a person would not alienate all of her property — even by giving the property to her child — and leave herself penniless. The effect of the halakhic presumptions in Text A and B scenarios is essentially to make the transfer, which was unconditional on its face, subject to conditions consistent with the presumptions.[38]

---

support her. *Rosh*, however, may believe that once there is a halakhic presumption that the woman is transferring the property just to keep her prospective husband from getting it — the presumption arising from the fact that she would not want to leave herself penniless in the case of divorce or widowhood — the *result* is that we say that she retained as much right in the property as she could while still preventing her husband from getting it.

36 This type of intellectual process — where one may have to take one step back in order, hopefully, to take several steps forward — is typical of Talmudic reasoning.

37 In a completely different context, for instance, *halakhah* generally recognizes that a debtor would be too embarrassed in front of his creditor to completely deny a legitimate debt. The debtor might, however, deny part of the debt. Consequently, if a debtor totally denies an asserted debt, nothing more is required of him unless the creditor brings at least one witness. On the other hand, if the debtor admits part of an alleged debt (*modeh b'miḳtsat*), the debtor is biblically required to take an oath denying that he owes any more than the amount he admitted. See *T.B. Bava Metsia* 3a; *Rambam, Mishneh Torah, Hilkhot Shevu'ot* 11:5; *Shulḥan Arukh, Ḥoshen Mishpaṭ* 87:1.

It is beyond the purview of this paper to survey the various types of halakhic presumptions and to question whether halakhic authorities may rely on any purported presumptions that, although not expressly articulated in the Talmud, appear cogent to them. See, generally, Haim Hermann Cohen, "Evidence," *Encyclopedia Judaica CD-ROM Edition* (distinguishing between *ḥazaḳot, umdenot*, etc.); R. Yeḥiel Zevi Ben Yoṣef Mordekhai Kahana (first half of 19th century), *Divrei Geonim, klal* 3.

38 Even commentators who do not take an explicit position as to whether the woman has a right to revoke a Text A or B transfer while she is married seem

*Rosh*, however, believes that just as there is a halakhic presumption that the woman would want to recover the property if she is divorced or widowed, there is also a presumption that she would want to be able to recover the property whenever she so desired, even while she is still married.[39] He demonstrates this by reference to Text D's first sentence, "But if the grantee does not acquire the property, the husband should acquire it," which seems seriously to suggest that the husband should in fact acquire the property. Yet, if the woman could not revoke the transfer during the marriage, *Rosh* argues, the grantee would acquire an interest that would prevent the husband from obtaining an interest in the property.[40]

---

generally to recognize that the halakhic presumption transforms what would otherwise be an unconditional transfer into a conditional or restricted transfer. *Rambam*, for instance, appears to treat a Text A or B transfer as a transfer on the condition that the property be reconveyed to the woman under certain circumstances (*matanah al menat lihahzir*) . See Avraham Yeshayahu Karelitz (*Ḥazon Ish*; 1878–1953), *Ḥazon Ish*, *Even ha-Ezer - Nashim*, *Hilkhot Ketubot*, *ṣiman* 76(9), discussing *Rambam*, *Mishneh Torah*, *Hilkhot Zekhiyah* 6:13. See also *Ḥelḳat Meḥoḳeḳ*, *Shulḥan Arukh*, *Even ha-Ezer* 90, *ṣif ḳoṭon* 23 (reports that *Ran* explains that the reason the grantee keeps the property if the woman predeceases her husband while still married is that the halakhic presumption makes it as if she has specified that the transfer to the grantee should, in such an event, be valid); *Beit Shmuel*, *Shulḥan Arukh*, *Even ha-Ezer* 90, *ṣif ḳoṭon* 32 (same).

39 If the right to recover the property while married were limited to situations in which the woman and her husband became impoverished, the right could arguably be understood as subsumed within the halakhic presumption discussed in Text B, not to leave oneself penniless. Nevertheless, because the *Rosh* does not so limit the right, it seems that another basis must be found for this rule.

*Rosh* implicitly argues that the overall halakhic presumption in Texts A and B is that the woman is only transferring her property to keep it from being automatically, and involuntarily, subjected to her prospective husband's marital rights; she retains all rights to the property that are not necessary to accomplish this objective. The more particularized rules, therefore, such as her ability to regain the property upon being widowed or divorced, merely flow from this overall presumption. *Rosh* seems to believe that the right to revoke the transfer during the marriage, and thereby voluntarily subject the property to her husband's interests, is similarly consistent with the overall presumption.

40 *Rosh*, Commentary to *T.B. Bava Batra*, chapter 9, *ṣiman* 30. *Rashba* also cites the first sentence of Text D as proof that the woman has a right to revoke the transfer even while married. See R. Betzalel Ashkenazy, *Shiṭah Meḳubetzet* III, at 170 (citing *Rashba*). Similarly, a Toṣafist, referred to as

According to *Rosh*, Text D's answer to the question it poses accepts the assumption that the woman, even while married, could revoke the transfer. It also assumes that the existence of this right would, without more, be enough to allow the husband to acquire an interest in the property transferred. Nevertheless, Text D explains that, in the marital setting, there is a unique reason why the husband does not obtain rights in the property. The sages rabbinically declared that the transferred property was to be treated in the same way as property the husband did not know about at the time of the marriage. Just as the husband does not acquire rights in property that was unknown to him, so he does not acquire rights in this property that was transferred.

What does this mean for creditor-debtor law? A creditor's rights to a debtor's property appears analogous to the husband's rights to his wife's property.[41] It would therefore seem to follow that if a debtor made the type of transfer discussed in Texts A and B prior to borrowing money from a creditor, the debtor would have a right to recover the property from his grantee. Furthermore, the debtor's right to recover the property would mean that the property never fully left the debtor's possession and the creditor would be able to foreclose on the property. In fact, this is the *Rosh's* analysis regarding protective transfers made by debtors.[42] Although a husband cannot assert rights in the property transferred in Texts A and B, this is only because of the special rabbinic rule mentioned in Text D. That rule was only made with respect to husbands and wives and not as to creditors and debtors.

---

"*Ri*," at least initially, cites the first sentence of Text D as proof that the woman has the right to revoke even while she is still married. See *Toṣafot, T.B. Bava Batra* 151a, s.v. *Galiya Da'atah.* It appears that "*Ri*" stands for R. Yitzḥaḳ b. Shmuel of Dampierre (*Ri ha-Zaḳen:* d.c. 1185). It is said that of all of the *Toṣafists* only the name of Rabbenu Tam is mentioned more often than that of *Ri ha-Zaḳen*. See R. Hersh Goldwurm (ed.), *The Rishonim* (Brooklyn, N.Y.: Mesorah Publications, Ltd., 1982), at 132. Nevertheless, a gloss on the commentary of Rav Yeshayah ben Mali d'Trani (*Toṣafot Rid*; 1180-1260), *T.B. Ketubot* 79a, assumes that the "*Ri*" referred to in *T.B. Bava Batra* 151a, s.v. *Galiya Da'atah,* was *Toṣafot Rid*, not *Ri ha-Zaḳen*. The author of the gloss and the basis for his assumption is unclear.

41 All of the commentators recognize, and deal with, this apparent analogy. See, e.g., *Rosh, T.B. Ketubot*, chapter 8, *ṣiman* 3; *Shut ha-Rashba* II:312; Rabbenu Tam, *T.B. Ketubot* 79a, s.v. *Assa'um.*

42 *Rosh, T.B. Ketubot*, chapter 8, *ṣiman* 3.

*Rabbenu Tam's View*

Rabbenu Tam[43] also construes the question in Text D as applying to the case of texts A and B. Nonetheless, his interpretation of Text D leads to conclusions quite different from those of *Rosh*. Rabbenu Tam does not believe that the first sentence of Text D is seriously suggesting that the grantee does not acquire the property.[44] Instead, he argues that Text D's first

43 *Rashi* also maintains that Text D refers to the type of Text A and B transfer to which Shmuel refers. In commenting on the fact in text B that Shmuel says he would tear up a protective deed, *Rashi* states: "Later on the Talmud asks 'Since the deed is not a deed, how does it protect the property?'" It seems clear that *Rashi* is referring to the question posed by the Talmud in text D. Similarly, commenting on the first sentence of Text D, *Rashi* says:

> This question is asked to Shmuel in the case in which a person deeds away all of her property and he [Shmuel] says that [the grantee] does not acquire [the property]. Since the grantee does not acquire the property, what "protection" is there? Let the husband come and acquire the property and eat from its produce and inherit it if she [his wife] predeceases him.

See also R. Meir Shif (*Maharam Shif*), Commentary to *T.B. Ketubot* 79a (saying that *Rashi* construes Text D as applying to the case of Shmuel); *Rosh, T.B. Ketubot*, chapter 8, *ṣiman* 2 (same).

44 Some commentators support Rabbenu Tam's position by pointing out that, according to *Rosh*, the first sentence of Text D: (1) seems to be seriously suggesting that since, according to Shmuel, the grantee does not acquire ownership, the husband should acquire the property; and (2) seems to be suggesting this as an objection to what was said by Shmuel. They find this problematic, however, because how does the Talmud know that Shmuel would not agree to the suggestion? Perhaps the reason Shmuel would rip up a protective deed is because he thinks it is a complete nullity and, indeed, agrees that the husband should acquire the property. They contend that it may be this difficulty that led Rabbenu Tam to reject *Rosh's* interpretation. See, e.g., R. Meir Ha-Levi Schiff (*Maharam Schiff*), *T.B. Ketubot* 79a. Rabbenu Tam's approach avoids this purported problem. He construes the first sentence of Text D as assuming that it is unthinkable according to Shmuel, who calls the deed a "protective deed," that the husband would really acquire the property because, if the husband did acquire the property, the so-called "protective deed" would provide no protection!

However, it is not clear why these commentators believe the first line of Text D is difficult for *Rosh*. Even according to *Rosh*, the Talmud knows, before it asks its question, that the woman's purpose was to protect her property from her husband. According to *Rosh*, the Talmud is not asking a question to Shmuel *per se* based on the fact that Shmuel calls the deed a "protective deed." At this point in the Talmud, one might assume that Shmuel calls it that merely because this is what the transferor wants to

sentence fundamentally questions Shmuel's ruling that the grantee obtains no rights in the property by showing that this ruling leads to an untenable conclusion. If Shmuel is correct and the grantee does not obtain rights in the property, says Text D, then the husband ought to obtain rights in the property. Yet, according to Rabbenu Tam, the Talmud believes that the husband's obtaining rights in the property is absurd. After all, if the husband were to obtain rights in the property, the "protective deed," designed to protect the property from the husband, would actually provide no "protection." According to Rabbenu Tam, any halakhic presumption must be faithful to the accomplishment of the woman's objective of shielding the property from her husband. Consistent with this analysis, Rabbenu Tam believes that the first sentence of Text D is really arguing that the woman's grantee does acquire ownership of the property, and the woman cannot recover it from her grantee. Of course, Text D rebuts this argument by stating that Shmuel's ruling is consistent with accomplishment of the woman's objective because, even though the woman has the right to recover the property from the grantee, the sages prevented the husband from acquiring rights in the property by decreeing that the property should be treated the same way as property which was unknown to the husband at the time of the marriage.

What are the consequences of Rabbenu Tam's approach for debtor-creditor

---

accomplish, even if she is mistaken as to her ability to achieve this. See *Rosh*, *T.B. Ketubot*, chapter 8, *ṣiman* 3; R. Lorbeerbaum, *Netivot ha-Mishpaṭ*, *Shulḥan Arukh*, *Ḥoshen Mishpaṭ* 99, *ṣif ḳoṭon* 5 (citing *Rosh*). Instead, the Talmud is simply asking, "If the grantee does not acquire the property because the woman can revoke the transfer whenever she wants, should not the husband acquire the property and, if so, what protection does the woman accomplish?"

Although we mentioned at the outset that we would not canvass the opinions of all commentators, we will use this one issue to illustrate the breadth of opinion. *Rambam* believes that the first line of Text D does not apply to a Text A or B transfer of all of the woman's property because, in such a case, the interest the grantee acquires is so great that the phrase, "If the grantee does not acquire the property," makes no sense. See *Ran*, Commentary to *Rif*, *T.B. Ketubot* 37b. By contrast, other commentators believe that pursuant to a Text A or B transfer, the grantee receives no interest at all — not during the woman's marriage and not in the event that she dies while married. See, e.g., *Toṣafot Rid*, *T.B. Ketubot* 79a (indicating that he is retreating from an opinion he expressed earlier on the same page); R. Yeshaya of Trani II (*Riaz:* 1235-1300), cited by Yehoshua Boaz ben Shimon Barukh (16th century), *Shilṭei Giborim*, Commentary to *Rif*, *T.B. Ketubot* 37a, *ṣiman* 1.

law? The special rabbinic decree treating pre-marital property transferred by a prospective wife as if it were property that the husband did not know about is irrelevant to debtors and their respective creditors. As a result, based on the first sentence of Text D, it seems that the only way a debtor can "protect" his property by a transfer prior to incurring debt would be if the debtor's grantee were to acquire the property. Because Rabbenu Tam believes that there is a halakhic presumption that the transfer was accomplished in such a way as to effectuate the debtor's objective to keep the property from his creditors, Rabbenu Tam rules that the debtor's grantee does acquire the property. Consequently, the debtor cannot recover the property from the grantee, and the creditor cannot foreclose on the property in the hands of the grantee.[45]

*Rosh* describes Rabbenu Tam's position as follows:

> Rabbenu Shimshon, of blessed memory, writes that an incident came before Rabbenu Tam involving someone who wanted to borrow money and deeded all of his property to another so that his property would not become encumbered to his creditor, as well as a case in which a person deeded all of his property to another to prevent it from becoming encumbered to his [future] wife's marital rights. Rabbenu Tam ruled that these gifts were valid gifts. What is the reason that [the Talmud] says that a protective deed does not convey ownership [to the grantee]? It is because she [the transferor] does

45 *Toṣafot*, *T.B. Ketubot* 79a, s.v. *Assa'um*, states:

> A case involving a protective deed [*shṭar Mavriaḥ*] came before Rabbenu Tam in which a person wanted to borrow money but did not want his property to become encumbered to his creditor — and also a protective deed so that a prospective husband's property would not become encumbered to pay the marital rights [*ketubot ishto*] — and Rabbenu Tam ruled that the deed was valid and enforceable. It is only here, [in the case of a woman who transfers property in anticipation of marriage] in which the husband does not obtain rights because the property is like property the husband did not know about at the time of the marriage, that we say the woman surely intended the deed as a protective deed [yielding the halakhic presumption that she has the right to recover the property from the grantee]. But in these cases [that came before *Rabbenu Tam*], if the grantee did not acquire the property the creditor or wife would acquire it, and the property would not be protected, we say that the debtor intended to convey the property completely [and the grantee acquires it completely].

*Ran* cites this view of Rabbenu Tam and does not mention the view of *Rosh*. See *Ran*, Commentary on *Rif*, *T.B. Ketubot* 37b. *Mordekhai*, however, states that the view of Rabbenu Tam disagrees with the ruling of R. Eliezer of Metz. See *Mordekhai*, *Ṣefer Mordekhai L'Ketubot*, *ṣiman* 208. *Rosh* says that his own view had the support of R. Meir Ha-Levi and "all of the Torah giants of this land." *Rosh*, *T.B. Ketubot*, chapter 8, *ṣiman* 3. For a general discussion of the debate between *Rosh* and Rabbenu Tam, see, e.g., R. Yonatan Eybeshuetz (1690-1764), *Urim veTumim*, *Ḥoshen Mishpaṭ* 99.

> not intend to convey ownership. Her basic intention is that her husband not acquire rights in the property, and her husband does not acquire rights for we say that the rabbis make the property like property that the husband does not know about at the time of the marriage. Therefore, the grantee also does not acquire the property. But here [in the case of the debtor or the husband], where we cannot say this reason [for preventing the creditor from acquiring ownership, because the rabbis made no special rule as to property transferred to "protect" it from creditors or wives], if the grantee does not acquire the property, the creditor or wife will acquire it. Consequently, we do not call such a deed a "protective deed," because it does not provide any protection [from the creditor or wife]. Instead, we cannot say that the debtor intended to protect his property but, instead, intended to give it as a complete gift and the grantee acquires it.[46]

*Rosh* fundamentally disputes Rabbenu Tam's conclusion that the debtor must be understood to have completely transferred ownership to his grantee. Indeed, *Rosh* argues that, although the debtor would like to shield his property from collection by prospective creditors, if the debtor knew that this could only be accomplished by unconditionally transferring the property to a third party, he would not make the unconditional transfer.[47] This

46 *Rosh, T.B. Ketubot*, chapter 8, *ṣiman* 3.

47 *Rosh* states:

> Certainly the transferor intended to protect the property, for, as the Talmud [Text B] explains, a person would not leave himself penniless and give his property to someone else. But the transferor erred in thinking the transfer would protect the property even though the grantee did not thereby acquire ownership of it. Since the *halakhah* is that the protection does not work unless the grantee acquires ownership, and the grantee cannot acquire ownership because the transferor did not intend to transfer ownership, the property remains in the debtor's domain (*reshut*) and is encumbered to pay his wife's marital rights and [his debt] to the creditor. In addition, the basic rule [regarding protective deeds] is based on how we understand the transferor's psychology. This man [the transferor] meant to protect his property and thought that the protective deed would work even if the grantee did not acquire the property. When it becomes known to him [the transferor] that this is impossible but that either the grantee acquires the property or the property becomes encumbered to pay the creditor or his wife's marital rights, it is clear to us all [*anan sa'adei*] that he prefers that the grantee not acquire the property but that it remain in his own domain. [This way], he enjoys its use and income until the creditor takes and satisfies his claim from the property — and the transferor avoids being a "Borrower who is an evildoer and does not repay" [*Ps.* 37:21] — or his wife predeceases him, leaving him the property free and clear of her claims, rather than have the grantee acquire the property, causing the transferor to immediately lose the property without even having his debt paid. And this is the way ha-Rav Rabbenu Meir ha-Levi, of blessed memory, decided the *halakhah*, as well as the rest of the Torah giants of this land, and this is the correct conclusion.

conclusion, *Rosh* maintains, is mandated by the halakhic presumption, articulated in Text B, that a person would not give all of his property to another, leaving himself penniless.[48] *Rosh* bolsters this argument by pointing out that one is biblically obligated to repay a creditor. Consequently, he argues, a debtor would prefer repaying a creditor than having the money go to a third party. Moreover, it is possible that the debtor will anyway end up paying the creditor from subsequently acquired assets. Thus, the transfer, according to Rabbenu Tam, could disadvantage the debtor without any compensating benefit. Indeed, in the case of a person who transfers his property to avoid its becoming encumbered to pay his prospective wife's marital rights this possibility may be even greater. The marital rights in question arise only upon dissolution of the marriage. If the wife predeceases the husband, the husband may not have to pay anything at all. Surely he would prefer continuing to enjoy the property until dissolution of the marriage — and perhaps even thereafter, if his wife dies during the marriage — to losing the property immediately and unconditionally.

Interestingly, the debate between *Rosh* and Rabbenu Tam may be based, at least in part, on fundamentally different views as to how halakhic presumptions are formed. *Rosh* thinks that if the debtor knew that the only way he could halakhically prevent his creditor from reaching the property would be to transfer it without the ability to get it back, the debtor would not want to transfer it, and he cites Text C for support. *Rosh* argues that the halakhic presumption is in accordance with what the debtor would want to happen if he were aware of the halakhic consequences of his conduct.[49]

There is no reason to believe that Rabbenu Tam thinks that a debtor, in order to protect his property from a creditor, would transfer it even if the debtor knew that he would never be able to revoke the transfer and get the property back. Instead, it seems more likely that Rabbenu Tam simply assumes that what the debtor would want, if he knew the *halakhah,* is irrelevant. What seems to be important to Rabbenu Tam is the narrow, conscious objective the debtor has in mind when he transfers the property, namely, the goal of keeping the creditor from getting the property. In order to achieve this goal, says Rabbenu Tam, the transfer must be complete and unconditional and, therefore, the halakhic presumption is that the transfer is complete and unconditional.

48 *Ibid.*

49 *Ibid.*

The positions of Rabbenu Tam and *Rosh* seem in agreement on one point: if the woman retained a right to recover the transferred property whenever she wanted, even while she was still married, this reservation would be enough to allow the husband to foreclose on the property — and if a debtor retained a right to recover the transferred property whenever he wanted, his creditor would be able to foreclose on it. How do we see this? Because if this were not the case, if the woman or creditor could protect the property through such a conditional transfer, there should be a halakhic presumption that this is indeed what the transferor intended. Instead, Rabbenu Tam says that the *only* way for a debtor to protect his property from his creditor is by making an unconditional transfer to a grantee.

While the positions of *Rosh* and Rabbenu Tam differ from one another, each appears internally consistent. *Rosh* believes that one who transfers all of his property to avoid a creditor intends to, and effectively does, retain the right to recover the property from the grantee at any point in time. The retention of this right is ordinarily enough to allow the transferor's creditors the right to foreclose on the property as well. In the case of *nikhṣei melog*, however, the sages created an exception by treating the property transferred as if it were property about which the husband had no knowledge at the time of the marriage. Rabbenu Tam, on the other hand, believes that one who transfers all of his property to avoid a creditor generally does not retain any right to recover the property. Why? The retention of such a right would ordinarily permit the creditor to foreclose on the property and the transferor does not want the creditor to have such a right. The only exception pertains to *nikhṣei melog*, because, in light of the sages' decree, it is possible to retain a right to recover the property without allowing the husband to acquire the property.

### *Rashba's View*

The position of *Rashba*, however, is puzzling. He believes that the first sentence of Text D is asked at least in reference to Text A and Text B transfers. He maintains, as does *Rosh*, that the woman transferring all of her property in Texts A and B has the right to recover the property from the grantee at any time that she wants, even while she is still married. Nevertheless, *Rashba* agrees with Rabbenu Tam, arguing that the creditors of a debtor who transfers all of his property cannot foreclose on the transferred property.[50] How can these two positions be reconciled?

*Rashba* is quoted as saying that the first sentence of Text D

> implies that she [the woman] has a right to revoke, even while she is still married because, if not, how could it [Text D] suggest that the husband should obtain the property? While she would be married, the transfer would be valid and the grantee would be the owner![51]

As already explained, *Rosh* also learns from this same sentence that the woman has a right to revoke while still married. *Rosh*, however, sees it from the implication that if there were a right to revoke, this would be enough to enable creditors to foreclose. How does *Rashba*, who disagrees on this point, learn from Text D that the woman has a right to revoke?

One possible answer is that *Rashba* distinguishes between cases in which the right to revoke is exercised and those in which it is not yet exercised — and he interprets Text D as referring only to instances in which the woman has already *exercised* her right to revoke. Let us evaluate this possibility carefully.

First, of course, it is necessary to establish that this answer is consistent with what *Rashba* writes in his responsum. He writes:

> [T]he [transferred] property is not encumbered — not to the husband and not to a creditor — because it was protected from them, and the grantees acquire the property until the transferor revokes [the transfer].[52]

The phrase "until the transferor revokes [the transfer]" clearly serves to modify the phrase, "the grantees acquire the property." The issue is whether it also modifies the phrase, "the [transferred] property is not encumbered — not to the husband and not to a creditor — because they were protected from them." If it does modify this phrase, then *Rashba* would be ruling that, after the transfer is revoked, the property would become *nikhṣei melog*. This ruling would make it impossible for *Rashba* to interpret Text D as referring to a case in which the woman has revoked, because Text D clearly states that the husband does not obtain rights in the property. However, it is possible that "until the transferor revokes [the transfer]" only modifies the phrase immediately preceding it, "the grantees acquire the property." If so, *Rashba* could rule that revoking the transfer does not change the fact that the property was, and still is, protected against the husband's obtaining rights in it.

50 *Shut ha-Rashba* II:312; *Beit Yoṣef, Ḥoshen Mishpaṭ* 99, s.v. *Dinei Kotev Nikhoṣov* (quoting *Rashba*).

51 R. Betzalel Ashkenazy, *Shiṭah Meḳubetzet* III, at 170 (citing *Rashba*).

52 *Shut ha-Rashba* II:312.

But is it plausible that after the transfer is revoked, the husband will still not acquire rights in the property? One early commentator, R. Aharon ha-Levi *(Ra'ah*; c.1230-1300), interprets Text D this way.[53] According to *Ra'ah*, until and unless the transferor revokes, the grantee's acquisition is "complete" and Text D's question, "[b]ut if the acquirer ["*lokeaḥ*"] does not obtain ownership of the property ... ," would make no sense. Only after the transferor revokes the transfer and regains ownership of the property is there any chance for the husband to acquire rights in it. If the husband knows his wife owns the property, it should become *nikhṣei melog*. According to *Ra'ah*, just as the sages exempted property that was unknown to the husband from becoming *nikhṣei melog*, so the sages decreed that the property that was the subject of the wife's transfer should not become *nikhṣei melog*.

There are, nonetheless, several problems with this interpretation. One is that there is little conceptual similarity between *Ra'ah's* version of the decree in Text D and the law regarding property that is unknown to the husband. Property that is unknown to the husband is only temporarily excluded from becoming *nikhṣei melog*. As soon as the husband learns about the property, it becomes *nikhṣei melog*. According to *Ra'ah*, it seems that so long as the transfer is not revoked, there is no need for the decree because the property does not belong to the wife. Even after the transfer is revoked, there seems to be no need for a decree, according to *Ra'ah*, so long as the husband does not know about the revocation, because even though the property belongs to the wife, the property really is property that is unknown to the husband. Consequently, the sages' decree, in Text D, only applies when the husband does know that the wife owns the property. Furthermore, according to *Ra'ah*, the decree does not exclude the property from becoming *nikhṣei melog* on a temporary basis. On the contrary, the protection is permanent.

### *Ḥazon Ish's View*

*Rashba* could largely avoid these objections if he were to interpret Text D the way R. Avraham Yeshayahu Karelitz (*Ḥazon Ish*; 1878–1953) does. *Ḥazon Ish* argues that Text D refers to a woman who exercises her right to revoke in a specific way — not by retaking the property but by selling or giving the property to another grantee.[54] He says that Text D assumes that

53 See R. Aryeh Leib ha-Kohen Heller (1745-1813), *Avnei Miluim, Even ha-Ezer* 90, *ṣif koṭon* 7 (discussing the *Ra'ah's* views).

54 *Ḥazon Ish, Even ha-Ezer-Nashim, Hilkhot Ketubot, ṣiman* 76(5).

the woman's unexercised right to revoke would not be enough for the property to become *nikhṣei melog*. Once the wife actually revokes the property, however, retroactively, it is as if the property was never transferred. Instead, it always belonged to the woman and, retroactively, would seem to have become *nikhṣei melog* from the very start of the marriage.

What if the husband does not know that his wife has revoked the transfer? *Ḥazon Ish* tentatively suggests that, under these circumstances, the property might *actually* be property that is unknown to the husband. If so, even without the decree referred to in Text D, the property would not become *nikhṣei melog*.

*Ḥazon Ish* rejects this suggestion. He assumes that the husband knew all along that his wife had made this premarital transfer.[55] Thus, from the start of the marriage, the husband knew that if his wife revoked the transfer, the property would retroactively be hers. *Ḥazon Ish* says that even this limited knowledge would prevent the property from being called property unknown to the husband. *Ḥazon Ish* says that the point of the sages' decree is precisely to equate this limited knowledge with no knowledge at all. This view of the decree seems more closely linked to the concept of property unknown to the husband than the approach taken by *Ra'ah*.

In addition, if the husband learns that the wife has revoked the transfer and that, therefore, the property is hers, *Ḥazon Ish* believes that the property would become *nikhṣei melog*. The decree was only to treat the husband's imperfect knowledge as no knowledge. The decree does not invalidate actual knowledge. Consequently, according to *Ḥazon Ish*, neither the rule regarding property unknown to the husband nor the decree mentioned in Text D provides permanent protection from having the property become *nikhṣei melog*.

Of course, if the transfer is revoked and the wife regains the property, it seems likely that the husband will learn about it. Perhaps for this reason, *Ḥazon Ish* says that Text D is dealing with a case in which the wife revoked the original transfer not by revoking the transfer and repossessing the

---

Incidentally, to the extent that the case involves sale of the property to another, this interpretation arguably fits well with Text D's use of the word "*loḳeaḥ*" in the sentence, "But if the acquirer ["*loḳeaḥ*"] does not obtain ownership of the property, the husband should acquire it." Although it could be used for any "acquirer," it seems more readily to connote "purchaser."

55 This assumption is especially apt in a case in which the woman transferred all of her property. The fact that the woman entered into the marriage with no property of her own would probably lead the husband to discover the transfer.

property but, instead, by reconveying the property to a new grantee.

But even a reconveyance seems to work in two steps: (1) it revokes the original transfer, because she cannot give it to a new grantee unless she first reacquires possession herself; and then (2) it transfers the property to the new grantee. What if the husband knew about the reconveyance at the time it occurred? Would he then have the type of "direct knowledge" that his wife owns the property that would render the property *nikhṣei melog*? *Ḥazon Ish* offers two possible answers. First, he states that perhaps Text D refers to a case in which the husband did not learn about the reconveyance of the property until after it took place. Alternatively, he suggests that the two steps of the reconveyance occur simultaneously, and, therefore, it cannot be said that the husband "knew" that the property had become hers before it was reconveyed.

Although ingenious, *Ḥazon Ish's* approach is also troublesome. In Texts A, B and C, the Talmud had mentioned two categories of transfers: Texts A and B transfer of all of one's property without any express restrictions and Text C transfers part of one's property with an express, written restriction. Text D seems clearly to be asking a question[56] as to one or both of these categories. There is little reason to suspect that Text D is only asking about a subset of these categories — cases in which the woman has revoked by reconveying the property to a new grantee.[57] The *Ḥazon Ish's* position is especially problematic because there is no reason to believe that the purported subset is a common one.

There is yet another difficulty with concluding that Text D refers only to cases in which the woman has already revoked the transfer. The first sentence of Text D poses an objection to something that preceded it. According to *Rosh*, the question is, "if the grantee does not acquire the property, the husband should get it, and what protection was accomplished?" According to Rabbenu Tam, the question is, "surely the grantee must acquire it because, if not, the husband would acquire it and what protection was accomplished?" In each case, the Talmud assumes that it is obvious that everyone would agree that, in the case under discussion, the property must be protected from the husband. It is this assumption that makes it appropriate to pose an objection rather than to simply ask a question.

But if Text D is talking about a case in which the woman revoked the

56 Of course, according to *Rosh*, it is a serious question and according to Rabbenu Tam, it is a rhetorical question.

57 This difficulty applies to *Ra'ah's* view as well, for he, too, limits Text D to cases in which the woman has already revoked the transfer.

transfer, why is the Talmud so certain that, even after this revocation, the property should be protected from the husband? Given that the protection is provided because of the transfer, perhaps revocation of the transfer is retroactive and it is as if the transfer never took place. Even assuming that the bottom line rule was, as *Ra'ah* and *Ḥazon Ish* believe it to be, that the property may be protected even after the woman revokes the transfer, the question is how Text D could so strongly *assume* this to be the case, that, based on this assumption, it could pose its objection. Despite these problems, there seems to be no better way to explain how *Rashba* could rule both that, even while married, the woman had a right to revoke the transfer and, nonetheless, the property did not become *nikhṣei melog*.

What are the implications of *Rashba's* view for debtor-creditor law? The debtor, in our hypothetical case, who transfers all of his property before become indebted, would be entitled to revoke the transfer and regain his property. If he did so, however, his creditors would be able to foreclose on the property. This would seem true even according to *Ra'ah*, because the sages did not generally make a decree to help creditors. Their enactment seems to have been exclusively for the benefit of wives who transferred property prior to their marriage to prevent it from becoming *nikhṣei melog*. Creditors should still be able to foreclose on property their debtors transferred because, even according to *Ḥazon Ish*, the concept of "property unknown to the husband" is irrelevant to the property of debtors.

### *Text D As Applying to Text C Transfers of Part of One's Property*

A number of commentators do not believe that Text D applies to Text A and B transfers of all of one's property. Some of these authorities argue that in Text A and B transfers, the grantees immediately acquire a sufficiently strong ownership interest in the transferred property that the first sentence of Text D, "But if the grantee does not acquire the property, the husband should acquire it," makes no sense.[58]

58 Some of these authorities may think that the woman does not have the right to revoke the transfer while she is still married. In his commentary on *T.B. Bava Batra* 151a, *Rosh* points out that there is a difference in one word between his version of the text and the version of Rav Shmuel b. Meir (*Rashbam:* 1080-1158). *Rosh* states that according to *Rashbam's* version, with which *Rosh* disagrees, it would seem that the woman would not have a right to revoke during her marriage. See *Rosh*, *T.B. Bava Batra*, chapter 9, *ṣiman* 1. *Toṣafot Ri*, *Toṣafot*, *Bava Batra* 151a, s.v., *Galiya Da'atah*, makes

Instead, these authorities argue that Text D applies to Text C transfers, situations in which the transferor clearly expresses a desire to restrict the transfer. As mentioned earlier, *Rambam* explains that a Text C transfer does not immediately convey any rights to the grantee. It only conveys rights if, at some later time, the transferor announces that she wants the transfer to have been retroactively effective. Consequently, Text D's question is that, since the grantee does not immediately obtain rights to the property, the husband should acquire them as soon as the marriage takes place. Read this way, Text D provides no inkling as to whether a debtor's right to revoke an otherwise *completed* transfer would enable the debtor's creditors to foreclose on the transferred property.

However, according to *Rosh*, a Text C transfer takes place immediately but is subject to subsequent revocation by the woman. The argument for the transferor having a right to revoke in a Text C transaction seems at least as persuasive as in Text A or B situations. In the latter cases, the right to revoke is not at all explicitly mentioned at the time of the conveyance but is only a halakhic presumption based on the sages' knowledge of human nature. By contrast, in Text C's case, the desire to restrict is expressly written in the deed. Even if the written language in the Text C deed is not technically adequate to subject the transfer to a legal condition — an issue that is not entirely clear — it is certainly sufficient evidence of the transferor's intention to give rise to the same type of halakhic presumption that apply to Text A and B transfers.[59] Therefore, just as *Rosh* rules that a person's creditors can foreclose on property alienated through a Text A or B deed of all of one's property, *Rosh* should rule that a debtor's creditors can foreclose on property transferred pursuant to the type of deed mentioned in Text C. As a result, according to *Rosh*, Text D's question could be asked of the sages in Text C just as much as of Shmuel. This would explain why the Talmud waits until

---

the same observation regarding the import of this version of the text, although he seems to disagree with it. The texts of *Raḥ* and Rebbenu Gershom b. Yehudah (*Meor ha-Golah*; 960-1040) are also the same as the *Rashbam*'s. Other authorities, without explicitly taking a position as to whether the woman can revoke the transfer while still married, apparently believe that the grantee's right to keep the property, should the woman die while still married, is sufficient to make Text D's first sentence inapt. See, e.g., *Ran*, Commentary to *Rif, T.B. Ketubot* 37b (discussing the *Rambam's* view).

59 See, e.g., Avraham Yeshayahu Karelitz (*Ḥazon Ish*; 1878–1953), *Ḥazon Ish, Even ha-Ezer-Nashim, Hilkhot Ketubot, ṣiman* 73(7).

after Text C to pose this question.[60] The Talmud, first in Text C, asks a question of Shmuel. Then, in Text D, it asks a question of Shmuel and of Text C. Although it is puzzling that *Rosh* does not explain that Text D's question applies to Text C as well as to Shmuel, there is reason to believe that the *Rosh* believes this is true. Each seems to deal with halakhic presumptions, one based on the fact that the transferor retains no property for herself (and on her impending marriage) and the other based on the explicit words of the deed (and on the transferor's impending marriage).[61]

On the other hand, Rabbenu Tam's position is unclear as to whether a creditor could foreclose on property transferred pursuant to a Text C deed.[62] If Rabbenu Tam thinks that the language in the deed creates a formal condition to the transfer and Rabbenu Tam understands the condition to purport to effect an immediate transfer subject to the transferor's right to revoke at any time, it might well be that the express condition would "trump" any possible halakhic presumption.[63] If so, the result would be that

60 At least one commentator argues that according to *Rosh* it does not make sense for the Talmud to have waited and that this difficulty may have been the reason why R. Moses b. Naḥman (*Ramban* or Naḥmanides; 1194-1270) thinks Text D's question applies to Text C transfers and not to Text A and B transfers. See *Ḳorban Netanel*, Commentary to *Rosh*, *T.B. Ketubot*, chapter 8, *ṣiman* 60.

61 See, e.g., *ibid.*, at *ṣiman* 40 (arguing that, according to *Rosh*, the same laws apply).

62 Rabbenu Tam does not state whether Text D's question is asked on Text C as well as on Shmuel. This is somewhat surprising because, according to Rabbenu Tam, the question to Shmuel is based on the fact that Shmuel refers to the deed as a "protective deed" while, based on the question, the deed does not seem to provide any protection. This question, however, could be answered as the *Rosh* does, by saying that it is called a protective deed because the transferor intends to protect her property through this deed, even though the transferor is wrong as to her halakhic ability to do this. See *Rosh*, *T.B. Ketubot*, chapter 8, *ṣiman* 3. One cannot use this answer as to Text C, however, because the sages in the *Baraita* in Text C expressly instruct a woman who wants to protect her property to use the protective deed they describe. The sages, therefore, must think that this device actually works.

63 It seems more likely that there could be a halakhic presumption that creates conditions on what otherwise appears to be an unconditional transfer than that there would be a halakhic presumption that creating conditions on a transfer that *expressly* states that it is unconditional. Similarly, it seems more likely that there could be a halakhic presumption that creates conditions on what seems to be an unconditional transfer than that there is a halakhic presumption that would overrule express conditions such as an

the transferor would have the right to revoke, but, because of the transferor's reservation of this right, the transferor's creditor would be entitled to foreclose on the property.

If, however, Rabbenu Tam thinks that the words in the deed do not create a formal condition but merely evidence the transferor's intent to protect the property from his creditor, the question becomes more murky. One obvious possibility is that Rabbenu Tam would take the same position as he did as to Text A and B transfers: the grantee would acquire the property completely. The creditor could not foreclose on it, but the debtor could not get it back either. The only problem is that the words in the deed not only evidence the debtor's desire to protect the property from the creditor, but they clearly show that the debtor wants to be able to revoke the transfer whenever he wants. Of course, as previously discussed, according to Rabbenu Tam (and *Rosh*), it is impossible for the debtor to both protect the property from the creditor and retain the right to revoke the transfer whenever he wants. It is uncertain how Rabbenu Tam would resolve this conflict. In this instance, however, Rabbenu Tam might prefer the debtor's clearly expressed subjective intention to be able to revoke as evidence that the debtor only wants to protect the property from his creditor if he can revoke at any time. If so, Rabbenu Tam would agree that the debtor retains the right to revoke but that the creditor may also foreclose on the property.

According to *Rashba*, it would seem that Text D's question should apply to Text C transfers just as much as it applies to Text A and B transfers. Similarly, *Rashba* seems clearly to state that the same rules apply to these different types of transfers.[64]

## PART III — SUMMARY & IMPLICATIONS FOR DEBTOR-CREDITOR LAW

According to *Rosh*, the following propositions are true:

1. In Text A and B transfers and in Text C transfers, a debtor who transfers has a right to revoke the transfer.
2. A debtor's reservation of a right to revoke a transfer (whether arising from a halakhic presumption or, presumably, from an explicit condition in the transfer), is ordinarily enough to enable a creditor to foreclose on the transferred property.

---

explicit reservation of the right to revoke at any time.

64 *Shut ha-Rosh* II:312.

3. The point of the sages' decree referred in to Text D, however, is to prevent a husband from foreclosing on property his wife transferred while reserving a right to revoke.
4. The sages' decree does not provide any protection for a debtor who transfers property to protect it from his creditors. The debtor can revoke the transfer and, even before any such revocation, the debtor's creditors can foreclose on the property.
5. Text D deals with a case in which the wife reserves a right to revoke, but has not yet exercised that right. This is clear, because *Rosh* states that the objection is that the grantee does not acquire the property because of the wife's "right" to revoke, and he never says that she has in fact revoked the transfer.

Rabbenu Tam's view, however, differs as to part of proposition #1. Rabbenu Tam does not think that a debtor who makes a Text A or B transfer to a creditor has a right to revoke the property. As discussed in Part II, however, Rabbenu Tam may believe that a debtor who makes a Text C transfer has a right to revoke. Rabbenu Tam seems to believe proposition #2, that, where the debtor does have an enforceable right to revoke, the debtor's creditor also has a right to foreclose. Similarly, Rabbenu Tam seems to believe propositions #3 and #4. Nor is there any reason to think that Rabbenu Tam disagrees with proposition #5. Rabbenu Tam surely maintains that Text D applies at least to cases in which the woman did not yet exercise her right to revoke.

*Rashba* agrees with propositions #1 and #4 and seems to disagree as to propositions #2, #3 and #5. He appears to rule that the fact that a debtor reserves a right to revoke a transfer does not enable the debtor's creditors to foreclose on the property; such foreclosure is possible only if and when the debtor exercises the right to revoke. He seems to contends that the point of the sages' ruling in Text D is to protect the woman's property *after* she exercises her right to revoke — perhaps as *Ra'ah* or *Ḥazon Ish* interpret the case. Similarly, he construes Text D as a case in which the woman has exercised the right to revoke.

Of these three views, *Rashba's* provides the greatest incentive for debtors to engage in these types of transfers. According to him, by so transferring the property, debtors at least temporarily protect it from their creditors without losing the right to demand the property back. According to *Rosh*, there may be some practical benefit from these transfers, at least until the creditors find out about them and are able to foreclose. According to Rabbenu Tam, there is virtually no incentive to engage in a Text A or B transfer for, by doing so, the debtor permanently loses all rights to the property.

Of course, as mentioned at the outset, the *halakhah* in any particular case may well depend on any of a number of variables that we have not considered. Moreover, a variety of halakhic innovations have been introduced over the years in many communities that would significantly affect a specific outcome. We have not tried to arrive at the halakhic "bottom line." Rather, the much more modest goal of this mini case study has been to explore and experience how Talmudic authorities engage in the first step of the halakhic process — the analysis of, and the extrapolation from, Talmudic texts — and how they reach very different results.

# 12

## INCARCERATION FOR NON-PAYMENT OF DEBTS

by

YOSEF RIVLIN*

### *Background*

In formulas in promissory notes, the debtor promises that should he not repay the debt on time, the lender is entitled to harass him and to hand him over to the non-Jewish authorities: "And he is permitted to go to the authorities and to bribe them [to take action against me] and to disparage me;"[1] "And if peradventure I tarry in repaying him the money at the fixed time, he is free to apply to the authorities and bribe them to impose upon me fines and penalties ... and has the right to fine and harass me;"[2] "And if I refuse to repay this debt at the due time, he is free to compel and charge me in any court whether according to Jewish law or civil law and to press charges in a gentile court and to banish me."[3] Further, in a debt bill found in the Munich Talmud, MS 1343, reference is made to physical punishment: "And he will not be liable for any harassment inflicted upon me such as the plucking of my beard, the tearing out of my hair and any beating to recover the money."[4] It is to be noted that these expressions are not found in the early books of bills of R. Sa'adiah Gaon and R. Hai Gaon. We first come

a Associate Professor, Department of Talmud and Faculty of Law, Bar-Ilan University, Israel.

1 Y. Rivlin, *Bills and Contracts from Lucena (1020-1050)* (Hebrew), (Ramat-Gan: Bar-Ilan University Press, 1994), 120. See also 125 there.

2 *Ṣefer ha-Sheṭarot le-Rabbenu Yehuda ha-Barzeloni,* (Berlin: Ittskovski, 1898, reprinted Jerusalem, 1967), 68 [= A. Gulak, *Otsar ha-Sheṭarot ha-Nehugim be-Yisrael* (Jerusalem: Defus Hapo'alim, 1926), 224].

3 Gulak, *Otsar, ibid.*, 207.

4 Y. Rivlin, "Bill Forms in the Munich Talmud Manuscript" (Hebrew), *Shenaton ha-Mishpat ha-Ivri* 20 (1995-1997), 312.

across them in the southern Spanish town of Lucena in bills written at the beginning of the eleventh century, in Judah of Barcelona's book of bills dating from the twelfth century and in other bills from then onwards. The exact meaning of "to harass me" is not clear. One is not forced, naturally, to conclude that corporeal punishment — flagellation or incarceration — is indicated. The surrender of the offender to the authorities also does not necessarily imply harshness of detention even though it is not outside the realm of possibility. As is well known, incarceration on account of non — payment of debt was an accepted punishment adopted throughout the world, as Kohler held: "The debtor was held in custody and spent his time in harsh conditions ... This measure ... became more and more prevalent during the Middle ages."[5] However, it is possible that the act itself, of handing over the offender to non-Jewish courts which had more efficient methods for the collection of debts, resulted in the debt being paid without the need for incarceration. Indeed, as we learn from the written text, the surrender of the offender to the civil authorities was regarded as an efficient way to collect debts involving costs but not necessarily imprisonment.

In later bills there is more explicit reference to incarceration as punishment. Thus, we find it written in *Ṣefer Tiḳun Sheṭarot* of Joseph Gaon of the sixteenth century:

> And he submitted his body to the mentioned person and gave permission to all and sundry who come into possession of this bill to seize his body at all times, at any place, anywhere in the kingdom, and to place him in custody until he repays the mentioned money ... and he had further agreed that any kindnesses that will be done to him by any King, Queen, Minister, or any Lady, or anyone, will be of no avail until he has repaid all the mentioned money.[6]

## *Elon's Research*

The question is, what are the practical implications of these texts? For example, is the lender entitled to apply physical punishment to the borrower, and may the lender submit the borrower to the non-Jewish authorities so that they apply the rigours of the law?

5 J. Köhler, *Shakespeare vor dem Forum der Jurisprudenz* (Wurzberg: Stahel, 1883), 16.

6 Gulak, *Otsar, supra* n.2 at 211. See also F. Baer, *Die Juden im Christilchen Spanien, Urkunden und Regesten* (Vol.1: Berlin: Akademie Verlag, 1929; Vol.2: Berlin: Schocken Verlag, 1936), in vol. 1, 1060-1065.

Prof. Menahem Elon researched this subject thoroughly. The first edition of his work was published about forty years ago, and has lately been republished with few changes.[7]

In principle, one can accept Elon's conclusion that from the time of R. Isaac Ben Sheshet Perfeṭ in the fourteenth century, a definite change took place with regard to the imprisonment of debtors which became standard practice.[8] Nevertheless, his finding that, until this period, imprisonment for non-payment of debt was not practiced at all, requires further study.[9]

*The Cairo Geniza Material*

Among the vast corpus of Geniza documents, there is testimony of incarceration on account of debt. We read of the offender being brought into the custody of the Muslim court in order that he honor his debt. We know that:

> Non-Muslims appeared and argued in Muslim courts in person or were represented by a Muslim attorney ... In the great majority of cases mentioned in the Geniza, Jews made use of the Muslim judiciary ... It was common practice to make contracts before Muslim and Jewish authorities concurrently.[10]

This led, in many cases, to the imprisonment of the debtor. Goitein writes of the struggle of Jewish ecclesiastical courts against the evading of honoring debts, employing the weapons of banishment and, occasionally, even submitting the debtor to the Muslim court, which did not hesitate to incarcerate:

> Another means to secure payment was the severe punishment, including long imprisonment and torture meted out to tardy debtors when brought before a

7 M. Elon, *Freedom of the Debtor's Person in Jewish Law* (Heb.: Jerusalem: Magnes Press, 1964); M. Elon, *Human Dignity and Freedom in the Methods of Enforcement of Judgments* (Heb.: Jerusalem: Magnes Press, 1999).

8 Elon, *Freedom, ibid.*, 140ff. In the second part of this article, I cite some sources discussed by Elon, and think that upon their basis we can entirely accept Elon's explanations and conclusions.

9 Elon's commentaries to these sources seems to be tendentious and were not based on the Cairo Geniza researches.

10 S.D. Goitein, *A Mediterranean Society, The Jewish Communities of the Arab World as Portrayed in the Documents of the Cairo Geniza, 1-5* (Berkely, Los Angeles and London: University of California Press, 1967-1988); 6 (Index) (1993), in vol. IV, 400.

Muslim court. The Jewish court had no power for such measures, but also took a strong stand and, in extreme cases, went so far as to excommunicate a member evading his obligations or to reserve themselves the right to "extradite" him to the Muslim authorities.[11]

This documentation dates from the eleventh and twelfth centuries. Banishment and imprisonment were regarded as extreme measures. Hence, we find the head of the Jewish community himself intervening to arrange payment of the debt. The Nagidim Mevorah and Samuel ben Ḥananiah intervened successfully to have the loan repaid in small installments over a length of time resulting in the full repayment of the loan without sanctions.[12]

*Incarceration for Dishonoring a Loan*

The Talmud discusses the slaughtering of the Passover-offering for a person confined in a Jewish jail.[13] *Rashi* explains the circumstances of his confinement, "Such as one who is being pressed to divorce a forbidden woman or to repay money."[14] Elon surmises that the passage refers to a debt incurred involving taxes and not an ordinary debt. His reasoning is: "There is not a hint of imprisonment for non-payment of debts at this period."[15] However, granted that this was rare at *Rashi*'s time, there must have been occasions when incarceration followed the evasion of repayment of loans, which we have referred to above, and therefore *Rashi*'s words are not so cut

11 Goitein, *Mediterranean Society, ibid.*, vol. I, 259-260.

12 *Ibid.*, 260; 464, n.192. In a document from 1098 we find: "In case the debtor does not pay the sum agreed upon before the Jewish court, the latter will bring him before the government" — ULC Add 3422. The same formula is written in a document from 1145, ENA 4011, f.50. The Nagidim are mentioned in the documents: Bodl. MS. Heb. a3, f2; TS 13J18 f.25, Goitein, *ibid.*, n.193. As we know from the Cairo Geniza documents, simple folk did not always act according the *Halakhah*: see M.A. Friedman, "The minimum Mohar Payment as reflected in the Geniza Documents", *Proceedings of the American Academy for Jewish Research,* 43 (1976), 37-38; Y. Rivlin, *Inheritance and Wills in Jewish Law* (Heb.: Ramat-Gan: Bar-Ilan University Press, 1999), 90. Here we deal not with the simple people but with the Halakhic authorities and the Jewish court; as we know, they always acted according to Jewish law, enactments and customs.

13 *Pesaḥim* 91a.

14 *Rashi, ad. loc.* (s.v. *Beit ha-Aṣurin*).

15 Elon, *Freedom, supra* n.7 at 114, n.15.

and dried and could refer to an ordinary loan.

A responsum of R. Joseph ibn Migash (first half of the twelfth century) contains the following:

> Concerning what you asked: Does a person who was incarcerated because of a debt, or a tax which everyone has to pay, say the *Ha-Gomel* blessing, or is it [said] only by one who was imprisoned because of a grave matter or whose life was in danger?

The answer is:

> Since he was placed in a prison, incarcerated in jail without any freedom of action and his situation has changed in that he has freedom of action, he is obligated to say a blessing.[16]

Here the case is explicitly about imprisonment because of debt. One is, of course, not constrained to say that we are dealing with a debt that a Jew owes to a non-Jew and where he has been committed to prison by a non-Jewish court. It is reasonable to assume that we may be dealing with a Jew to Jew debt and where the confinement served the lender to speed up settlement.

Abraham ben David of Posquières, *Rabad* (twelfth century), the author of the *Hassagot*, writes with regard to sureties for a loan: "Let a body come in lieu of a body until he compromises with him."[17] The *Maggid Mishneh*, Vidal Yom Ṭov of Tolosa (fourteenth century) expresses amazement with the words of the *Rabad*, but, nonetheless, he also understood that the guarantor is imprisoned until the lender is reconciled.[18] And even if this explanation of *Rabad*'s words bristles with difficulties, one cannot entirely reject such an interpretation. Hence there is another source for showing that imprisonment was a possible penalty for dishonoring a loan. This means there are, at least, three different sources that underpin the view that a debt defaulter was kept in custody.

### *The Prohibition of Arrest*

Maimonides rules explicitly that it is forbidden to imprison: "and if the borrower has nothing [to repay] ... the borrower goes on his way scot-free and he is not apprehended."[19] R. Samuel Ṣardi (thirteenth century) supports

16 *Resp*. 90 (Jerusalem: Lev Sameach, 1991), 80.

17 *Malveh ve-Loveh* 25:14.

18 *Ad loc.*

19 *Malveh ve-Loveh* 20:1.

Maimonides and holds

> and we are not to incarcerate his body [of the borrower] ... but since it is known to the lender or to the Jewish court that the borrower is poor, it is forbidden for the *dayyan* to shame him by means of one of these acts.[20]

However, he adds that if there exists a doubt as to the ability of the borrower to repay, he is to be interrogated to determine if he is a swindler, but on no account may he enter the house of the debtor.

Elon deduces *a priori* from this ruling that incarceration is prohibited and there are those indeed who connected the prohibition against entering the debtor's house with that of inprisonment. But an examination of the sources shows that many of the Rishonim held that the reason why entry into a borrower's house was forbidden, was because of "invasion of privacy;"[21] hence there is no need to connect this to the prohibition of arrest.

Possibly, when the borrower had money to repay the debt but did not do so, even among Jews the sanction of imprisonment was occasionally employed. R. Jonah of Gerondi writes thus at the beginning of the thirteenth century: "And it is right to be zealous in remonstrating with the aggravators among our people in a number of places to put the borrower in manacles even when he is unable to repay the debt."[22] From this we are able to deduce that imprisonment was practiced among the Jewish people and his criticism is directed against placing those in custody who did not have the means to repay. Apparently, one can deduce that should the debtor have the wherewithal, but does not repay, he deserves a punishment.

These sources condemn incarceration explicitly. However, they are mainly directed toward a borrower who cannot repay the debt. As quoted "when the borrower does not have anything".

R. Solomon ben Abraham Adret, *Rashba* (thirteenth century), is quoted:

> Concerning what you asked: If a person pledged himself and his property and spirited away his property, is his body to be bound since he pledged it or not? Answer: His body is not mortgaged to be sold like a thief who is sold on account of his theft, since a person does not write so that he be pledged and made like a slave. But he is mortgaged like a borrower and his property is like guarantors ... [23]

From the words of Adret "since a person does not write so that he be pledged

20 *Ṣefer ha-Terumot* II, 1:2.

21 See *Semag* (*Ṣefer Mitzvot Gadol,* R. Moshe of Coucy) *Asayin,* 93.

22 *Sha'arei Teshuvah* III, 88.

23 *Resp.* I, 1069.

and made like a slave," it can be inferred that there is an impediment in the determination of the borrower and hence one cannot, upon the basis of this responsum, make wide generalizations. In sum, all that is said is that, in his obligation, the borrower did not intend to pledge his body, but had in mind only an ordinary obligation common to all borrowers.

A similar conclusion is to be drawn from a responsum of R. Asher ben Jeḥiel, *Rosh* (thirteenth-fourteenth centuries).

> And with regard to the other matter about which the sages wrestled in their minds vigorously, if any Jew be permitted to issue forth an IOU of another Jew, to seize forcibly his body upon the basis of the IOU, ... it is clear that if the borrower has no money to repay, the lender may not seize the borrower's body and subjugate him, nor may he sell it to recoup his debt.[24]

Apparently, one can deduce from this citation that only when the borrower does not have the means to repay the debt is he not to be seized, but should he have the wherewithal and spirits it away or repudiates the debt, he can be detained. This is simply how Rabbi Eliezer Waldenberg understood the *Rosh*:

> But in any case we learn this from the latter part of the *Rosh*, since after he has explained that he cannot be subjugated physically he concludes and writes: "And hence why should he be seized since he is not allowed to subjugate, nor is he allowed to harass him." — The reason of the *Rosh* is that since he cannot arrest him, there is no use in his seizing him since he cannot subjugate him nor harass him, and this is relevant if he does not have the means to pay. However, if he does have the means to repay it is reasonable to seize him, since he will not be free in his actions and it will pressure him to agree to reimburse him.[25]

There were, indeed, other attitudes, but there can be no doubt that in the case of a borrower who does not honor his debt though he has the means to repay, incarceration was not considered halakhically untenable. One must remember that, during the whole period discussed here, the scribes who wrote the promissory notes were accustomed to incorporate formulas which were binding on the borrowers. Gulak, for example, includes a formula, apparently from Castille: "And he transferred control of his body to the mentioned one ... that he can seize his body at will ..."[26] And in a bill from the end of the fourteenth century: "And we will be bound, oppressed and seized according to his desires, and we will not leave until all the above-

24 *Resp*. 68:10.

25 *Resp. Tsits Eliezer* XVI, 59.

26 Gulak, *Otsar, supra* n.2 at 211.

mentioned are carried out."[27] Despite all that has been said, seizure on account of a debt was not common.

*Change and Adaptation*

The above cases constituted the basic idea of incarceration as a punishment, which crystallized and became more and more the norm. R. Isaac ben Sheshet Perfeṭ, the *Ribash* says:

> Question: Reuben who borrowed from Simeon, and pledged himself absolutely, i.e. physical seizure and subjugated himself to give unalienated chattels, to pay the Alfarda tax as customary in the Kingdom of Aragon. Should he not be in possession of unalienated chattels, his body is to be seized. Now Simeon. the lender, has demanded repayment of his loan from Reuben, the borrower, but the latter does not have [the means to repay the debt]. Simeon desires that the borrower be bodily seized as stipulated, but the borrower argues: It is illegal to be bodily seized and there is no Biblical sanction that a Jew be seized for any pledge. In sum, who is right?[28]

In his responsum the *Ribash* says that, in principle, the borrower is right and the condition stipulated is not binding. Basing himself on the responsum of the *Rosh* mentioned above, he rules that the condition is of no avail as regards bodily subjugation. The *Ribash* describes the custom which has taken root in Saragossa to incarcerate a debtor who had pledged himself, and even in the absence of the borrower's undertaking, he would still be liable to be arrested unless he produced a suitable surety. The *Ribash* wanted to declare himself against, but it was explained to him that there is no alternative, and, because of swindlers, these measures have to be enforced. Further on, he explains the considerations for allowing these steps, and he differentiates and states that if the borrower had the means to repay, they may seize him bodily whether he has committed himself or not. However, should he not have the wherewithal:

> I see no legal loophole to enable his bodily seizure since he has no means to pay unless he swore to place himself in jail and not to leave it until he has repaid, and this is a kind of ostages[29] by the instrument of which he is bodily seized as he swore in order to uphold his oath.[30]

27 Baer, *supra* n.6 at 739.

28 *Resp*. 484.

29 See below note 31.

30 *Resp*. 484.

What can be deduced from the *Ribash* is that there were indeed cases of imprisonment because of a debt, especially where the debtor had the means to pay and eluded repayment. We have seen that the Sages who preceded the *Ribash* supported such a step against the defaulter. However, this was not so widespread and many lenders suffered losses. The obligations which the borrower took upon himself, according to the wording of the notes, including the oath that the lender is allowed to subdue and oppress, constituted an important instrument for carrying out incarceration because of a debt. The *Ribash* designated this procedure by the word "ostages".[31] It appears in the works of a number of Sages not in connection with debt. Adret does mention it in connection with a debt:

> And if he swore to him, that if by a certain date he had not repaid the debt, he should stand *ostages* till he repays him, he has to fulfil his oath and to stand by the *ostages*.[32]

On the essence of "ostages" Baer writes that we are speaking of a detention site outside the town.[33] It seems that it was much used when new arbitrators were appointed. As the *Rashba* writes, "When the time arrives to appoint others in their place they stand in the ostages and eat of their own till their assent is finalized."[34] This means when the term of the appointment of others in their place is reached, they have to leave the city and to wait at the detention site outside it until the new appointments are made.

In fourteenth century Germany, too, winds of change began to blow. Alexander Suslin ha-Kohen of Frankfurt, cites proof from the Talmud. "Abba b. Martha owed money to the house of the Resh Galutha ... they distressed him,"[35] making the point that a person who has means and yet does not repay is to be incarcerated.[36] R. Yoseph ben Solomon Colon, the

31 It comes from the old French. See '*hostage*', in *The World Book Dictionary,* vol. I, ed. C.L. Barnhart, R.K. Barnhart (Chicago: World Book-Childcraft International, 1978), 1022; *Webster's Third New International Dictionary,* vol. I (1968), 1094.

32 *Resp. Rashba ha-Meyuḥaṣot la-Ramban,* 246.

33 Y. Baer, *Toledot ha-Yehudim bi-Ṣefarad ha-Notsrit* (Tel-Aviv: Am Oved, 1959). 135; 503 n.35. See B.Z. Dinur, *Yisrael ba-Golah,* II, 2 (Tel-Aviv: Dvir, 1966), 329-330.

34 *Resp.* V, 284.

35 *Shabbath* 121b.

36 *Aggudah, Shabbath, ad loc.* R. Alexander (fourteenth century) served in a number of German communities: Worms, Cologne, Frankfurt am Main and Erfurt.

*Mahariḳ* (fifteenth century), also cites the Italian custom "to seize the defaulter who refuses to pay a pledge and to imprison him by the hand of a non-Jew." He goes on to express opposition to handing over the defaulter's money to the non-Jew.[37]

We have also Provencal sources and, moreover, some of them in the manuscripts of the *Orḥot Ḥayyim* of R. Aaron ben Jacob Ha-Kohen of Lunel (second half of the thirteenth and first half of the fourteenth centuries). There is a collection of bills of which there is one with the title "A pledge with guarantors, oath and ostages."[38] This provides us with opportunity to trace ostages in the context of a loan.

### *Ostages Bill*

A Promissory Note with Guarantors, Oaths and Ostages[39]

> We,[40] the witnesses [who have signed at the bottom of this deed] know [that the borrower and the guarantors[41] came before us and said: be our witnesses with an acquisition[42]] that I wanted with my own volition or we wanted with our own volition,[43] without compulsion but with a whole heart and desirable mind, and we obliged ourselves and our properties a complete obligation with a full acquisition from now, such and such *dinars*, such coins, with full weight, legal tender in this place today. We fixed dates for the installment payments in a fixed place to him or to his attorney without refusal, delay or omission on this issue such and such *dinars* on the fixed date or to pay it at the end of the year which begins now. And we mortgage to him and to his attorneys, a complete mortgage with a full acquisition from now for the mentioned loan, all our property which we bought and which we shall buy,

37 *Resp.* 127.

38 Manuscript *Moscow-Ginzburg 107/10,* Ha-Makhon le-Tatslumei Kitvei Yad, Jerusalem, mic. 6787, 240-249.

39 This is the exact title of the bill. R. Moshe Hershler published it in *Genuzot Yerushalayim* III (5751), 129-160. This was an edition of the New York JTS manuscript (Rab. 664, acc. o185). Hershler did not know that this bill and the whole collection was composed by R. Aaron ha-Cohen of Lunel. Hershler's edition contains many mistakes. A new edition of the Moscow manuscript will be published by me in another place; there I will show the differences between the two editions. I include here a few extracts from the long bill.

40 On the preamble formula of the bill, see Rivlin, *Lucena, supra* n.1 at 86-88.

41 On loans and securities, see Rivlin, *Lucena*, *supra* n.1 at 46-64.

42 On the acquisition in the bill, see Rivlin, *Lucena*, *supra* n.1 at 95-96.

43 On the formula of free will see Rivlin, *Lucena*, *supra* n.1 at 96-97.

real property and, by them, other property. They will be responsible, pledged and mortgaged to him and to his attorneys to collect from them the mentioned loan on the fixed dates ... We brought guarantors ... and they said: Be our witnesses by performing a complete acquisition. Write it by using the best formulas of right and sign it, and deliver it to the mentioned lender. It will serve him and his attorneys as good evidence and right proof because we wanted of our own volition to be the guarantors for the mentioned *dinars*. And in our presence, they swore a severe oath in the name of G-d, without cheating and without any pretext for regret, that if they will not repay the entire loan, they will stand in "ostages" in a certain place, and they will not ever leave it until the lender will get all his money. They include in their oath, that if for a reason of compulsion they will not be able to stay in the fixed place, they promise that immediately after the compulsion is over they will stand in the "ostages" and stay there until the loan is paid. We acquired from them with an instrument with which it is proper to acquire.

These are the points which arise from the bill:

1. The borrower pledges all his property to the lender.
2. The borrower provides guarantors from whom the lender can draw money at the first request.
3. The borrower and the guarantors undertake on a severe oath that if the debt is not honored in time, they willingly will enter custody until the loan is repaid in full.

It is possible that the *Ribash*'s ruling took root but in the *Taḳanot* (regulations) of those expelled from Spain that reached the shores of North Africa which obviously reflected the norm of the countries they had forcibly left, for it was written there: "He shall not place him under lock and key even though it is stated so in the document."[44] However, in practice, the expelled continued to incorporate this wording in the debtor's bill reinforced by an oath, and this practice, we are taught, was not only in vogue in southern France during the fourteenth century but also continued in North Africa at least until the sixteenth century.[45]

### *Aḥaronim*

We find this trend ever-increasing especially during the later half of the

44 *Kerem Ḥamer,* II, #22 (Livorno, 1869).

45 Manuscript, *Tiḳun Ṣoferim,* New York, no. 0393, Makhon Ben Zvi, no. 1869. I would like to thank Prof. M. Benayahu, for giving me this manuscript. On the importance of this collection and its deeds, see Y. Rivlin, "Formularies from North Africa", *Aṣufot* (accepted for publication).

sixteenth century. Isaac ben Samuel Adarbi, one of the foremost halakhic authorities of Salonika, rules that if the borrower swears that he does not have the means, the lender does not have authority to detain him as Maimonides had written.[46] The later Sages also understood Maimonides as referring to where the borrower does not have the means to repay. There is no proof from his ruling that the borrower cannot be detained should the borrower have the means to repay.[47] Samuel ben Moses de Medina writes: "It seems to me that there is a hint permitting detaining one who owes but does not repay,"[48] and he cites *Rashi*'s comment on Pesaḥim (cited above). Another responsum of de Medina is quoted in *Paḥad Yitsḥaḳ* of R. Isaac Lampronti.[49]

> There is no doubt that if the borrower has property to repay but does not want to repay, that he is detained in prison ... but even if it is clear to us that he is able to repay but a small sum over the period ... but he does not want to do it ... he is confined in prison.

R. Elijah ben Ḥayyim of Constantinople, *Ranaḥ* (second half of the sixteenth century and beginning of the seventeenth century), reviews the opinions of all his Rabbinical predecessors holding the view that the debtor is not to be detained, but adds that this is specifically so only if the borrower does not have the means to repay," but if he does have the means to repay but does not want to do so, and the Jewish court is unable to seize his property, he is incarcerated until he repays his debt."[50] He further explains that the view of Adret is that no proviso helps, but, in principle, if he has the means but does not repay, he is detained.[51]

R. Yom Ṭov ben Aḳiva Tsaḥalon (1559-1620) ruled that detention for non-payment of a loan is a legitimate step.[52]

46 *Resp. Divrei Rivot,* 302.

47 See *Resp. Ḥiḳeḳei Lev,* II, *Ḥoshen Mishpaṭ,* 5.

48 *Resp. Maharashdam,* 390.

49 Letter B, s.v. *Ba'al Ḥov pri'ato Mitsva* (Venecia, 1750), 44a.

50 *Resp. Ranaḥ,* 58.

51 Elon's attitude to *Ranaḥ*'s explanations (Elon, *supra* n.7 at 163 n.196) imply indirect criticism. From Elon's point of view, the *Rashba* and other Rishonim did not give permision to incarcerate the borrower. Every scholar is at liberty, of course, to explain the sources according to his own view, and it is legitimate and well accepted. This criticism can be applied to Elon's method too. As we wrote, his attempt to show that there is not a hint of incarceration is not based on a real explanation of the sources.

52 *Resp, Maharitats,* 94.

A similar development took place in Poland and Germany. R. Moshe ben Israel Isserles, the *Rema*, and R. Solomon ben Jeḥiel Luria, *Maharshal* (sixteenth century), simply held that a borrower who has the means but does not repay is detained.[53] R. Yom Ṭov Lipmann Heller (second half of the sixteenth century, the first half of the seventeenth century) wrote that the punishment of imprisoning a defaulting borrower is to be regulated.[54] During the seventeenth century many *Taḳanot* were in force in Poland and Germany concerning borrowers with means to repay, and the punishment of detention became customary. What characterizes these regulations is that their originators did not explain the words of the Rishonim and relied on their own authority because of the many breaches of the law and the increase of evaders of loan repayments.[55] Judah Aryeh Modena (seventeenth century) instituted similar measures in Italy.[56]

During the eighteenth and nineteenth centuries this trend became the practice in all communities, i.e. the detention of a defaulter whose ability to repay the debt was not in doubt. The question now is: Is there a possibility of detaining one who does not have the means to repay? R. Ḥayyim Palache, *Habif* (Izmir, Turkey), compiled a comprehensive discussion on this issue and he, like his predecessor, R. Elijah ben Ḥayyim, the *Ranaḥ*, proves that the core-idea was already inherent in the words of the Rishonim.[57] The German Sages such as R. Gershon Ashkenazi, "*Ha-Gershuni*" (seventeenth century) and R. Jonathan Eybeschutz (eighteenth century) in his book *Urim ve-Tummim*, explain the words of the Rishonim in the same above mentioned way, namely, that there is freedom to impose incarceration on one who has the means to repay but does not do so.[58]

From the twentieth century, too, we have a wide-ranging responsum from the pen of Rabbi Eliezer Waldenberg of Jerusalem, where he reviews the opinions of his predecessors and simply concludes that most Rishonim permit detention for defaulting repayment of a loan when the borrower has the wherewithal to repay the loan but chooses not to do so.[59]

53 *Rema, Shulḥan Arukh, Ḥoshen Mishpaṭ* 97:15. *Maharshal*, *Yam Shel Shelomo, Baba Kamma, ha-Ḥovel*, ch.65.

54 *Pilpula Ḥarifta* on the *Rosh*, *Baba Metsi'a* 85, #38. 2.

55 See Elon, *Freedom*, *supra* n.7 at 173ff.

56 *Resp. Ziḳnei Yehudah* (ed. S. Simonsohn), 108 (Jerusalem: Mossad Harav Kook, 1956), 156.

57 See *Resp. Ḥiḳeḳei Lev*, *supra* n.47.

58 See on *Shulḥan Arukh, Ḥoshen Mishpaṭ*, 97.

59 *Tsits Eliezer, ibid*; E.Y. Waldenberg, "Ma'asar ke-Emtsai u-ke-Onesh", *ha-*

*Summary*

In sum, we conclude, from the material assembled, that many Rishonim held the opinion that it was permissible to incarcerate a defaulter not prepared to honor his debt. However, even those who thought that under no circumstances was it permissible to do so, the bill's wording was enlisted to force detention upon the borrower because of his commitment and oath.

Adret and Perfeṭ mentioned "ostages" — a term unknown until the discovery of the bill in the *Orḥot Ḥayyim.* The text of the document describes the obligation of a borrower and his oath, that if he does not repay his debt, he will commit himself into detention and stay there until he has completely repaid his debt.

The fact that the formula of the *Orḥot Ḥayyim* found its way also to North Africa and served the local scribes there, teaches us that this bill also helped the sages to enforce incarceration of an evading defaulter.

*Torah ve-ha-Medinah* II (1950), 31-35; L.Y. Kaminer, "Onesh ha-Ma'asar be-Yisrael", *Teḥumin* IX (1988), 143-146. For a different opinion see *Ase Lekha Rav,* R. Ḥayyim David ha-Levi, III, 57.

# 13

# THE RISE AND DECLINE OF THE LAW OF THE REBELLIOUS WIFE IN MEDIEVAL JEWISH LAW

by

ELIMELECH WESTREICH*

The ruling now prevalent is that a woman initiating divorce proceedings according to Jewish law is required to submit a ground, chosen from a defined list appearing in the Talmud; barring such a ground, the husband cannot be coerced to grant a divorce.[1] This approach originates in a mishnah stating that "the woman is put away with her consent or without it, but a husband can put away his wife solely by his consent."[2] This formulation also appears in the last codification of Jewish Law, the *Shulḥan Arukh,* and is fully endorsed by R. Moses Isserles, who represents Ashkenazi tradition.[3] Yet, between the talmudic period and the time close to the *Shulḥan Arukh,* Jewish law had sustained a divorce regime enabling the woman to coerce her husband to grant a divorce without submitting a defined ground. These proceedings were based on the law on the rebellious woman, which originates

* Professor of Jewish Law and Family Law, Tel-Aviv University, Faculty of Law. This research was supported by The Tel-Aviv University Fund for Research and by the Center for Jewish Law Studies, Shaarei Mishpaṭ College. A Hebrew version was published in *Shenaton Ha-Mishpaṭ Ha-Ivri* XXI (1998-2000), 123-147.

1 For a summary of the ground, see Benzion Shereschewsky, *Family Law in Israel* [Hebrew] (Jerusalem: Rubin Mass, 1992, 4th ed.), 295-308.

2 *M. Yevamot* 14:1.

3 *Shulḥan Arukh, Even ha-Ezer*, ch. 77. This section, which sums up the rulings on the rebellious wife, does not even mention the possibility of coercing the husband to divorce on the strength of this ground. In contrast, the two previous codes, *Ṣefer ha-Ṭurim (Even ha-Ezer,* ch. 77) and *The Code of Maimonides, The Book of Women*, tr. Isaac Klein (New Haven, Yale University Press, 1972), *Laws of Marriage* 14:8, do speak of this suit as an available option, although they do not always agree with it.

in the Talmud and was expanded at the dawn of the geonic period to serve the woman as a broad and generalized ground. The rebellious woman ground spread throughout the East and to the large European centers in Spain and Ashkenaz to become the prevalent law enforced by all. What led to the decline of such a significant ground to the point that the *Shulḥan Arukh*, written in the second half of the sixteenth century, never even mentions it? This article attempts to trace the changes in the validity of the rebellious woman ground, from its beginnings in Northern Europe all the way to North Africa, pointing to a possible link between its rise and fall on the one hand, and the Gentile surroundings on the other.

Rebellion in the Mishnah[4] and in the Talmud[5] refers to the refusal of one of the spouses to fulfill a duty laid down in the marriage contract [*ketubah*], and primarily the duty of cohabitation. The Mishnah discusses both the rebellious woman and the rebellious man, and the Amoraim engaged in a dispute as to whether rebellion concerns only cohabitation or also a refusal to work.[6] It appears that the ruling considers that rebellion is only pertinent to cohabitation,[7] and this will also be the approach endorsed in this article. The core of the discussion on the rebellious woman in both the Mishnah and the Talmud focuses on the economic sanctions to be imposed on the woman who rebels against her husband, and on their enforcement.

The husband, according to the Talmud had no need for the rebellious woman ground in order to support divorce claims or obtain a license to marry another wife. We did find, however, that the Talmud relates to the possible existence of a divorce suit based on the woman's rebellion. Evidence appears at three different levels of halakhic sources: the first is the Talmud itself, the second are geonic writings, and the third are the commentaries of the early Rishonim. In the talmudic discussion on the rebellious woman, a saying is cited drawing a distinction between two types of rebellious women, one who says, "I like him but wish to torment him," and another who says, "he is repulsive to me." The printed version of the Talmud reads as follows:

4 *Ketubot* 5:7.

5 *BT Ketubot* 63a-64a.

6 The discussion in the Babylonian Talmud opens with a question: "Rebel in what [respect]? R. Huna replied: [In respect] of cohabitation. R. Jose b. Ḥanina replied: In respect of work."

7 R. Isaac Alfasi, *Ketubot* 63b. Maimonides, *Laws of Marriage* 14:8; *Ṭur Shulḥan Arukh, Even ha-Ezer* ch.77. Among the early authorities, only R. Eliezer b. Joel ha-Levi (*Ravyah*) sided with R. Jose b. R. Ḥanina, who holds that a woman is rebellious if she refuses to work.

> What is to be understood by "a rebellious woman"? Amemar said: "One who says: 'I like him but wish to torment him.' If she said, however, 'He is repulsive to me,' she is not coerced (לא כייפינן לה)." Mar Zuṭra ruled: "She is coerced (כייפינן לה)."[8]

According to this version, the dispute between Amemar and Mar Zuṭra hinges on whether the rebellious woman is coerced to retreat from her rebellion. In contrast, the version in the Leningrad-Phirkovits Ms. reads as follows: "What is to be understood by 'a rebellious woman'? Amemar said: One who says: 'I like him.' But if she said, 'He is repulsive to me,' he is coerced (כייפינן ליה)."[9] In the latter version, the subject in Amemar's saying is the husband, and, therefore, if the rebellious woman says, "he is repulsive to me," she can coerce her husband to grant her a divorce on this suit.

The view that the Talmud itself is the source providing the rebellious woman with a divorce suit appears in geonic writings. This is extensively discussed in an article by Yeraḥmiel Brody[10] on the legislative activity of the Geonim. His conclusion is that, according to the Geonim, the source of the halakha coercing the husband to grant a divorce to his rebellious wife is the Talmud itself. Several geonic writings indeed state so specifically. Rav Sherira Gaon, a prominent figure who provides copious and precise information on the history of the Geonim and their halakhic and public endeavor,[11] explains the Talmud as follows:

> and their ruling was that she is suspended without a divorce for twelve months, since she may retract, and after twelve months the husband is coerced to write her a divorce.[12]

R. Isaac Alfasi, active in the second half of the eleventh century, was the most prominent halakhist in Spain after the geonic period. In his treatise, *Ṣefer Ha-Halakhot*, widespread throughout Spain (where he took refuge late in his life), he explicitly states that the ruling coercing the husband to

8 *BT Ketubot* 63b.

9 *BT Ketubot*, with *Maṣoret ha-Shaṣ ha-Shalem* (R. Moshe Hershler editor, Jerusalem, 1977), 88, in the section on variant versions. This manuscript is marked there as ל״פ.

10 Yeraḥmiel Brody, "Were the Geonim Legislators?" (Hebrew), *Shenaton Ha-Mishpaṭ Ha-Ivri* 11-12 (1984-1986), 298-300.

11 His well-known treatise, *Iggeret Rav Sherira Gaon*, is the most important source of information on the geonic period and on preceding eras, and excels in providing rich and accurate information.

12 *Otsar ha-Geonim, Ketubot* (Responsa Section), sec. 479, p.192. The source of the responsum is *Geonim Responsa Sha'are Tsedeḳ,* 56a, ch.4, sec.15.

divorce his rebellious wife originates in the geonic ordinance rather than in the Talmud itself. Discussing the issue of a woman who has pledged a certain sum as a dowry and is unable to meet her commitment, he relates the dispute between Admon and the sages (according to R. Jose b. R. Judah) on whether she should continue waiting until her hair grew gray, or can tell her fiancé to either marry her or set her free.[13] Alfasi then added:

> As for what our rabbis have enacted on the rebellious wife, to grant her a divorce immediately regardless of whether it was her father or she who says he pledged either to marry me or set me free, he is *coerced* to divorce her against his will.

Clearly, then, according to Alfasi, the husband is compelled to divorce his rebellious wife, and the source of this ruling is the geonic ordinance.

What type of rebellious woman is the subject of the geonic ordinance — the one claiming, "I want him," the one claiming, "he is repulsive to me," or both? Although this is a crucial question, a comprehensive discussion of it is beyond the scope of this paper. Let me note that both types of rebellious women have been the subject of various interpretations in the course of the centuries, and changes in the meaning ascribed to each of these types may have been intended to solve problems faced by halakhists ruling on these issues. I hold that the rebellious woman claiming, "I want him" is the woman who refuses cohabitation with her husband but is interested in continuing the marriage. In contrast, the rebellious woman claiming, "he is repulsive to me" is the one interested in divorce and, therefore, she also refuses cohabitation. "He is repulsive to me" is merely the reverse of "I want him." Alfasi indeed uses the expression "I do not want him" as an alternative to "he is repulsive to me."[14]

Due to Alfasi's prominent status in Spain and his direct and close links with geonic sources, we find that, from the beginning of the eleventh century, divorce was coerced in Spain on the rebellious wife ground.

Like Alfasi, Maimonides also ruled that a man is coerced to divorce his rebellious wife, but supported this ruling relying on evidence from the Talmud itself. In his Code, the ruling is worded as follows:

> The wife who prevents her husband from having intercourse with her is called "a rebellious wife," and should be questioned as to the reason for her rebelliousness. If she says, "I have come to loathe him, and I cannot willingly submit to his intercourse," he must be compelled to divorce her immediately, for she is not like a captive woman who must submit to a man

13 *BT Ketubot* 109a.

14 *BT Ketubot* 63b.

that is hateful to her.[15]

On the one hand, Maimonides strengthened the rebellious woman ground by anchoring it in the Talmud itself rather than in the geonic ordinance. On the other hand, he weakened it by characterizing the rebellious woman claiming, "he is repulsive to me" as actually saying she cannot have conjugal relations with her husband on emotional grounds. In any event, the view of these two prominent halakhists shaped Jewish law in the Spanish domain for centuries to come, until the impact of later Ashkenazi influence began to register.

The ruling that the husband is coerced to divorce on the rebellious woman ground had already made its way into Ashkenazi surroundings during the geonic period, and is manifest in the rulings of R. Gershom, one of the early Ashkenazi authorities active around 1000 CE.[16] A question addressed to him dealt with the case of a man who took a second wife, against the wishes of his first wife, who then demanded a divorce and her *ketubah*.[17] R. Gershom ruled that, according to the Talmud, taking a second wife does not constitute grounds for divorce in favor of the first wife because the ruling follows Raba, who stated: "A man may marry wives in addition to his first wife,"[18] and the woman's claim must thus be rejected in this case. R. Gershom argues, however, that the talmudic ruling is no longer valid and "Should she want to divorce without her *ketubah* and against his wishes, he is coerced to grant her a divorce."

After two generations, *Rashi* endorsed the ruling coercing the husband to grant a divorce to his rebellious wife, but claimed that this ruling originated in the Talmud. According to his interpretation of the Talmud, the rebellious woman claiming, "I want him" is indirectly coerced to stay with her husband

15 Maimonides, *Laws of Marriage* (=*Ishut*) 14:8.

16 Abraham Grossman, *The Early Sages of Ashkenaz: Their Lives, Leadership and Works* (900-1096) [Hebrew] (Jerusalem: Magnes Press, 1989, 2nd ed.), 111, sets the date of R. Gershom's death at 1028, and estimates his date of birth c. 950-960. R. Gershom's main activity, therefore, took place in the first quarter of the eleventh century.

17 Ephraim Kupfer, *Responsa et Decisiones* (Jerusalem: Mekize Nirdamim, 1973), sec.147; *Responsa of the Maharam of Rottenburg,* (Prague) sec.865. *Hagahot Maimoniot*, Constantinople edn., *Ishut*, 14:8, cites another responsum by R. Gershom on this matter, dealing with a man coerced to divorce his rebellious wife. Although some Tosafists wonder whether R. Gershom held that the husband is actually coerced to divorce, this responsum fully clarifies that R. Gershom did indeed endorse this view.

18 *BT Yevamot* 65a.

by the threat of a gradual decrease in her *ketubah*.[19] In contrast, the rebellious woman claiming, "he is repulsive to me" is not coerced to stay, and *Rashi* implies that the husband is coerced to divorce her.[20] Although this was the reading of *Rashi* prevailing among the Tosafists,[21] some understood him differently.[22] *Rashi* seems to have followed a course similar to that of Maimonides, who had relied on the talmudic ruling for coercing divorce in the case of the rebellious woman. R Samuel b. Meir (*Rashbam*), *Rashi*'s grandson, was even more explicit.[23] Ruling on a case in Paris in which a woman had rebelled against her husband, he stated that the man should be coerced to divorce.[24] Several other sages mentioned in the question, members of the Paris court, joined *Rashbam* in this responsum.

This responsum preceded a turning point in the rulings coercing the man to divorce his rebellious wife, for, when *Rashbam*'s verdict reached his brother, R. Tam, he, in the uncompromising style that was his trademark, vehemently rejected the ruling coercing the husband to divorce his rebellious wife. In the view of R. Tam, the two sources in halakhic literature widely adduced to justify coercion — the geonic ordinance and the reading of the Talmud — were completely inadequate. Rashi's interpretation of the Talmud, which was well-known to him, appeared mistaken to R. Tam, and he therefore concluded that nothing could be learned from the Talmud on this count. Regarding the geonic ordinance, R. Tam held that the Geonim had exceeded their authority when instituting ordinances of this type. He held that the authority to authorize suits coercing a husband to divorce his wife was confined to the talmudic sages; they had drawn up a closed list of grounds, and nothing should be added to it. Babylonian Geonim had no authority to legislate new grounds beyond those explicitly mentioned in the Talmud, hence his conclusion that a husband cannot be forced to divorce his rebellious wife.[25]

19 *Rashi*, *Ketubot* 63b, s.v. "*de-amrah ba'ena lei.*"

20 *Rashi*, *Ketubot* 63b, s.v. "*aval amrah me'is alai.*"

21 *Toṣafot*, *Ketubot* 63b, s.v. "*aval amrah me'is alai*" (at the opening). See also *Hagahot Maimoniot*, *Ishut*, 14:6.

22 *Toṣafot*, *Ketubot* 63b, s.v. "*aval amrah me'is alai*" (at the end). See also *Hagahot Maimoniot*, Constantinople edn., *Ishut*, 14:8.

23 *Ṭur*, *Even ha-Ezer*, ch.77.

24 *Ṣefer ha-Yashar*, Responsa Section, edited by Shragah Rosenthal (Berlin: n.p., 1898), sec.24.

25 This view of R. Tam is also mentioned in *Toṣafot*, *Ketubot* 63b, s.v. "*aval amrah me'is alai.*"

Echoes of R. Tam's criticism reached the South of France close to his times. R. Isaac b. Abba Mari of Marseilles, in the *Ṣefer ha-Ittur* (1179),[26] cites the geonic ordinance on the rebellious woman stating that "whatever she is holding is taken away from her, and he is coerced to give her a divorce immediately" and, by his testimony, "this was the practice for six hundred years." But he was already aware of R. Tam's view, and wrote as follows:

> R. Jacob's (=Tam's) innovation was that, according to the Talmud, the husband is not coerced to divorce against his will, but we do enforce coercion according to the later rabbinical ordinance, because all the rabbis agreed to this.[27]

R. Isaac accepted R. Tam's interpretation of the Talmud, preferring it to Rashi's. He rejected, however, R. Tam's position concerning the geonic ordinance and, unlike him, ruled that the Geonim had not exceeded their authority in their ordinance on the rebellious woman, which is fully valid.

R. Zeraḥiah ha-Levi Gerondi (*Razah*), also active in Provence, took a significant step toward adopting the approach represented by R. Tam. He wrote of the geonic ordinance on the rebellious woman cited by Alfasi, qualifying it as follows:

> The ordinance issued at the [geonic] academy, therefore, ruling that a divorce resting on a rebellious woman suit is granted immediately, was an emergency measure, due to circumstances they had witnessed in their times, but in later times we apply the talmudic ruling.[28]

Naḥmanides, who lived in the North of Spain and was active in the middle of the 13th century, considered R. Zeraḥiah's argument an elegant evasion, covering his patent opposition to the geonic ordinance.[29] In his novellae on the Talmud he writes:

> I would not, God forbid, dispute the geonic ordinance, for who am I to question and change a practice adopted by the Geonim from my rabbis.[30] Furthermore, I challenge those who claim that it is improper to follow their ordinance and that we should adopt talmudic law instead, and claim that we

26 Ephraim E. Urbach, *The Toṣafists* [Hebrew] (Jerusalem: Bialik Institute, 1986), 100.

27 *Ṣefer ha-Ittur*, under *Mered*, vol.1, 58d.

28 *Ha-Maor ha-Gadol, Ketubot* 63b, s.v. *katav ha-Rif zal, ha-din hu dina de-Gemara be-moredet.*

29 Naḥmanides, *Milḥamot Adonai*, *Ketubot* 27a, s.v. *katav ha-Rif ha-din hu dina de-Gemara.*

30 In another version: "for many years".

> should heed them and act according to their ordinance.[31]

Ultimately, however, he added the following sentence, which goes beyond his recommendation, stating, "presently, we must be very wary on this issue and refrain altogether from acting on this ordinance, which has already been rescinded because of the wantonness of the times."

Naḥmanides' approach was indeed helpful in facilitating the next step, namely, forbidding the use of the geonic ordinance altogether. R. Solomon b. Adret (*Rashba*), Naḥmanides' disciple, who, like his teacher, was active in Northern Spain in the last quarter of the thirteenth century and in the first decade of the fourteenth century, adopted this policy. His position was that the rebellious woman ground could not be used to justify coercion, neither according to talmudic law nor according to the geonic ordinance.

In locations where rulings tended to follow Maimonides or Alfasi who, as noted, had adopted the geonic ordinance on the rebellious woman, *Rashba* did not preclude adopting the rebellious woman ground. He writes

> In any event, if the custom in those places was to follow Maimonides, let them do so, because you know that the Geonim had also said that the husband is coerced to divorce his rebellious wife, and we have no strength to dispute or dismiss their views in those places that adopted them.[32]

*Rashba* appears to be referring here to various places in Castile or Southern Spain, such as the kingdom of Granada, where the tendency was to rely on the rebellious woman ground in their rulings. These areas, which were strongly influenced by Moslem culture or even directly under Moslem rule, were not yet ready to reject the rebellious woman ground, unlike areas in Northern Spain, which had long ago been conquered by Christians and where Christian culture was dominant.

There were probably intermediate areas between Northern Spain, where the rebellious woman ground was ruled out by the end of the thirteenth century, and Southern Spain, where it was still enforced in practice. In Toledo, for instance, the capital of Castile at the center of Spain, the rebellious woman ground was not eradicated *de jure*, but was no longer enforced.[33]

The rebellious woman ground underwent further and hastened erosion in Spain with the arrival of R. Asher b. Jeḥiel (*Asheri*), an Ashkenazi sage who

31 *Ketubot* 63b.

32 *Rashba*, *Responsa*, Part 2, sec.276.

33 *Asheri*, *Responsa*, ch.43, sec.13.

immigrated to Spain in 1305.[34] Upon his arrival, he found that the prevalent practice in the kingdom of Castile and in other places in Southern Spain was to coerce divorce on the rebellious woman ground. According to his testimony,

> from my arrival to this country, I have prevented them throughout the land of Castile from coercing any man to divorce his wife upon her saying that she does not want him.[35]

At some stage, he became involved in an intense controversy with a sage named R. Jacob Alfasi from the city of Cordoba, in Southern Castile, a city the Christians had conquered about fifty years previously.[36] R. Jacob Alfasi had issued a ruling coercing a man to divorce on the strength of a rebellious wife ground. *Asheri* opened by noting that "our teachers, the sages of Ashkenaz and France, go to the furthest extreme to avoid coercing divorce because they agree with R. Tam and his main arguments, and find it proper to rely on them."[37]

*Asheri* rejected Maimonides' approach, which had relied on his interpretation of the Talmud, and he also dismissed the geonic ordinance on the rebellious wife, as cited by Alfasi. Contrary to R. Tam, however, he did not question the very authority of the geonim to issue such an ordinance, and merely claimed that the ordinance was invalid in contemporary Spain, on two counts. The first was that the ordinance had not really taken root in Spain, and had only become known to Spanish Jews through Alfasi's books. Second, the ordinance had been meant to protect Jewish women, and "now it appears that the situation has turned; the daughters of Israel in this generation are impudent — hence, it is best to desist from coercion."

Contrary to *Rashba*, *Asheri* ordered Spanish Jews to accept R. Tam's view, and demanded that they desist from the practice of coercing husbands to divorce their rebellious wives. His approach was uncompromising, and he ruled, "all endeavors relying on this ground multiply bastards in Israel." But he could not ignore past episodes when men had been coerced to grant

34 Abraham H. Freiman, *Rosh: R. Asher b. Yeḥiel and his Descendants* [Hebrew], tr. from German Menahem Eldar (Jerusalem: Mossad Harav Kook, 1986), 29.

35 *Asheri*, *Responsa*, ch.43, sec.9.

36 Cordoba was conquered in 1236, and Seville in 1248. See L.P. Harvey, *Islamic Spain 1250 to 1500* (Chicago: University of Chicago Press, 1990), 11.

37 *Asheri*, *Responsa*, ch.43, sec.8. Parts of this section are inseparable from sec.9, and deal with the same question.

divorces following local custom. In such cases, his stance was that the children were not bastards, since "this is my ruling only for the future, but concerning the past, if they have relied on our teacher Moses, what is done is done." This is a surprising stance, extremely interesting from the perspective of legal theory, but beyond the scope of the present discussion.[38]

Spanish Jews were thereby denied the geonic ordinance as a legal source upon which they could rely to coerce divorce on the rebellious wife ground; they were only left with Maimonides' law, which from then on served as the most prevalent form of support among those seeking to preserve their older tradition.

*Rashba*'s disciple, R. Vidal de Tolosa, who wrote the *Maggid Mishneh* commentary on Maimonides' Code, was already more resolute in his opposition and adopted *Asheri*'s approach, perhaps even under the latter's influence.[39] At this time in Castile, R. Jacob b. Asheri, author of the *Ṣefer ha-Ṭurim*, ruled in favor of his father and against Maimonides.

The approach of these halakhists, however, did not close the matter. In last third of the fourteenth century, some communities in Spain were still following Maimonides in their rulings, after they had accepted his code as the compelling norm. The most prominent halakhists active in the kingdom of Aragon, such as R. Nissim Gerondi (*Ran*), who lived in Barcelona a generation later,[40] and R. Ephraim Vidal,[41] were not decisive and unequivocal in rejecting as invalid the ordinance concerning the rebellious woman.

The move from Aragon to Algeria of two prominent figures such as R. Isaac ben Sheshet Perfeṭ (*Ribash*) and R. Simeon Duran at the end of the fourteenth century brought them directly into contact with Jewish communities living in a distinctively Moslem environment where the rebellious wife suit was accepted without question. They engaged in a determined struggle to impose the legal tradition they had brought with them from Northern Spain and, for this purpose, they subverted the legal basis enabling the use of Maimonides' ruling by instating a qualifying ordinance. For *Ribash* this closed the issue, since he held that a divorce coerced on a

38 On this and on *Asheri*'s position on the rebellious woman see my article, "Judicial Decisions by Rabenu Asher b. Yeḥiel in Spain", in *Studies in Halakha and Jewish Thought Presented to R. Prof. Menachem Emanuel Rackman on his 80th Anniversary,* edited by Moshe Beer (Ramat Gan: Bar-Ilan University Press, 1994), 162-168.

39 *Maggid Mishneh, Laws of Marriage*, ch.8, sec.8.

40 *Teshuvot ha-RaN* (ed. Feldman (Jerusalem, 1984), sec.62.

41 *Tashbez, Responsa*, Part 2, sec.256.

claim of "repulsion" was invalid even *ex post factum*.[42] In contrast, R. Simeon left open a slim chance of implementing the rebellious woman ground if the woman married after obtaining a divorce on these grounds.[43] Possibly, in Algeria and elsewhere in North Africa, R. Simeon's position was accepted because his descendants also served in prominent rabbinical positions for several generations after him.

This ordinance by *Ribash* and R. Simeon not to follow Maimonides regarding the rebellious woman claiming "repulsion" persisted even two generations later, as attested by R. Simeon's grandson:

> Here, in Algeria, the original rabbis, our teachers *Ribash* and R. Simeon, agreed to follow the code of Maimonides except on three issues: on the rebellious woman claiming "he is repulsive to me."[44] ·

Neither Maimonides' high standing nor the fact that his ruling on the rebellious woman claiming "repulsion" was deeply entrenched in North African communities were sufficient to withstand the pressure of these two prominent halakhists, *Ribash* and R. Simeon, who brought the juridical tradition of Christian Spain to this typically Moslem environment.

The course of the process unfolding over several centuries is quite clear. The erosion in the rebellious woman ground proceeded along the two axes of time and space. As we move forward in time, the ground of the rebellious woman, which allows coercing the husband to grant a divorce, is progressively eroded — the further South we move, the later in time the erosion. To explain this development, let us consider the main point in the rebellious woman plea. The origins of this ruling, or at least its strong entrenchment, are clearly related to specific circumstances of time and place — the onset of the Moslem conquest of Babylon in the second half of the seventh century. Halakhic sources explicitly indicate that the aim of this ruling was to prevent malicious manipulations in Moslem courts that forced Jewish men to grant a divorce demanded by women claiming "repulsion."[45] We know that Moslem law acknowledges a law similar to the rebellious wife plea, and allows the wife to divorce her husband if a suitable clause was made part of the marriage contract. This step could reflect the influence of Moslem law, which had become dominant in Babylon and could also be a result of deliberate

42 *Ribash, Responsa*, sec.104.

43 *Supra* note 41.

44 *Responsa Yakhin U-Boaz*, Part 2, sec.23.

45 *Hilkhot ha-Rosh*, *Ketubot* 85, sec.35. Brody, "Were the Geonim Legislators?", *supra* n.10 at 295.

government interference designed to limit the authority of Jewish courts. In any event, the geonic ordinance clearly originated as a result of factors that, although directly affecting Jewish circumstances, were extraneous to *Halakhah*. The waning of the rebellious wife ground was not related to a single, defined event; rather, it moved along time and place in a protracted process that was not always linear.

I hold that the influence of the Gentile environment also affected the decline of the rebellious woman ground, ultimately leading to its abolition. This influence, however, is indirect, as Jewish society internalizes the social norms of the Gentile environment as a result of a prolonged encounter, and projects them onto Jewish law through a complex mutual relationship whose stages cannot be traced.[46] The external environmental factor is Christian society and its prevalent legal and social norms concerning marriage and divorce. R. Tam's view constellated as Christian society became monogamous and imposed Catholic laws making divorce impossible.[47] In these circumstances, it is very hard to uphold divorce claims raised by the husband — and it was indeed at this stage that R. Gershom's ban became a powerful legal factor — and even more so to uphold a blameless divorce initiated by the wife. From here onward, the process of erosion moved along the lines of advance of Christian society, which gradually conquered and dominated areas that had so far been under Moslem influence and control, at least in Spain.

46 In this vein, scholars resort to different versions of these terms, including environmental stimulus or inspiration, but this issue is beyond the scope of this paper.

47 J.A. Brundage, *Law, Sex, and Christian Society in Medieval Europe* (Chicago: University of Chicago Press, 1987), 176-228.

14

# MENTAL DISEASE IN DIVORCE LAW IN THE RESPONSA LITERATURE AND IN RABBINICAL COURT RULINGS IN ISRAEL

by

SAMUEL WOLFMAN*

## *Scope of the Paper*

Mental disease, especially in mild and moderate forms, not like most physical handicaps, can frequently be hidden from the surrounding society, even from close persons, in work, school etc. When it comes to matrimonial matters, such diseases can also be hidden from a future spouse. Consequently it is quite easy to conceive of a case where such a disease is uncovered only after marriage by the party from whom the disease was hidden.

Hidden handicaps are referred to in the Mishnah, as *mumin shebaṣeter,*[1] and Rav Naḥman, commentating on that Mishnah in the Talmud,[2] uses epilepsy as an example to illustrate such a hidden handicap. The similarity between epilepsy and mental diseases, lies in the fact that between attacks, patients can lead normal lives; thus the disease can be hidden, most of the time, from the community. The legal outcome can be a divorce claim, based on the bad faith bargain, *meḳaḥ ṭa'ut* principle, which may void the marriage bond.

* The author is a graduate of the Tel-Aviv University Law School and the Talmud Department at the Faculty of Jewish Studies and Humanities (MA) and is a research student (for Ph.D.) in the Talmud Department at the Faculty of Jewish Studies and Humanities, Tel-Aviv University. He serves as legal counsel and director of the medical-pharmaceutical division of Agis Industries (an Israeli pharmaceutical corporation).

1 Mishnah *Ketubot* 7:8.

2 *Ketubot* 76b-77a.

Mental disease in family life has some unique disrupting aspects on the marital bond, even more than physical handicaps, in the sense that it may disturb the basic emotional communication between the spouses. Additionally, the mentally ill spouse may, at times, be governed by uncontrollable urges and impulses, up to a point where the physical safety of other family members is compromised.

The issue of mental diseases is, unfortunately, not a remote or infrequent problem. The prevalence of major affective disorders -schizophrenia- in the general western population is 1%.[3] The average prevalence figures for major depression in medical publications vary in the medical epidemiological literature. According to some sources, such prevalence is between 2% and 17%,[4] while according to others, it ranges from 10-25% for women and 5-12% for men.[5]

As we are dealing with such a high prevalence, it is only reasonable to conclude that mental disturbances, as causes for divorce claims, are not at all remote anecdotal cases, but rather, are frequent causes of marriage breakups. The Halakhic sages had to deal with in many claims of this nature which were brought before them.

The issue of mental diseases in divorce law actually deals with two different topics: The first one, is the competence question, namely, is a divorce of or by a mentally ill person valid? The second topic deals with mental disease as marriage breaking and as a cause for divorce enforcement on the ill spouse.

Although this article will refer to the competence of the mentally ill person to marry and divorce, still, the main discussion will deal with the issue of mental disease as a cause for divorce enforcement.

### *Halakhic Terms for the Mentally Ill Person*

1. *Shoṭe'*: The most common halakhic term used to describe the mentally ill person is *shoṭe'*. It is different from the commonly used Hebrew word which has a very broad meaning in the spoken Hebrew language,

3 American Psychiatric Association, *Diagnostic and Statistical Manual of Mental Disorders - DSM IV*, American Psychiatric Association, 1994.

4 E. Edward Beckham, William R. Leber, *Handbook of Depression*, Second Edition (New York: The Guilford Press, 1995), 17.

5 M.M. Weissman et al., "Cross National Epidemiology of Major Depression and Bipolar Disorders," *Journal of the American Medical Association* (1996) 276-293.

referring to a stupid person or to a fool. This is the common Talmudic term found in the basic description of mental disease symptoms.[6]

2. *Ruaḥ Ḳetzara*[7] — Short tempered: Mentioned by the Talmud as a disqualifying handicap of the *Cohen* for serving in the temple; it is explained by Rashi in that passage as Devil's Mood.
3. *Ruaḥ Ra'a* — Evil Mood: Mentioned in the Talmud[8] and explained there by Rashi as insanity governed by the devil forces[9] or even by paranoiac drives[10]. Also, Evil Mood — *Ruaḥ Ra'a* — is found in the codification literature of Maimonides[11] and Ḳaro.[12]
4. *Etim Ḥalim Etim Shoṭe':*[13] This is a Talmudic description of a mentally relapsing/remitting state, where the sick person at times is perfectly normal and at other times is completely dissociated from reality.
5. *Bar Shaṭia:*[14] This is another Talmudic description of the mental patient who is at times disease-free in remission and is perfectly competent to perform commercial transactions, even sell all his assets. However when he is in a mental disease state, his actions are void and have no legal consequence.
6. *Sha'amumit / Meshu'amemet:*[15] The meaning of these two words is bored and indifferent. The Talmud refers to this diagnosis in regard to a slave girl who is sold to a new owner; *Rashi* there explains these terms as insanity.
7. *Ḳordiaḳoṣ*: This term is mentioned in a few Talmudic references. In the context of divorce it says,[16] "He who was seized by *ḳordiaḳoṣ* and said write and serve a *geṭ* to my wife, did not say anything."[17] As it seems,

6 *Ḥagiga* 3b. The detailed description of the *shoṭe'* will be elaborated below.

7 *Bekhorot* 44b.

8 In quite a few places such as in *Eruvin* 41b or in *Ta'anit* 22b.

9 *Eruvin* 41b.

10 *Ta'anit* 22b. *Rashi* does not use, of course, the term *paranoid*. However, the topic discussed there fits into such a description, as the issue deals with a person forced to run away by enemies or by *his own spirit*.

11 *Mishneh Torah, Gerushin* 2:14.

12 *Shulḥan Arukh, Even Ha'ezer* 121:1.

13 *Rosh Hashana* 28a.

14 *Yevamot* 31a.

15 *Baba Metzia* 80a.

16 *Giṭin* 67b.

17 Meaning that his saying (or his appointing a messenger for serving the *geṭ*) is void.

the reason for invalidation of that person's act is that he does not, at that time, have discretion and an understanding of reality, which are preconditions for a husband's competence to divorce his wife.

It is difficult, however, to draw a clear-cut conclusion, from that passage, that, although being dissociated from reality, *ḳordiaḳoṣ* is actually a mental disease. It is rather a temporary state described by Shmuel, in that passage, as a person, who drinks new wine from a vat and is overcome by *ḳordiaḳoṣ*, a demon, causing the symptoms. *Rashi*, in his commentaries on the passage, holds that it is a state of mind caused by excessive wine drinking.

Maimonides in his Mishnah commentary to this passage attributes the symptoms to overfilling of the brain chambers and refers to this syndrom as epilepsy.

In light of the above, *ḳordiaḳoṣ* should not be included in the mental disease terminology list. However, in light of the analogy with mental dissociative presenting symptoms, we found it appropriate to mention this syndrome.

A different approach can be found in an article published in the psychiatric literature of the last century,[18] where *ḳordiaḳoṣ* is perceived as delirium caused by organic brain syndrome.[19] Certainly, that is not temporary, but, rather, is a long-standing dissociative state of mind.

It should be mentioned that all the above terms and more, some very descriptive, are quoted in most of the commentaries, codes and responsa.

### *The Halakhic Definition of the Mentally Ill*

The initial description of the mentally ill person is illustrated in quite a few Talmudic sources, for example, in the Babylonian Talmud in *Ḥagiga*[20] and in the Jerusalem Talmud in *Terumot*[21] and in *Giṭin.*[22] According to the Baraita in *Ḥagiga,*[23] a person with mental illness behaves in a bizarre manner

18 L.D. Hankoff, M.D., *American Journal of Psychiatry* 129:2 (August, 1972), 147.

19 The term organic brain syndrome is very seldom used nowadays. The present term used in medicine is dementia.

20 *Ḥagiga* 3b-4a.

21 *Terumot* 2a.

22 *Giṭin* 38a.

23 The Baraita itself asks: "Who is the *shoṭe'*?" without specifying the

in three forms: He walks outside at night all by himself; he sleeps overnight in the graveyard[24] and he rends/tears his clothes.

The Talmudic sages Rav Huna and Rav Yoḥanan debate whether, for the purpose of definition, all above three behaviors need to be exercised by that person, or whether a person can be declared insane if only one bizarre behavior is practiced by him.

Rav Papa, in that passage, adds a fourth possible form from another Baraita: "Who is a *shoṭe*'? He who loses/destroys/wastes[25] what people give him."

Maimonides,[26] when discussing the testimonial competence of witnesses, defines the incompetent *shoṭe'* in the following manner: "He is not only as one who has bizarre manners, such as walking naked, breaking appliances and throwing stones, but is also, as anybody who is insane with his mind, always distorted at least in one area, although he may talk like a normal person on other matters."

It is interesting to note that Maimonides includes in the list of the incompetent witnesses, not only the insane, but also the epileptic, as well as the fool and the hasty. However, the common denominator for all is that all of them should present some degree of insanity and/or incompetence in matters requiring discretion.

Also, it should be noted, that Maimonides did not list any of the four symptoms mentioned above in *Ḥagiga*, but mentioned three other behavioral patterns and referred more to general patterns. Some of the commentators, such as R. Joseph Ḳaro in *Bet Yoṣef*[27] already noted it. It seems that R. Ḳaro gathered that the conclusion to be drawn from that deviation of Maimonides is that the list in *Ḥagiga*, is not a closed list, but rather serves as an example.

It is also important to note the concluding sentence in Maimonides'

---

relevance for which this question is asked. However, *Rashi* there does refer to that topic when he explains that the relevance is the question of personal competence for *Mitzvot* (no liability in transgressions) as well as of competence for commercial transactions.

24 Being oblivious to the danger of lurking spirits.

25 The direct translation of the Talmud word "*me'a'bed*" means to lose; however, the actual meaning of this symptom may be more in the area of wasting what he is given by people.

26 *Mishneh Torah*, *Edut* 9:9-10.

27 *Bet Yoṣef, Ḥoshen Mishpaṭ* 35:8.

statement,[28] where he states that "all of the above symptoms cannot be described in a comprehensive manner in writing, as the mental state should be determined in the end by the presiding *dayan.*"

Based on the above, it is quite clear that the *halakhah*, prior to discussing the material rules relevant to the mentally ill person, tries to clarify first, who is that *Shoṭe'*, that insane, mentally ill person. Also it is obvious that insanity and mental incompetence are not at all easily defined.

When addressing the issue of mental disease in divorce law, it should be noted that in each case brought before the sages, there is a preliminary question, which usually does not exist when dealing with physical handicaps. This question needs to be answered before any halakhic debate is undertaken. The question to be asked, when dealing with a divorce motion due to mental reasons, is does the said person suffer from a mental disease, or is it merely a behavioral malfunction or behavioral disturbance with no effect on the cognitivity or discretionary ability of the person.

Also, it should be born in mind that this difficult issue was faced not only by the halakhic sages. Even modern psychiatry cannot, in some cases, come to a consensus on this matter. This is reflected in medical papers and in opinions of experts in courts about questions of temporary insanity, uncontrollable urges or regarding the question of forced mental hospitalization. An example of this difficulty, can be demonstrated by examining the symptom of losing things which is mentioned in the basic definition in *Ḥagiga.* Is it really a psychiatric disorder, or is it dementia either of the Alzheimer type or perhaps just senile dementia?

### *Mental Disease and Competence to Marry*

Although, the main problematic area of insanity in family law is the divorce issue, one has to bear in mind that the basic problem of lack of discretion starts already at the marriage stage. Indeed, this issue may be less of a practical problem, due to the fact, that in most cases, an obvious disease and noticeable symptoms will prevent the "normal" party to engage in such wedlock in the first place.

On the other hand, when it is a case of a hidden disease, intentionally or in good faith,[29] then the problem may pop out sometime soon after the

28 *Supra* n.27 at 35:10.

29 A disease could be concealed from a future spouse by intention. On the other hand, some diseases may have masked symptoms so that they are concealed

marriage, or in other cases, only at a very late stage, so again it becomes a divorce problem. In this context it is well addressed in the *Mishneh Torah*, in the *Ṭur*, in the *Shulḥan Arukh*, as well as in the responsa.

A good and thorough discussion can be found in a responsum of R. Yitsḥaḳ Elḥanan Spector, chief Rabbi of Kovna in the 19th century.[30] The question dealt with there is the validity of the *geṭ* of a mentally ill husband. In this case the *geṭ* was approved by a rabbinical court which was not aware of the fact that the husband had been psychotic and severely depressed and had a history of mental hospitalization even during his marriage period. This sage indeed approved the discontinuation of the marriage and the release of the woman to marry, based on two arguments:

The first was the ratification of the *geṭ* due to the fact that the husband had many remission periods. In fact, most days he was in remission, and majority overrules minority. In consequence, the *geṭ* was valid, as the husband had the required discretion needed for divorce.

The second and more interesting argument, was the actual voidance of the marriage retroactively due to the incompetence of the *Shoṭe'*, the insane person, to marry.

Indeed, there is a doubt, when judging, retroactively, the mental condition of a person at the time and moment of the wedding. However, in that case, there was some testimonial evidence that, at the time of the wedding, the husband behaved somewhat strangely and he looked (the expression in the responsum is "shining eyes"), to a certain extent, like an insane person.

On the other hand, the bride, at the time of the wedding, still had the unmarried status presumption (*ḥezḳat pnuia*), therefore, her non-doubtful presumption overweighs his doubtful ability to marry due to incompetence.

The consequence, in that case, was that the woman remained in her non-married status and the marriage was void.

### *Legal Competence of a Mentally Ill Person to Divorce*

The strict uncompromized halakhic rule which is rooted in the Torah — *De'oraita* — requires that the act of divorce, in particular the handing over or servicing of the *geṭ*, is preconditioned with the absolutely free will of the *geṭ*

---

from the future spouse in good faith, as even the sick person may not be aware of his disease at the early stages.

30 R. Yitsḥaḳ Elḥanan Spector, *Sh'elot Ut'shuvot Ein Yitsḥaḳ*, 2 (The Responsa Project, Bar-Ilan University, Version 8, 2000), *Even Ha'ezer* 7.

server, the husband. Without such free will the *geṭ* is considered a *geṭ*-under-coercion, a *geṭ me'oo'ṣe'*, and is not valid at all.

This rule, that the husband must have free-will, has however some exceptions, which are discussed in the Mishnah and in the Talmud in *Ketubot* Chapter 7, *Ha'me'dir*. It lists two diseases/handicaps of the husband as sufficient enough reasons to force him to divorce his wife.[31]

The first disease is "*sheḥin*", which is already mentioned as one of the ten plagues brought upon Pharaoh in Egypt, and represents a severe, repulsive skin disease similar to psoriasis or leprosy.[32]

The other disease is termed as "*polipos*" and is regarded by the Talmudic commentators as very severe bad breath.

Therefore, in the case of such exceptions, the husband is allegedly forced to divorce his wife, even when he does not want to do so. It is important to note, however, that despite the *halakhah* in this Mishnah, in practice it is not an easy procedure to follow, and the halakhic sages throughout the generations tried to limit such forcing of husbands to the most extreme and exceptional cases.

However, the general free will requirement is the basic prevailing rule, that is, that the *Bet Din* not approve a divorce unless it is convinced that there is the free consent of the husband.

After Rabenu Gershom's *ḥerem*, the wife's consent as well, was considered a precondition for the divorce.

Consequently, it is difficult from a halakhic point of view, to validate a divorce when either of the parties is dissociated from reality and cannot exercise the necessary discretion.

This rule is debated in the Talmud, in *Yevamot.*[33] The Mishnah states that "when a woman becomes insane, the husband cannot divorce her, and when the husband becomes deaf or insane, he cannot divorce her forever.

The Talmud, when discussing this Mishnah, concludes that in actuality, the problematic issue is only when the husband is dissociated from the discretion necessary for *geṭ* servicing. As for the woman, at least before R. Gershom, there is no need for her discretion or consent for receiving the *geṭ*. However, due to an ordinance of the sages, (*taḳanat ḥakhamim*) the insane wife is not sent away. This ordinance was instituted, in order to protect her

31 *Mishnah* 7.

32 Although it is certain that *sh'ḥin* is a severe skin disease, the exact nature of *sh'ḥin*, or its connection to a modern defined disease, has not yet been fully determined by sages or doctors.

33 *Yevamot* 112b.

from abuse by immoral persons who might take advantage of her poor discretion and her inability to judge reality.

Abaye explains that this conclusion can be derived from the phrasing of the Mishnah: "cannot divorce" is used in reference to an insane wife, whereas "cannot divorce her forever" is used in the case of the insane husband. Accordingly, in the case of the husband, it is a Torah rule (*de'oraita*) that when the husband is insane, he cannot divorce *forever,* but in the case of the wife, the Mishnah does not use the word forever, meaning that, in fact, there is a possibility according to the Torah, of divorcing her without her will; however the sages made an ordinance (*taḳanat ḥakhamim*) preventing it.

The above had been codified in the *Mishneh Torah* of Maimonides[34] as well as in the *Shulḥan Arukh* of R. Ḳaro[35] The rule is set by Maimonides as follows: "It is the sages' ordinance that the husband of an insane woman cannot divorce her until she recovers since she is not able to protect herself against abuse by the immoral. Therefore, he should let her stay married to him and provide her with food (alimony), while he is allowed to marry another woman. On the other hand, he is relieved from his other marital obligations to her as a sane person cannot live with the insane in the same house."

It seems from the above, that mental disease or insanity, can bring marriage life to a deadlock when the insane party is in a state of constant dissociation from the surrounding environment and is not able to judge reality.

Indeed, when the wife is the sick spouse, there is always the solution suggested by Maimonides and adopted by quite a few sages along the generations, namely, that the husband is allowed to marry another woman. However, when it is the husband, who is in a constant state of dissociation from reality, then it is very difficult to find a halakhic solution that will release the wife from her sick husband's bonds.

All the above, refers to a constant dissociative state of mind. However, the issue of mental diseases in marital life, is quite different when the nature of the disease is of the progressive-remitting type. In this case, the diseased person has periods of remissions, when his behavior is quite normal, enabling him to use discretion like any other normal person. This is the situation called *etim ḥalim ve'etim shoṭe'* in the halakhic literature.

As patients in such periods of remission function with full understanding

34 *Mishneh Torah, Gerushin* 10:23.

35 *Shulḥan Arukh, Even Ha'ezer* 119:6.

of reality and are fully competent, they can use their discretion to consent to the divorce process, both to service or to receive the *geṭ*, thus fulfilling the basic free will halakhic requirement.

The issue that arises in these cases submitted to the sages is the question of whether or not to accept the divorce claim of a healthy person to force a divorce on a mentally ill spouse since life with the ill spouse, during the mentally-ill period, can become simply unbearable.

It should be noted that the above, including the definition of *shoṭe'*, refer to major affective disorders (mostly represented by schizophrenia), when the ill person is totally dissociated and has no reality perception.

However there is also that other group of mental diseases which raises similar questions, the non- dissociative diseases such as depression, anxiety, panic disorders, obsessive-compulsive disorders, etc. The characteristic feature of these diseases is that the ill person is fully aware to his disease, but cannot help himself. That is contrary to the dissociated person who lives in his own imaginary world and is not aware at all that his world is not the real one. These non-dissociative diseases are considered "soft" mental ailments, or neurosis (as opposed to psychosis). Nevertheless they may present as well a major threat to family life.

It is true that the severity of the disturbance in these cases may be different and significantly reduced compared to diseases such as schizophrenia. However, according to medical literature, the overall lifetime prevalence of major depressive disorders is 10-25% for women and 5-12% for men[36] (referring to all levels of severity).[37] Consequently, it is easy to understand that depressive disorders may, as well, represent a significant portion of the mental disease problem in halakhic divorce law. Here, the question is not so much in the area of discretion, reality understanding, or legal competence. The problem in this case is whether the *halakhah* can allow divorce enforcement, when the mental disease, though not dissociative, makes life with the sick spouse unbearable.

### *Non Pre-marriage Disclosure of Mental Diseases in the Mishnah and the Talmud: Bad Faith — meḳaḥ ṭa'ut*

The issue of a bad faith bargain — *meḳaḥ ṭa'ut* — which is mostly

36 See above note 5.

37 According to this source, the prevalence of *very severe* depression of the bipolar type ranges between 0.4% and 1.6% in the general population.

raised with regard to commercial matters, may also present serious consequences in the validation or ratification of the marriage bond. This is due to the fact that, according to *halakhah*, a precondition for the validity of a marriage is the consent of the husband to marry that particular wife as presented to him, as well as her consent to marry that particular husband as presented to her. The mental illness of a spouse revealed only after marriage, may provide a reason for a claim of false representation and that the party had not consented to marry such a handicapped person. This issue, although not specifically referred to as a mental disease, is addressed in the Mishnah in *Ketubot,*[38] which deals with the general issue of the wife's handicaps, and a husband's claim of a bad bargain, "*mekaḥ ṭa'ut.*"

The rule is that if the handicap had been known to the husband before the wedding, then he is estopped from claiming a bad bargain. However, if it is a hidden handicap, one of which he could not have been aware of before the wedding, "*mum she'baṣeter,*" then, indeed, he could claim that he had been the victim of a bad bargain. Rav Naḥman, in the Talmud,[39] brings epilepsy — "*nikhpe*'" — as an example of a handicap that a person could conceal from his spouse before the marriage.[40]

The analogy to mental disease is quite obvious, be it a major affective disease of the remitting/relapsing type, or be it one of the non-psychotic "softer" diseases, such as depression, anxiety, obsessive-compulsive or panic disorders. The common denominator in all of these diseases, like in the case of *nikhpe'*, is that it is quite easy to conceal them before the wedding, but through daily living with one's spouse, they come to light.

Another Mishnah in *Ketubot*[41] presents the mistaken consent rule by stating that a precondition to a marriage, set by the husband, that the wife has no handicaps, voids the marriage when such is revealed later on. However, a marriage without such an explicit precondition does not void the marriage, but, rather, serves as a reason for divorcing the wife without paying

38 *Mishnah, Ketubot* 7:8.

39 *Ketubot* 76b.

40 Most of the time, most epileptic patients lead normal lives while the epileptic seizures which appear occasionally in attacks are quite spaced from each other. *Rashi*, in that Talmud passage, adds to Rav Naḥman's statement that the epileptic attacks appear in regular known periods (in fact, the epileptic patient may have a prodromal period when he feels the imminent attack before it appears) so that he can avoid the presence of people when the attack takes place.

41 *Ketubot* 7:7.

her *ketuba*.

As for the definition of such handicaps, the Mishnah refers to a list of handicaps which disqualify a *Cohen* from serving at the temple services as detailed in another Mishnah in *Bekhorot*.[42]

It should be noted, that mental diseases, or *shoṭe'*, are not specifically listed as *Cohen* handicaps in that *Bekhorot* Mishnah. However, the Mishnah list refers to "short mood" or "short tempered", explained by *Rashi*, as "devil's mood", which can be interpreted as insanity. It is possible that the Mishnah refers to psychotic phenomena where the *Cohen* hears "devil's voices".

In conclusion, according to the Mishnah, a mental disease, which a woman had contracted before her wedding and was revealed only after the marriage, may, allegedly, serve as a reason, either for complete voidance of the marriage, or for divorcing her, without paying her *Ketuba*.

*Talmudic Differences between Husband and Wife in Regard to Mental Diseases*

The above selection from the Mishnah deals only with case of the handicapped wife. However, a different set of rules applied when the husband is the mentally ill spouse. The basic difference between the husband and wife in divorce rules, before the ordinance of Rabenu Gershom (*ḥerem*) was issued, was that the precondition for divorce by spousal consent applied only to the husband serving the *geṭ*. Consequently, at that tine, a *geṭ* could not be forced on the husband against his will, whereas the will of the wife did not play a role; thus, in the period before R. Gershom, a *geṭ* could be forced on her.[43]

Accordingly, if a husband, under the court's coercion, served his wife a *geṭ*, the divorce was void, or at least doubtful, so that if the woman remarried, her new marriage was sinful and the children of that second union, were "*mamzerim*".

Following this rule, another Mishnah in *Ketubot*[44] referred to a husband who contracted handicaps after marriage. This Mishnah stated clearly that he should not be forced to divorce his wife.

It should be noted, however, that the above basic rule, namely, that the husband should not be forced to divorce his wife, was not a consensus. In

42 *Mishnah Bekhorot* 7 (the entire chapter).

43 *Mishneh Torah, Gerushin* 1:1-2.

44 *Mishnah Ketubot* 7:9.

fact, the Mishnah presents a disagreement between the sages regarding a possible exception to this rule in the case of major handicaps (*mumim gedolim*) where R. Shimon ben Gamliel does allow such enforcement.[45]

The Talmud explains and gives representative examples of major handicaps such as blindness, amputated arms or broken legs.

Comparing this Mishnah,[46] with the Mishnah mentioned above where, in the case of exceptional conditions, the husband could be forced,[47] one may notice a common denominator: the list of handicaps refers only to physical ones. There is no reference to mental diseases of the husband.

The fact that mental diseases are not mentioned at all in the above two Mishnayot, may point to two conclusions:

1. The Talmud does not regard mental diseases as major handicaps, neither like *sh'ḥin* or *polipos*[48] which may justify divorce enforcement on the husband, nor even like a broken leg, which, according to R. Shimon ben Gamliel, may be a good reason to force the husband.
2. There is a distinction between the husband and wife with regard to mental diseases. According to the previous conclusion, there are no circumstances, even according R. Shimon ben Gamliel, when mental disease could serve as a cause for divorce. However when referring to a wife's handicaps, the former Mishnah[49] states that all handicaps disqualifying a *Cohen* for Temple services, as set in the Mishnah in *Bekhorot,*[50] are also considered handicaps which allow divorcing the wife.
3. In summary, as far as Talmudic law is concerned, mental diseases are

45 The commentators in the Talmud debate the question as to whether the final rule (*halakhah*) is according to R. Shimon ben Gamliel or according to most of the sages — *ḥakhamim* — opposing him, namely, that there is no way to force the husband to divorce, even when he is the one who has contracted those major handicaps.

46 See above note 44.

47 *Mishnah Ketubot* 7:10, regarding the two diseases/handicaps of the husband, *sh'ḥin* and *polipos*, which are sufficient reasons to force him to divorce his wife.

48 Some Rishonim (R. Ya'aḳov ben Meir Tam, France 1100-1171 [Rabenu Tam], R. Asher ben Yeḥiel, France and Spain 1250-1327 [the *Rosh*]) regard these two diseases as a rigid closed list that rules out any other handicap or disease.

49 See above note 41.

50 See above note 42.

not regarded as major handicaps in the case of the husband, but they are considered marriage breaking handicaps, when the mentally ill person is the wife.

*Mental Illness As a Cause for Divorce in the Post-Talmudic Era*

One of the first guiding references, cited in almost every responsum dealing with this issue, are the words of R. Asher b. Yeḥiel (the *Rosh*).[51] He dealt with the case of a woman who requested a divorce due to the insanity of her husband which progressed to the point of jeopardizing her physical safety. Also she claimed, that he might regress into a dissociative state, and she then would become an a*gunah* forever.[52]

The *Rosh*'s ruling refers to the Mishnah in *Ketubot* discussed in the previous chapter;[53] he regards *sh'ḥin* and *polipos* mentioned there as a closed list of handicaps serving as a reason for divorce enforcement on the husband. Also, the *Rosh* cites another Mishnah in the same chapter stating that "a husband, who contracted handicaps, should not be forced to divorce his wife."[54]

All of the above, brings the *Rosh* to the conclusion that, in that case, the husband should not be forced to grant a divorce. As for the wife's problem, he suggests that either the wife use all of her persuasive talents to convince the husband to divorce her by consent, or that she accept him with his disease and consume his assets.

It is obvious, that the *Rosh* holds that husband's mental disease is not a strong enough reason to force divorce upon him, as insanity is not included in the closed list of handicaps in the Mishnah in *Ketubot*.

However, R. Joseph Trani (the *Ma'Ha'Rit*),[55] when dealing with a question about epilepsy, found a contradictory ruling by the *Rosh*,[56] one in

51 R. Asher ben Yeḥiel, *Sh'elot Ut'shuvot Ha'Rosh* (The Responsa Project, Bar-Ilan University, Version 8, 2000), 43:3.

52 Since he may lose completely the ability for discretion and free will. Also see *supra* note 25 at 4, regarding the *Mishnah* in *Yevamot*: "When the husband becomes insane, he cannot divorce his wife forever."

53 *Mishnah Ketubot* 7:10.

54 *Mishnah Ketubot* 7:9.

55 R. Joseph Trani, Zfat-Kushta (Turkey), 1568-1639, *Sh'elot Ut'shuvot Ma'Ha'Rit* (The Responsa Project, Bar-Ilan University, Version 8, 2000), 1:113.

56 *Sh'elot Ut'shuvot Ha'Rosh*, 42 (the entire *Klal*).

which the *Rosh* ruled that epilepsy is a sufficient reason for a husband to be forced to grant a *geṭ*, even though it is not included in that closed list of the above Mishnah.

Therefore, the *Ma'Ha'Rit*, concludes, that indeed the *Rosh* holds that insanity, like epilepsy, is a good enough reason for husband *geṭ* enforcement, since both are major handicaps (*mumim gedolim*). According to the *Ma'Ha'Rit*, that conclusion may be deduced from the fact that even bad breath, which is much less severe than insanity, is a *geṭ* enforcement reason.

As for the above mentioned responsum, where, allegedly, the *Rosh* ruled categorically against *geṭ* enforcement, *Ma'Ha'Rit* holds that that case dealt not with real insanity, but rather with a bad cultured, bad tempered and mindless husband. Such a "handicap", as much as it disturbs marriage life, cannot be considered a major disease and therefore cannot serve as good enough reason for *geṭ* enforcement on the husband.

In spite of the above, the *Ma'Ha'rit* himself, in his concluding remarks in that responsum, opined that in light of the severity of the matter, it is best to avoid enforced divorce[57] of the epileptic or of the insane. He also refers to R. Eliezer b. Joel Halevi (the *Ra'Bi'ia*)[58] who holds categorically, that insanity is not a sufficient enough reason for such enforcement, since it is not included in the Mishnah list.

Many sages do not accept that *Rosh* ruling as interpreted by the *Ma'Ha'rit*.

The *Shulḥan* Arukh[59] cites the above-mentioned *Rosh* progressive insanity case and rules, very clearly, that the husband should not be forced to divorce, as insanity is not within the closed list of *geṭ* enforcement handicaps.

Two other Rishonim, the *Ra'Bi'ia* and R. Mordekhai b. Hillel (the *Mordekhai*), mentioned also in the commentary on the *Shulḥan Arukh* by R. Moses Isserles (the *Rema*),[60] and cited also by R. Moses Ṣofer (the *Ḥatam Ṣofer*),[61] although dealing with epilepsy, rule that any handicap not included

57 He uses the wording: "Every person should run away from divorce enforcement, like one who is running away from a snake."

58 See below notes 60-61 and the relevant text.

59 *Shulḥan Arukh Even Ha'Eżer* 154:5: "A person who develops a very bizarre daily behavior and his wife asks for divorce enforcement on him due to her fear that he might kill her in his madness, must not be forced to divorce, as his case is not included within the closed list of the sages."

60 There, in that passage in *Even Ha' Ezer.*

61 R. Moshe Ṣofer, 1762-1839, *Sh'elot Ut'shuvot Ḥatam Ṣofer* (The Responsa

in the closed Mishnah list cannot serve as a reason for *geṭ* enforcement on a husband. Consequently, these two Rishonim, are cited by quite a few *poṣḳim*, including the *Ḥatam Ṣofer* who holds that mental diseases cannot serve as sufficient enough reason for *geṭ* enforcement on the husband, since they are not included in the Mishnah list.

Another reference for the divorce claim of a wife due to a mental disease of the husband, is Maimonides, who is cited quite often in the responsa literature dealing with this issue. It should be noted that Maimonides does not refer directly to the issue of husband *geṭ* enforcement due to mental disease, since his *halakhah* deals with the general issue of divorce enforcement due to repulsion — *me'iṣ alai*. Accordingly, Maimonides[62] sets the rule that a repulsion claim by the wife is a legitimate claim, which should be acknowledged, accepted and consequently used to enforce a divorce on a husband[63].

One of the most frequent, almost always built-in arguments, used in divorce claims due to mental disease, is the claim of repulsion, *me'iṣ alai*. Therefore, it is easy to understand why the above general *halakhah* of Maimonides[64] is cited by many scholars as a *geṭ* enforcement reference in such cases.

As for the claim of a husband for divorce enforcement on his mentally ill wife, the debate is between either strict adherance to R. Gershom's *ḥerem* and not enforcing a *geṭ* on her in any case, or accepting his claim due to the fact that he is repulsed and cannot live with her anymore, like the case of the repulsed wife.

Another solution, in the case of a husband whose wife is mentally ill, which is suggested by quite a few sages,[65] is to allow the husband to marry

---

Project, Bar-Ilan University, Version 8, 2000), 3, *Even Ha'ezer* 1:116.6.

62 *Mishneh Torah, Ishut* 14: 8.

63 The *halakhah* there states the following: "The wife who deprives her husband of sexual relations is called a rebellious wife. If, when asked the reason for her rebelling, she says that she is repulsed by him and cannot have intimate relations with him, the husband is forced to divorce her since she is not his prisoner and cannot be forced to have sexual relations with a person she hates."

64 In fact, Maimonides was not the first to set this rule. Long before him, during the period of the Geonim, Rav Sherira set the rule of divorce enforcement on a husband whose wife did not want to live with him. See Benjamin Lewin, *Otzar HaGe'onim, Ḥeleḳ Ha'teshuvot, Ketubot* 191-192.

65 Mostly Sefardim who did not accept R. Gershom's *ḥerem*.

another woman. That is also in line with the Talmud in *Yevamot* and Maimonides in Divorce law, which approve such a solution when the wife is totally insane and cannot exercise discretion.[66] It should be emphasized, however, that the sages did not often exercise this solution of approval for marriage with another woman, and especially not in cases when the wife is in a remitting/relapsing state and can perfectly well use discretion when she is not under a psychotic attack.

In summary: The debate regarding the question as to whether a mental disease should be regarded as a major handicap (*mum gadol*), severe enough for divorce enforcement, dates back already to the period of the Rishonim (*Rosh*, *Ra'Bi'ia*, *Mordekhai*, *Ma'Ha'rit* and Maimonides). The above discussed rulings of the Rishonim have been cited in the responsa literature throughout the generations, even up to the present time, as will be discussed below.

### *Non Dissociative Mental Diseases in Divorce Law in the Responsa Literature*

Non dissociative mental disorders, such as depression and anxiety, are charachterized by the fact, that the ill person has full awareness of reality and his mental competence is not damaged. Moreover, in most of the cases, though he may be fully aware of his mental problem, he is not able to overcome his presenting symptoms, be they excessive worries and fears in anxiety, or inner urges, including obsession and compulsion which are regarded as part of depression.

The Talmud itself, in *Ḥagiga*,[67] when debating whether a *shoṭe'* needs to fulfill all three bizarre behavioral criteria to be considered insane, proposes that if only one strange behavior is evident, then perhaps that person could not be declared as *shoṭe'* since there might be a good reason, other than insanity, for that bizarre behavior.

One of the bizarre behavior patterns of the *shoṭe'* is that "he walks outside at night all by himself." The Talmud gives a possible reason for that person's behavior; it is due to "gandripas". *Rashi*, in his commentary on the passage, says that, according to what he heard, *gandripas* is an anxiety

66 In fact, R. Gershom's *ḥerem* includes also the prohibition to marry two women. However the sages who rule for such a solution, hold that the *ḥerem* is lifted in such a case. See below at the section on court rulings.

67 *Supra* note 23 at 4 and related text.

disease.[68] Consequently, one could argue that indeed, non-dissociative disorders are referred to in the Talmud; however they are not considered mental diseases.

The responsa literature, or at least the responsa of the Rishonim, does not differentiate between major affective disorders, where the person is totally or partially dissociated from reality, and minor "softer" diseases, such as depression and anxiety, where the person is fully aware of his disease, but cannot overcome his inner urges.[69]

Accordingly, one can find in quite a few responsa, descriptions of depressed[70] or agitated persons who are defined by the halakhic sage as insane, without differentiating those cases from those of the dissociative, reality-remote persons.

An example of the above can be found in the responsum of the *Rosh* cited above.[71] That responsum deals with the case of a woman who claims that her husband suffers from progressive foolishness and madness, and the *Rosh* rules that the husband should not be forced to divorce his suffering wife.

However the *Ma'Ha'Rit*, explains that in fact it is not insanity but rather a case of bad temper or of a problematic personality.

Still the *Rosh* regards this case as madness.

It can be deduced from the above, that any disease which is not real insanity, such as anxiety or depression, is not a sufficient reason for *geṭ* enforcement.

In should be noted, however, that as far as the personal competence to marry and divorce is concerned, the attitude of the *halakhah* towards the mental patient, still differs between dissociative and non-dissociative persons.[72]

68 It should be noted, however, that eventually, *Rashi* explains that "*gandripas*" is excessive body temperature, so that that person is not insane at all. All he wanted is to walk outside in the cold night temperature to cool himself, a perfectly sane and normal behaviour.

69 The modern terminology will appear only in very modern responsa as well as in the 20th century rabbinical courts rulings which already adopted modern medical terminology.

70 In fact, even the original symptoms described in the *Mishnah* in *Ḥagiga* (see note 23) such as walking alone at night or sleeping in the graveyard, may refer to depression and not necessarily to a psychosis.

71 *Sh'elot Ut'shuvot Ha'Rosh* (The Responsa Project, Bar-Ilan University, Version 8, 2000), #42.

72 The differentiation is between the person who is in constant dissociation

In contrast to the responsa of the Rishonim, there is a reference to the "very sad" or depressed patient in the late responsa literature, mostly from the *Ḥatam Ṣofer* period.[73]

The *Ḥatam Ṣofer*[74] describes a divorce claim against a husband who lost a lot of money, defining him as a "melancholic" or "black bile", *mara sh'ḥora*. It seems to be a description of a reactive depression case,[75] resulting from the financial loss.

Although that case deals with the wife's request for a divorce due to the depressive/melancholic state of her husband, still the *Ḥatam Ṣofer* discusses also the question of the husband's competence. In such a case, he gathers that even if the person does act strangely, as long as he can exercise discretion, and as long as he talks and answers with logic and sense, then he is like any other sane person. The outcome of that case had been a non-enforcement ruling, and the wife's claim to force her husband to serve her a *geṭ* was denied.

This *Ḥatam Ṣofer* responsum is quoted and discussed in many late responsa as well as in rabbinical court rulings.

One such interesting responsum of the present generation was written by R. Eliezer Waldenberg, a former *dayan* at the rabbinical high court in Jerusalem. In his collection of responsa *Tzitz Eliezer,*[76] he comments on the *Ḥatam Ṣofer* responsum, deducing from its wording that the case described in the *Ḥatam Ṣofer* responsum, is a "sad mood" case that had not yet progressed into full blown insanity. According to *Tzitz Eliezer*, mere fear of a progression of the "Sad Mood" into insanity still does not justify *geṭ* enforcement – which is the actual rational of the *Ḥatam Ṣofer* ruling.

However, full blown insanity, as well as a person who is under remission but had suffered proven insanity attacks in the past, is considered by R. Waldenberg to be subject to a major handicap and such a husband should be forced to divorce his wife.

The interesting part in that responsum is that it can be gathered from it that this *poṣeḳ* regards "sad mood" or depression, at least in some cases, as a

---

from reality, who can never be competent and the mental remitting/relapsing person, who is fully competent while he is in remission.

73 End 18th-beginning 19th century (1762-1839).

74 *Sh'elot Ut'shuvot Ḥatam Ṣofer* 4, *Even Ha'Ezer* 2.

75 The *Ḥatam Ṣofer* elaborates on the sadness of that person, causing him rage and odd behavior.

76 *Sh'elot Ut'shuvot Tzitz Eliezer* (The Responsa Project, Bar-Ilan University, Version 8, 2000), 6:42, *Orḥot Mishpaṭim*.

preliminary stage of insanity. Accordingly, his wording leads to the conclusion that depression is a progressive disease that may progress eventually into a full blown mental, dissociative disease.

Another "black bile" case is described by R. Shalom Mordekhai Ha'Cohen Shevadron (the *Ma'Harsham*) in the 19th century.[77] In his responsum,[78] *Ma'Harsham* describes a very depressed person who, at times, is very self centered and has difficulties even with talking. Here too, the debate is not so much regarding the depression as a cause for divorce, but rather one of checking the competence of that depressed person to serve the *geṭ*. The *Ma'Harsham* discusses the particular features of that case in a way that leads to the conclusion that all presenting symptoms of that depressed person, including talking to himself, still do not make him incompetent as he can use discretion.

A third example for depression in the responsa literature, is a case described at the beginning of the 20th century by *Nose' Ha'efod*.[79] The case described in this responsum,[80] deals with depression caused probably by progressive blindness. That person is described as one who repeats sentences and talks about irrelevant matters. Here too, the term is "black bile" *mara sh'ḥora*. The ruling in this case, refers to the responsum of the *Ḥatam Ṣofer*[81] and states that, although a "black bile" person is very sad and moody, still as long as he can use discretion, he is competent to serve a *geṭ*.

In summary: Depression has been described in the responsa of last 200 years as a very severe sadness called "black bile", *mara she'hora*. The debate of the scholars is whether such depression diminishes the personal competence of the ill person for marriage or divorce.

As it seems, most of the sages agree that the mere fact that a person suffers from such sadness does not diminish his competence to marry or divorce as long as he understands reality and can use discretion. Moreover, even when there are times when he seems dissociated temporarily from his surrounding, he is still considered competent since he can use discretion most of the time.

77 R. Shalom Mordechai Ha'Cohen Shvadron, Galicia, 1835-1911.

78 *Sh'elot Ut'shuvot Ma'Harsham* (The Responsa Project, Bar-Ilan University, Version 8, 2000), 7:164.

79 R. David Pipiano, Chief Rabbi of Bulgaria, 1851-1925.

80 *Sh'elot Ut'shuvot Nose' Ha'efod* (The Responsa Project, Bar-Ilan University, Version 8, 2000), 4.

81 See notes 75-77.

## *Mental Disease as a Problematic Field in Rabbinical Courts Ruling in Israel*

Rabbinical court rulings in Israel regarding mental disease in divorce claims reflect two problematic areas in *halakhah.*

The first is a basic problem in the halakhic judicial system that does not apply the binding precedent rule. The result is that rabbinical courts may base their rulings on a number of different Rishonim or on the opinions found in a variety of responsa so that different courts may come up with different rulings in similar cases.

The second area reflects the halakhic problematic dilemma regarding the validity of a *get* served under coercion.

It is important to note, that this dilemma exists also in physical diseases and handicaps. However, when dealing with mental diseases, there is an additional problem. In most bodily physical diseases, the mere existence of the disease is usually a factual, non-debatable matter. However, when it comes to mental diseases, the court, in many cases, needs to first clarify a preliminary question, namely, can the claimed symptoms be defined as mental disease — *shote'*, or do they merely reflect bad temper and behavioral changes which cannot be considered a mental disease.

In this respect, one should refer to the fact that even Maimonides, when discussing the qualifications of witnesses to testify,[82] refers the above question to the discretion of the presiding *dayan*. Therefore, when discussing the mentally ill witness,[83] he states in his concluding sentence: "All of the above cannot be described in a comprehensive manner in writing and is determined by the presiding *dayan.*"[84]

And indeed, in many cases, the court is dealing with contradicting medical/psychiatric expert opinions, where the plaintiff's medical experts state that the defendant is mentally ill while the defendant's experts determine that the bizarre behavior is no more than a personality disorder. In fact, the question of mental competence, or the question as to whether the presenting symptoms are part of a mental disease, is thoroughly discussed not only in *halakhah*, but also in many areas of the modern judicial system.

Examples of such debates are seen in the Israeli criminal proceedings when a defendant's competence to stand trial for criminal activity is brought into question. According to the Israeli criminal law, punishment for murder

82 *Mishneh Torah, Edut,* chapter 9.

83 *Supra* n.82 at 9:9.

84 *Supra* n.82 at 9:10.

could be reduced when the felony has been performed in a state where, "due to severe mental disorder or a defect in cognitive skills, the defendant's capability had been significantly limited, however, not to an absolute inability to understand what he is doing, or to understand the felonious nature of his deed, or to avoid doing it."[85]

The fact that even the modern Israeli legislature did not set clear-cut definitions and specifications as to the competence of mentally limited criminals demonstrates the deep problematic nature of the problem. Consequently, when researching criminal court cases in Israel, one may find a lot of inner debates among judges who have made rulings contradicting the opinions of psychiatric experts.

Such a debate took place in a murder case, where the defendant killed his friend after an argument about a tape recorder.[86] In that case, the judges, both in the district court as well as in the supreme appeal court, discussed the question as to whether a personality disorder can be deemed equivalent to a severe mental disease.

In another case, where the defendant had murdered his girlfriend,[87] the court had to deal with the question of a borderline personality which caused the defendant to have psychotic attacks which prevented him from controlling or understanding his deeds.

In a third case, where the defendant was indicted for killing his wife and for attempting to kill his son,[88] the court had to deal with different experts' diagnoses such as cyclic personality disorders versus a passive-aggressive personality. It is interesting to note, that in that case, the court referred to the "visibility" of such a personality disorder, which might be analogous to the obvious vs. hidden handicaps[89] described above in the Talmud.[90]

When examining the above mentioned question, dealt with already in the 13th and 16th centuries by the *Rosh* and *Ma'ha'rit*,[91] one cannot avoid noticing the similarity of the debate which took place among the medieval sages and that which still goes on today in the modern judicial system. As in previous generations, the question is still discussed in current day courts as

85 Criminal law, clause 300A.

86 CC 1011/97, *State of Israel* v. *Meir Elimelech.*

87 CC 214/91, *State of Israel* v. *Gilad Shemen.*

88 CC 256/95, *State of Israel* v. *Surany.*

89 *Mum galui vs. mum she'ba'ṣeter.*

90 See above, notes 2-3.

91 See above notes 51-57 and related text.

to whether an alleged insane husband is really a mentally ill person or is merely displaying "bad behavior" or "mindlessness" which might be referred to, in modern terminology, as a personality disorder.

### *Court Rulings When the Husband is the Mentally Ill Spouse*

From the halakhic standpoint, the case of the ill husband is a major core problem since *geṭ* coercion is a strict Torah transgression. Therefore, it is not surprising to find many contradictory arguments in the same case emphasizing, on one hand, the strict Torah transgression of releasing a married woman, an *eshet ish,* to the world, while, on the other hand, trying to avoid the agonizing woman from becoming an abandoned wife, an *agunah.*[92]

However, despite the empathy that the *dayanim* show towards the "trapped" wife, still, at least in the early rulings of the rabbinical courts in Israel, the tendency of the courts has been to reject motions for divorce enforcement on a mentally ill husband.

The background to that tendency had been the full adoption by the courts of the *Ḥatam Ṣofer*'s[93] approach and the strict interpretation of the *Rosh*'s ruling, as well as those *Ra'Bi'ia* and the *Mordekhai*. According to those rulings, no handicaps, other than those mentioned in the closed Mishnah list, could serve as a reason for forcing a husband to grant a *geṭ.*

Such is the case, in a ruling from the early 1950's[94] where the court rejected a wife's claim for a divorce from her mentally ill husband. She claimed that his mental state deteriorated, that he had more attacks and that he had beaten her and the children. The treating doctors testified that indeed he suffered an insanity attack, however, they said that he was under treatment and able to maintain married life.

Despite his mental disease, the court considered *geṭ* enforcement to be coercion, which voids the validity of a *geṭ.*

It should be noted however, that the court requested the husband not to abuse his vested power and that he show generosity towards his wife.

92 In fact, such a woman is not abandoned by her husband and is not a real *Agunah.* However, as the husband is not competent and is not able to serve a *geṭ*, her status is very similar to the *Agunah* who, on the one hand, does not have a husband with whom she can live, and, on the other hand, is trapped in her marriage and cannot marry another man.

93 See above note 62 and related text.

94 PDR 1, p.65.

However, all this could be done only out of his good will and not by enforcement.

Contrary to the above ruling, in later rabbinical courts rulings, some courts did find creative ways to solve the problem of a wife who was not able to live under the same roof with her mentally ill husband.

Following are a few examples:

A. In a rabbinical high court decision, given in 1962,[95] the court discussed the appeal of a woman against a district court which rejected her motion to enforce a *geṭ* on her epileptic husband. Though that case dealt with epilepsy, the rational of the ruling can be applied, as well, to a mentally diseased husband. In fact, a great portion of the court written ruling referred to the *Rosh* and to the insane husband.

After discussing the various contradictory rulings of the sages (*Rosh*, *Ra'bi'ia* and others), the court held that a majority of the opinions of the sages holds that a husband may be forced to divorce his wife. The rational, according to the court, was that the alternative was to leave that woman practically as an abandoned and deserted wife. Under these circumstances, it seemed right to the court to enforce the *geṭ* on the husband, release his poor wife and not leave her as an *agunah* for life.[96]

It should be pointed out, however, that in its final ruling, the court avoided the necessity of deciding the question of *geṭ* enforcement due to the disease. In its conclusion, it ruled that if enforcement is to be granted, it should be based on the fact that the husband could not support his wife, as his disease had limited his working capabilities.[97]

We should take note that despite the use of this circuitous reasoning and despite its reluctance to base its ruling on the husband's mental handicap, the court did, indeed, find a creative way, to apply a different halakhic argument

95 Case no. 184/320: PDR 4, p.166.

96 There, on page 168. The court uses quite a few strong statements, such as: "although some Rishonim may void such a *geṭ*, still, when it is a case of major desertion ("*Igun Gadol*"), such a *geṭ* may be regarded as good enough to release her to remarry." (The court refers to *She'elot Ut'shuvot Pitḥei Teshuvah*, 120). Another point the court makes is that in case a majority of opinions approve enforcement, such enforcement overrules the strict *Giṭin* rules.

97 The high court returned the case to the district court to check the welfare support to which the family is entitled. The instructions given to the district court had, indeed, been to approve divorce enforcement on the husband, but only in case such welfare could not support the family's needs.

to force a mentally ill husband to grant his wife a divorce.

This court case is a good example of the problematic depth of the debate with which the courts have to deal. While reading that court case, it is obvious that the *dayanim* do refer to the severe consequence of the abandoned wife, the *agunah*, however, they still hesitate to enforce divorce on the husband based only on the handicaps argument.

B. Another district court decision,[98] given in 1971, dealt with a woman's divorce claim, against her husband who had been hospitalized in a mental institution after trying to kill her.

The court referred to the contradiction in the *Rosh*'s ruling regarding non-*geṭ*-enforcement in the case of a mentally diseased husband as opposed to enforcement in the case of the epileptic husband. Also the court cited the *Hagra*, who stated that if a wife accepted her husband's handicap, it is a reason for not forcing a *geṭ* upon that husband. As the circumstances in that case, pointed to such an acceptance, the wife was estopped, or prevented from claiming that she was severely disturbed by her husband's handicap since she herself proved, by her behavior, that she could bear to live with him. Such an estoppel, formed by her former consent, has the halakhic term "*savra vekibla*", meaning that after she considered the matter and accepted it, she cannot claim against it.

Accordingly, the court concluded that the reasoning behind the *Rosh*'s contradictory rulings could be explained in a different way than the *Ma'Ha'rit*, in the following manner: In the case of the progressive mental disease, where the *Rosh* ruled against husband enforcement,[99] the woman had married her husband despite his handicap which had been known to her before the wedding. Therefore it was reasonable to apply the estoppel principle, *ṣavra veḳibla.*[100]

98 PDR 8, p.216.

99 See above notes 51-54 and relevant text.

100 The *dayanim* in that court came up with a very interesting argument regarding estoppel – *ṣavra veḳibla* – in cases similar to this one. They based the classification of major and minor handicaps on a presumption derived from the individual behavior of the sufferer. Accordingly, a minor handicap, *mum ḳaṭan*, is a handicap that an individual could live with and could adjust to it. On the other hand, a major handicap, *mum gadol*, is such a handicap that no spouse could live with. According to this argument, if a husband's handicap was known to the wife before the marriage and was accepted by her, then even if, for the majority of people, such a handicap is considered a major handicap, for her it should be considered a minor one

On the other hand, in the case of the epileptic, where the *Rosh* approved the enforcement claim against the husband, the husband had contracted the disease after wedding. In such a case, the *Rosh* ruled that one could not force the poor wife to remain a living widow with an epileptic husband. In this way the court actually made an analogy between the epilepsy case dealt with by the *Rosh* and the mental case that came before it.

For the matter itself, which dealt with the wife's divorce motion based on her husband's proven mental disease, with a high probability of violence, the court ruled that the husband should be forced to serve the *geṭ* to his wife.

However, from reading the court's ruling, it is difficult to draw a clear-cut conclusion regarding the court's stand on the distinction between major and minor handicaps *(mumim gedolim* vs. *mumim ḳeṭanim)* as far as insanity is concerned. It seems that the court found a good reason for granting the wife's motion even though it might be subject to criticism because insanity was not included in the closed Mishnah list. The reasoning of the court for the creative solution it came to, in this case, might have been the danger and jeopardy to the wife's physical safety due to the husband's mental disease which had been expressed in violence and even in an attempt to kill her.

C. The above ruling was repeated by the 1981 ruling of another court[101] confirming *geṭ* enforcement on a very violent husband. Although his mental state did not meet the strict definition of the insane person, the *shoṭe'*, the court went further and made an analogy between the woman, the plaintiff and an *eved kena'ani*, a Canaanite slave, whom one is prohibited from turning in to his master. In a similar manner, the court said that "we cannot turn over this poor woman to her violent husband, and we have to release her from him."

The court's opinion, is well summarized in the concluding section of that ruling, as follows:

- He, who becomes insane and is dangerous to his family should be forced to serve a *geṭ* to his wife.
- A husband who endangers his wife should be forced to serve her a *geṭ*.
- However, when the danger can be prevented by other means, divorce

---

since she herself proved by her acceptance that she is ready to live with that handicapped husband.

101 PDR 12, p.3.

enforcement should not be used.

- A court should do whatever it can to release a woman from constant danger and fear resulting from her husband's insanity.

D. In another court ruling,[102] the court voided a marriage based on medical testimony that the husband was admitted to a mental institution long before the wedding. The legal reasoning: bad faith, *meḳaḥ ṭa'ut.* Here too, the court avoided the question as to whether the Mishnah list is just an example or is it a closed list. Also, the court avoided ruling on the question of major or minor handicap, although, it did refer to that issue by stating that insanity is a major handicap.

E. Another example of rabbinical court thinking was presented in a responsum written by R. Eliezer Waldebberg, who served as a *dayan* in the rabbinical high court in Jerusalem.[103] In fact, that responsum is based on a rabbinical high court ruling that he had served as the presiding *dayan*.

The case dealt with a schizophrenic husband who, when under attack, had become violent, damaging property, beating, and also threatening to kill his wife and children. As it turned out, that husband had been treated for mental disorders prior to his marriage, and, after his marriage, had been admitted twice into a mental institution.

Based on the above facts, the wife sued her husband for divorce enforcement; but the husband refused, claiming that he had been cured and was perfectly normal. The doctors' opinion, presented to the court, could not rule out the possibility of a future relapse in his mental condition.

R. Waldenberg, after a very extensive analysis of the different sages' opinions, states very clearly that such insanity, endangering the wife's safety, is considered a major handicap and a prime reason for divorce enforcement. He even argues with the common understanding that, according to the *Ḥatam Ṣofer*,[104] divorce can never be enforced on a mentally ill husband. Paradoxically, he finds support in the *Ḥatam Ṣofer*'s responsum on divorce enforcement previously discussed. The *Ḥatam Ṣofer*, when rationalizing his reluctance to rule for divorce enforcement on the epileptic, opines that the epileptic does not endanger his wife, since epilepsy is not contagious.

102 PDR 15, p.1.

103 *Sh'elot Ut'shuvot Tzitz Eliezer* (The Responsa Project, Bar-Ilan University, Version 8, 2000), 6:42, *Orḥot Mishpaṭim*, # A.

104 See above note 60 and the related text.

However, in the case discussed by R. Waldenberg, the insane husband, when under attack, represents a real danger to his wife, even though, at the time of the court ruling, he was in complete remission. R. Waldenberg's conclusion is, therefore, that the concern for the physical safety of the wife overrules the alleged transgression.[105] Consequently, that wife should be saved from such a possible danger and the schizophrenic husband must be forced to divorce his wife.

It is quite obvious that the common denominator in the above rulings was the search for creative solutions to ease the agony of women whose husbands' mental diseases made their lives unbearable.

*Conclusions Regarding Court Rulings When the Husband Is the Mentally Ill Spouse*

The above rabbinical court cases lead to several conclusions regarding divorce enforcement on the mentally ill husband.

1. Although in the past, the rabbinical courts in Israel were rather strict and took the *leḥumra* standpoint, the current general trend is mostly to find creative solutions that will solve the human problem. Thus, the current rulings tend to enable a wife to receive her *geṭ* and not stay as a prisoner with her mentally ill, sometimes violent, husband.
2. When the husband's disease is of the violent type, endangering the safety of the wife and children, the question of coercion is secondary to the physical safety of the family. The reasoning of the courts is that the severity of the danger is higher than the severity of the transgression,[106] meaning that the danger is more important and overrules the transgression.
3. Insanity is considered by most of the *dayanim* to be a major handicap, *mum gadol,* which is a sufficient reason for forcing a husband to divorce his wife.
4. A possible factor in the courts' rulings to enforce divorce on a mentally ill husband lies in the fear that, in the present generation, when such a wife cannot officially release herself from the marriage bond, she might look for relations with another man, thereby violating a major basic Torah law of *eshet ish* (a married woman).

105 *Ḥamira ṣakanta me'iṣura.*

106 The court used the same expression as in the previous note.

5. Quite a few of the courts have stated that an insane husband's condition is even worse than *sh'ḥin.*[107] a major skin disease included in the closed Mishnah list. This is due to the fact that the *sh'ḥin* affected husband could be forced to serve a *geṭ*, while in the case of the mentally ill, the poor wife depends on his good will; hence she should be helped by the court.
6. Also, some courts opined that insanity is worst than epilepsy, since an epileptic attack, in most cases, is a relatively limited, short term attack, lasting only a few hours. An insanity attack, on the other hand, may last for weeks, months or, sometimes, years.[108]
7. The above rulings, may serve as precedent setting in the sense that perhaps the Mishnah list for enforceable divorce on the husband,[109] is not a closed list, but, rather, is a representative list that should be applied to a variety of major diseases and handicaps.
8. In spite of the above conclusions, if a rabbinical court can find a good reason to enforce divorce on the mentally ill husband — other than just insanity as a major handicap — it will prefer using that other reason. Different reasons used by the rabbinical courts are, in fact, creative solutions to avoid actualy contradicting the rulings of Rishonim and other sages who opposed and did not support *geṭ* enforcement on the husband.

*The Problem of the Mentally Ill Wife*

As already stated above, application of the strict halakhic rules of the Torah and Talmud regarding divorce enforcement include a major basic difference between the case of the mentally ill husband and that of the mentally ill wife. That difference has diminished, at least partially, since R, Gershom's *ḥerem* against the forcing of a wife to accept a divorce against her will; however, it certainly has not disappeared altogether. In fact, despite the relative "equalization" between the husband and wife regarding the consent condition, from both sides, there still are a few major differences between the motion of a wife for enforcement of a divorce against her husband and a husband's motion to enforce such a divorce on his wife.

107 For example, PDR 15, p.1, conclusion 10 (p.2).

108 *Sh'elot Ut'shuvot Tzitz Eliezer* (The Responsa Project, Bar-Ilan University, Version 8, 2000); see above note 103.

109 That list includes only two diseases: *sh'ḥin* and *polipos*.

One major difference is that in the husband's case, no coercion or compulsion measures to end the marriage may be taken by the court against a husband unless the husband personally serves the *geṭ* to his wife or to her proxy (which may be the court). It is different in the case of the wife since, at least according to the Talmudic law, her agreement is not necessary at all. In fact, if a *geṭ* is thrown into her arms, the divorce is valid, even if she screams and protests that she does not want to be divorced. Consequently, according to Talmudic law, in the case of the wife, there is no need, in the first place, to use any coercion or compulsion measures.

Another difference lies in the fact that under certain circumstances, even after R. Gershom's *ḥerem,* a husband with the problem of a recalcitrant wife may be solved by granting him special permission to marry another woman. Such a measure could be enacted also in the case of the insane wife who cannot understand reality and has no discretion. No such permit can be granted to the wife of an ill husband. As long as her first marriage has not expired, either by *geṭ* serving or by her husband's death, she cannot marry another man.

A third difference in the woman's position, when compared with that of the husband, is that the husband has financial obligations towards his wife. A wife has no such obligations toward her husband. Therefore, major debates in divorce enforcement cases center about the question as to whether the *geṭ* enforced husband should also be enforced to pay his wife her *ketubah.*[110]

A fourth difference may be noticed in the degree of danger to which the mentally ill spouse exposes his family. While the insane wife is also perfectly capable of harming and damaging her husband and children, still, most of the claims of violence come from the wife in reference to the husband's aggressive violence. Consequently, one may regard such a motion coming from a wife as more urgent than a husband's motion, for although living with an insane wife may indeed be unbearable, at least, in most cases, it can hardly be defined as dangerous.

In practice, although there is no prohibition in the Torah against enforcing a *geṭ* on a wife, still most of the rabbinical courts in our generation tend to apply R. Gershom's ordinance, and do not allow *geṭ* coercion on the wife.

On the other hand, insanity is considered a handicap in women, as the

110 A similar debate is raised abount the question as to whether the enforced wife still has the right to receive her *Ketubah* and alimony.

Mishnah in *Ketubot*[111] states that all disqualifying handicaps of *Cohanim* are considered handicaps in women.[112]

It is important to emphasize that the discussion here refers to the mental relapsing/remitting cases, where a wife has perfectly sane periods. A wife who is in a state of permanent insanity, totally dissociated from reality, is in a completely different situation since she has no legal competence to receive or to keep a *geṭ* in her possession.[113]

One of the basic halakhic sources, cited frequently in the courts' rulings, is the *Shulḥan Arukh*[114] where it is stated that an epileptic wife can be forced to receive her *geṭ* and where the ordinance of R. Gershom, which bars divorce coercion on a wife, does not apply in such a case. The rational for this is supplied by the *Rosh* who is cited there as stating that, certainly, R. Gershom's intention was not to create a preference for women whereby, in cases of major handicaps, handicapped men could be forced to grant a divorce, while in the case of handicapped wives, husbands were "stuck" with them for life.

The *Rema* in that paragraph adds that such wife enforcement can apply only in major handicaps; however, when it is not a major disease, she should not be forced to receive a *geṭ* and be divorced from her husband. It is obvious that the *Rema* considered R. Gershom's *ḥerem* to be a very serious and binding rule, almost like a Torah rule that cannot be turned around unless there is a very serious reason to do so.

### *Rabbinical Court Rulings When the Wife Is the Mentally Ill Spouse*

In principle, the trend nowadays in the rabbinical courts is to find halakhic solutions that can equalize the status of the wife and the husband. Therefore, in cases of major diseases, the *geṭ* is enforced on both, husband as well as wife, while in non-major diseases, neither the wife nor the husband are subject to an enforced divorce.

Following are some rabbinical court cases as well as citations/ conclusions from such rulings which refer to Rishonim and Aḥaronim and

111 *Ketubot* 72b.

112 See above note 42 and related text.

113 Even if she could keep the *geṭ*, but could not exercise discretion to protect herself, she cannot be divorced; see *Mishneh Torah, Gerushin* 6:23, also R. Ḳaro, *Shulḥan Arukh, Even Ha'ezer* 119:6.

114 *Shulḥan Arukh, Even Ha'ezer* 117:11.

can serve as guidelines. Also, those rulings, may illustrate standpoints and viewpoints of the presiding *dayanim*:

1. In a district rabbinical court ruling given in 1970,[115] the court granted a husband's motion to enforce a divorce on his schizophrenic wife who claimed that her mental state was no more than depression and transient bad-mood attacks. According to the evidence presented to the court, the wife's pre-marital psychiatric hospitalizations had been concealed from the husband. Her mental attacks had been explained to him as sever headaches.

The court held that:

A. Insanity is considered a major handicap (*mum gadol*).
B. A mental disease which had relapsed several times in the past is presumed likely to relapse again. Therefore, even if the wife is currently symptom free, her state is still considered a major handicap.
C. A wife who has deceived her husband, concealing her disease from him, could be forced to be served a *geṭ*.
D. If the wife refuses to receive the *geṭ*, the court may disregard R. Gershom's *ḥerem* and grant the husband a permit to marry another woman.[116]

Based on the above, the court ruled that a divorce should be forced on the wife. However, if she refuses to divorce him, her husband could marry another woman.

2. In a 1979 rabbinical high court ruling,[117] the court dealt with a husband's divorce motion due to symptoms of mental disease displayed by his wife only after they had already married. The medical diagnosis stated that she was suffering from paranoidic schizophrenia. Despite that, the husband continued living with her another three years until she was admitted to a psychiatric institution without any time set for her release. Also, the doctors recommended that, due to heredity risk, she should not get

115 PDR 8, p.174.

116 It is worth noting that the court found the additional marriage permit a better solution in that particular case as the wife herself asked for this ruling. Her rationale had been to avoid becoming a divorced woman with all of the economic and social consequences entailed. By making this decision, the court actually took into account the ill wife's agony and vulnerability and did not stick to the strict rule of *geṭ* enforcement in major handicaps.

117 PDR 14, p.3.

pregnant.[118]

It appeared that the wife had a history of psychiatric hospitalization, the first time at the age of 14; this information had been concealed from her husband.

It should be emphasized that despite her hospitalization, she had not been totally dissociated from reality and could understand the essence of a divorce and a *geṭ*.

The district court which first dealt with that case held that the husband could be granted a permit to marry another woman, however, he was required to bear her hospitalization costs. Also, he was obligated to pay her alimony, if and when, she is released from the hospital.

The high court confirmed the lower court ruling regarding permission to marry another woman; however, it rejected the ruling regarding the husband's obligations to pay alimony to his wife.

This court ruling was very comprehensive and referred to many responsa which dealt with similar cases. Consequently, the following conclusions, which also are listed as such in that ruling, can, perhaps, serve as guidelines in this area of the mentally ill wife.

A. There is a consensus that R. Gershom's ordinance does not apply when a wife is insane, hospitalized in a mental institution and cannot function as a wife.[119]

B. R. Gershom's ordinance applies only in a case of a minor handicap (*mum ḳaṭan*), but does not apply when a wife's handicap is a major one *(mum gadol)*.

C. Concealing diseases which have existed before marriage may serve as grounds for divorce enforcement, both on the man, as well as on the woman; in such cases R. Gershom's ordinance does not apply.

D. Even if a husband lived with his wife after he discovered the handicap, he can still sue for divorce and is not stopped from making such a claim.[120]

118 In such a case, the husband had a good halakhic claim, that he could not fulfill the *mitzva* of *p'ru u'r'vu*, producing offspring.

119 This conclusion, as well as the following ones, are listed in a conclusion list of the court ruling.

120 The rationale for this ruling, is explained in the following way: In the Talmudic period, when a husband had no restriction on divorcing his wife if he wanted to, the fact that he continued living with her after revealing her disease could work against him since he most probably agreed and chose to accept his wife handicaps. However, after R.Gershom's *ḥerem*, when he knew that he could not force a divorce on her, his continuing to live with

3. A similar ruling can be noticed in another rabbinical district court case in Jerusalem.[121] Here too, the husband sued to enforce divorce on his mentally ill wife as her pre-marital illness had been concealed from him. The court debated whether the evidence presented indeed supported the husband's claim that the illness had already existed before their wedding and whether she could be forced to be served a *geṭ*, in any case, due to the severity of her illness.

Like in the previous cases, here too, the court accepted the husband's motion and ruled that he could marry another woman.

The conclusions from this court case, are quite in line with the those of the previous ones, however it is worthwhile to quote a few of its conclusions:

A. Major handicaps contracted by a woman after marriage are a valid reason for *geṭ* enforcement on her, and R. Gershom's ordinance does not apply in such a case. In instances of minor handicaps, however, R. Gershom's ordinance does apply and she may not be forced to divorce her husband.

B. Mental disease is a major handicap (*mum gadol*) and one is not expected to accept living under one roof with such an ill spouse.[122]

C. In the case of a wife whose mental disease has a pattern of relapsing and remitting, the husband is allowed to divorce his wife or to marry another woman. In such a case, there is no violation of R. Gershom's ordinance.

D. Even when the wife is in remission, repeated mental attacks in the past create a presumption of insanity which gives a reason for divorce enforcement.

### *Conclusions Regarding Court Rulings When the Wife Is the Mentally Ill Spouse*

The above presented rabbinical court cases lead to the following conclusions regarding divorce enforcement on mentally ill wives:

1. There is a similarity between husbands and wives in cases of

---

her was not by choice and therefore could not serve as an estoppel against him.

121 PDR 15, p.88.

122 The court used Maimonides' expression: "No person could live with a snake in same proximity."

concealing the mental disease from the other side. In both instances, divorce can be enforced.

2. While in the mentally ill husband's case there is only one alternative, divorce enforcement, when it is the wife who is the mentally ill, there is another alternative, permission for the husband to marry another woman without being divorced from his mentally ill wife.
3. R. Gershom's ordinance does not apply when the wife has contracted major handicaps or diseases (*mumim gedolim*).
4. Based on the previous conclusion, it can be stated that when the wife is mentally ill, then neither *geṭ* enforcement on the wife, nor granting the husband permission to marry another woman, are violations of R. Gershom's ordinance since it does not apply in such cases.

*General Conclusions Regarding the Issue of Mental Disease in Halakhic Divorce Law*

The incompetence of the insane person to marry is a consensus in *halakhah* rooted already in the Talmud.[123] Rami Bar Ḥama states there the reason why even *Rabanan*, the sages,[124] have not enacted any ordinance for the marriage of the insane man and woman, as "one cannot live with a snake in the same proximity."

However, the more serious problematic area is the divorce stage, where the two main questions to be answered are in regard to the competence of the insane to divorce and the question of *geṭ* enforcement on the mentally ill spouse.

The problem of insanity in family life, is a very severe and complex one that may destroy intimacy and family relations between the spouses. As it is not a rare and uncommon phenomenon, the *halakhah*, as a judicial system, had to cope with the numerous claims for divorce or for the voiding of marriage which were brought before the sages.

123 *Yevamot* 112b.

124 The passage there deals with the issue of the validity of the marriage of a deaf person. According to the strict rule of the *Torah*, such a marriage has no effect and is void, however, it is the sages' ordinance which gives validity to the marriage of the deaf. As for the insane, it is a different rule since an insane person cannot exercise the necessary discretion, and even the sages, *rabanan,* did not enact any ordinance to ratify such a marriage.

On one hand, it can be gathered from the responsa cited in this paper, as well as from the rabbinical court cases, that many *dayanim* are quite open and receptive to the human agony of the normal spouse who cannot bear living with his/her mentally ill spouse under the same roof. The result is expressed in their attempts to find creative solutions to release the suffering spouse from the marriage bond.

However, and despite the above, there still are certain cases when even the most liberal rabbinical courts will not be able to release a poor woman whose husband is in a totally disoriented mental disease state and cannot even understand the meaning of divorce. That is due to the fact that, not like in other legal systems, divorce, according to *halakhah*, cannot be valid and legally binding unless the husband personally, or through a proxy, serves and delivers a *geṭ* to his wife. No rabbinical court, could declare that a marriage had terminated when such a husband is reluctant to serve a *geṭ*. In other words, no court decision could replace the necessary serving of a *geṭ* on his wife.

Consequently, it seems that the issue of mental disease in halakhic family law, especially the question of divorce enforcement, will continue to occupy both the *dayanim* at the rabbinical courts as well as halakhic scholars and students for many years to come.